SOCIAL ENTREPRENEURSHIP AND MICROFINANCE

JONATHAN H. WESTOVER, EDITOR

SOCIAL ENTREPRENEURSHIP AND MICROFINANCE

JONATHAN H. WESTOVER, EDITOR

COMMON GROUND

First published in 2013 in Champaign, Illinois, USA
by Common Ground Publishing LLC
as part of The Organization book series

Library of Congress Cataloging-in-Publication Data

Social entrepreneurship and microfinance / Jonathan H. Westover, editor.
    pages cm
 Includes bibliographical references and index.
 ISBN 978-1-61229-245-8 (pbk : alk. paper) -- ISBN 978-1-61229-246-5 (pdf)
 1. Social entrepreneurship. 2. Microfinance. I. Westover, Jonathan H.

 HD60.S6293 2013
 658.4'08--dc23

                          2013025257

Cover Image Credit: Phillip Kalantzis-Cope

Table of Contents

Part 3: Social Entrepreneurship and Microfinance Education

Part 4: Cases in Social Entrepreneurship

Acknowledgements

I want to thank Common Ground Publishing for providing me with a venue for publishing this edited compilation. Additionally, I would like to thank the many individuals who contributed their own research to this edited work. Of course, this book would not be possible without each of their important contributions. Most of all, I would like to publically thank my beloved wife, Jacque, and my six wonderful children (Sara, Amber, Lia, Kaylie, David, and Brayden) for all of their love and support!

Contributor Information
(In Order of Contribution Appearance)

Dr. Jonathan H. Westover

Jonathan H. Westover, Ph.D. is an Assistant Professor of Management and Director of Academic Service Learning at Utah Valley University, specializing in international human resource management and business strategy. He received his Doctorate of Philosophy and Master of Science degrees in the Sociology of Work and Organizations from the University of Utah. He also received his Master of Public Administration degree (emphasis in human resource management) from the Marriott School of Management at Brigham Young University. He was a Fulbright Scholar at Belarusian State University in Minsk, Belarus and has been visiting professor at the University of Science and Technology of China, in Hefei, China. Additionally, he has worked as a part-time faculty member in both the Organizational Leadership and Strategy Department and Romney Institute of Public Management in the Marriott School of Management at BYU, as a part-time faculty member in the Management Department in the David Eccles School of Business at the University of Utah.. His ongoing research examines issues of globalization, labor transformation, social entrepreneurship and microfinance, work-quality characteristics, and the determinants of job satisfaction cross-nationally.

Dr. Martin Brueckner

Martin Brueckner is a lecturer at the Institute for Social Sustainability in the School of Management and Governance at Murdoch University in Perth, Western Australia. In this capacity he teaches both undergraduate and postgraduate classes in the area of sustainability management, economics of sustainability and sustainability theory. Martin's research focuses on industry-community relations and sustainable communities as well as environmental policy-making and regional sustainability. His work is concerned with questions of social and environmental justice, corporate governance and corporate social responsibility.

Sally Paulin

Sally Paulin is a lecturer in Sustainability in the School of Management and Givernance at Murdoch University. Her research interest is in the area of social sustainability with special emphasis on community engagement and participation as well as volunteering and the experiences of community groups. Sally is also interested in the areas of sustainable waste management and resource recovery, sustainable agriculture and the importance of acknowledging lay and local knowledge when looking for solutions to complex problems.

Jenna Burleson-Davis

Jenna Burleson-Davis was an associate lecturer with the School of Management at Curtin University of Technology, as well as an Adjunct Lecturer at Portland

State University in the United States. While at Curtin, she conducted research on social enterprise in Western Australia. Jenna has lectured in the subjects of Management, Strategic Management, and Business Sustainability, and has worked in both not-for-profit and private enterprise. Her key research interest is in the area of social enterprise, seeking solutions that can holistically improve the human condition.

Prof. Samir Chatterjee
Samir Ranjan Chatterjee is a Professor of International Management at Curtin University, Australia. He has authored and co-authored 12 books,30 book Chapter and about 160 refereed papers in Scholarly journals and International Conference proceedings.

Brigita Baltaca
B.Baltaca is an Assistant Professor in Management at BA School of Business & Finance, Latvia, specializing in leadership and marketing. Additionally she is actively participating in faculty mobility within Europe. Recently she had been delivering classes at Haute Ecole EPHEC University College and Leuven University College in Belgium as well as coordinating international student projects. Her previous professional experience includes such positions as Bank Leading Project Analyst, Training Officer and Director of internationally supported development projects in Latvia in the area of cooperative finance. She holds a Master of Public Administration from the University of Latvia and currently is a doctoral degree candidate at the Faculty of Economics, University of Latvia. She is also an author of a series of publications on the role of credit unions in the economy of Latvia.

Dr. Sam Wells
Sam Wells graduated from the University of Adelaide in 1978 with 1st Class Honours in History. As South Australia's 1979 Rhodes Scholar, he completed his doctorate at Oxford in 1983. Sam spent 18 years in corporate human resource management and organisational development. He established his own consulting business in 2001 and continues to advise CEOs and executive teams on cultivating organisations in which employees at all levels can 'be everything they are'. For five years from 2007, he was MBA Director in the University of Adelaide Business School. Sam's research and personal interests focus on sustainability, both in its broadest sense, and as it applies to organisations and the management of people within organisations.

Stephanie Betz
Stephanie Betz graduated from the University of Corporate Education in Mannheim with a focus on Industry/Aviation in 2002. After six years in the Aviation industry at a major German airport, she undertook her Master of Business Administration at the University of Adelaide, with electives in Global Business, Entrepreneurship and Organisational Sustainability. Steff returned to her roots in the European Aviation Industry in 2006. She worked for the European Parliament in Industry and Trade as an intern. Since May 2007 she has

worked as a consultant focusing on strategy, organisational change and site development. Steff's research and personal interests focus on sustainability, currently in the aviation industry and its visions for the future.

Dr. Roni Kaufman

Roni Kaufman is a Senior Lecturer with the Spitzer Department of Social Work, Ben-Gurion University of the Negev, Israel.

Dr. Amos Avgar

Amos Avgar worked for twelve years as the JDC Director of Welfare Programs in the Former Soviet Union (FSU) and was the architect of the *Hesed* Movement, a network of 178 *Hesed* welfare centers that was developed across the FSU serving at their peak over 250,000 people. In 2003, Amos was appointed to the position of Chief Program Officer at New York Headquarters and currently is the Chief Operating Officer of Tag International Development and resides in Jerusalem.

Dr. Julia Mirsky

Julia Mirsky, Ph.D. is a Psychologist and a Professor with the Spitzer Department of Social Work, Ben-Gurion University of the Negev, Israel.

Dr. Joanne Neal

Concordia University College of Alberta, Canada

Jennifer Butler

Jennifer Butler is a Ph.D. Candidate at National Chengchi University where she studies International Development. She received her BA in Political Science from Texas A&M Corpus Christi and her MA in International Relations from St. Mary's University. Her current research encompasses educational economics and development, and investigates the impact that financial education and financial literacy have on financial inclusion through microfinance and entrepreneurship.

Dr. Yogendra Acharya

Dr. Yogendra Prasad ACHARYA is an academic and works for York University in Canada . He holds a PhD from The University of Melbourne, Australia. Dr Acharya is an MBA and a lawyer. Yogendra teaches quantitative and applied research methods, economics, finance, organizational behavior, and elements of law at York University. Some of his areas of specialization are: Social Entrepreneurship and Microfinance, Development Studies, Economics, Finance, and Organizational Behavior. Yogendra has 18 years of industry experience in the development and banking sector as a Management Expert. He has published a book on sustainable microfinance and poverty alleviation. Dr Acharya has also worked for the University of Toronto and community colleges in Ontario as a sessional faculty.

Dr. Salim Lakha

Dr Salim Lakha has multidisciplinary qualifications including economics, urban studies and anthropology. He was the coordinator and senior lecturer in the Development Studies Program at The University of Melbourne from 2001-2009. In 2011 he was a Visiting Senior Research Fellow at the Asia Research Institute, National University of Singapore. He is currently an Honorary Senior Fellow in the School of Social and Political Sciences (University of Melbourne). His research interests include international migration, Indian diaspora, globalization, and governance, democratization and development. His area of specialization is India.

Dr. Anthony Marcus

Anthony Marcus has a PhD in Anthropology from the City University of New York and has done research on poverty, livelihoods development, gender, kinship, social capital, and ethnic conflict in the Republic of Maldives, Cuba, Guatemala, Nepal, the United States, Indonesia, and Sri Lanka. He was one of the founders of the School of International Development of Melbourne University that provided Australia's first online MA/Ph.D and has consulted for the United Nations and the Red Cross. He is currently at John Jay College of Criminal Justice of the City University of New York, where he studies human trafficking, teenage prostitution, prisoner reentry, and the victimization of undocumented Latino migrants.

Popy Begum

Popy Begum, John Jay College of Criminal Justice of the City University of New York, USA

Dr. Hong Son Nghiem

Dr Nghiem is a research fellow at the Centre of National Research on Disability and Rehabilitation Medicine (CONROD), the University of Queensland, Australia. He has conducted substantial empirical research and consulting work in development sector in Vietnam with NGOs, donors and government agencies. His research interests include applied econometrics, development economics and health economics.

James Laurenceson

Senior Lecturer, School of Economics at University of Queensland. James Laurenceson is currently a Senior Lecturer in Economics at The University of Queensland. He has previously also held appointments at Shimonoseki City University in Japan and Shandong University in China. His research focuses exclusively on the Chinese economy and has been published in international, peer-reviewed journals such as China Economic Review, China Economic Journal, Journal of Chinese Economics and Business Studies, China and World Economy and Frontiers of Economics in China.

Dr. Jianhong Xue

Jianhong Xue is a professor of Agricultural and Environmental Economics at Northwest A&F University in Yangling, China, specializing in economics of agribusiness organization, food safety, population adiposity, and entrepreneurship. He received a Bachelor's of Science in Business Administration, a Master's of Science and a Ph.D. in Agricultural Economics with an emphasis in Agribusiness Management from the University of Missouri-Columbia. He taught Agricultural Economics at Carleton University in Ottawa, Canada shortly prior to join the Faculty of Economics and Management at Northwest A&F University. He recently received support from National Social Science Foundation for his research on entrepreneurship and support from Chinese Ministry of Education for his collaboration with distinguished oversea scholars. His research interests focus on using interdisciplinary approaches on current and potential social problems. His ongoing research examines the relationship between the characteristics of food supply chain and food safety in China, the impacts and causes of population adiposity, the problem of professional imposed economic transactions, and entrepreneurship in college and university graduates.

Dr. Vijaya Sherry Chand

His areas of interest include innovation, education systems, the non-profit sector, and sustainable development. He worked in social development organizations for eleven years before joining academics in 1993. His current research interests include antecedents of individual workplace innovation, the consequences of innovative work performance of teachers for learning climate and children's motivation, domain mapping of individual educational workplace innovations; other areas of interest include teacher development, ecological knowledge of school children, decentralized management of basic education, sustainable development planning, and development/ social entrepreneurship. He is the winner of the Hewlett-Packard Sustainability & Social Innovation Award (2012), for educational innovation. He is the Editor of *Vikalpa*: *The Journal for Decision Makers*, the journal of the Indian Institute of Management, Ahmedabad, India, where he is Professor at the Ravi J. Matthai Centre for Educational Innovation.

Prof. Yehuda Bar Shalom

Prof. Bar Shalom has done research in the following topics: Social entrepreneurship, psycho social- approaches in education, Arab-Jewish relations, Jewish identity, religious and secular encounter in Israel, relations between ethnic groups in Israel, Jewish Identity, Israel Diaspora relations and multicultural education. He served as Chair of the Education department, Head of the tenure committee and Dean of students at the David Yellin Academic College in Jerusalem. He is co-founder of the Social Entrepreneurship network with Eyal Bloch and he also teaches at the Tel Aviv University Overseas school. His book, *Educating Israel: Educational entrepreneurship in Israel's multicultural society*, has been published by Palgrave macmillan in 2006.

Eyal Bloch

Eyal has many years of experience both as formal and informal educator. Initiated many new programs on multiculturalism and co-existence. Co-founder of the Social Entrepreneurship Network and Co-founder of "All in Peace".

Yonatan Glaser

Yonatan Glaser is the founding Director of B'Zedek ('in Justice'), an initiative to activate and train Israeli youth and tertiary students in social change and social justice. A serial social and educational entrepreneur, Mr. Glaser was a co-founder of Netzer Olami, an International progressive Jewish-Zionist Youth Movement active in 13 countries. He later founded Hiburim, an Israeli non-profit that worked to weave together the Jewish and liberal humanistic traditions in Israeli schools. Mr. Glaser has worked in formal and informal education settings with Israeli and Jewish Diaspora youth leaders, teachers and School Principals. He has taught, initiated new educational programs, developed curriculum and led educational interventions, worked for the Israeli Ministry of Education and participated in the Ministry's Citizens for 21st Century Conference. Holding Law and Economics degrees from Melbourne University (Australia), Mr. Glaser earned his MA in Jewish Philosophy from Hebrew University (Israel). He is a graduate of Israel's prestigious School of Educational Leadership. Mr. Glaser served the (Jewish) Reform Movement in North America as its Central Educational Shaliach (Emissary) from 2003- 5.

Prof. Ethel Brundin

Ethel Brundin is Professor in Entrepreneurship and Business Development at the Department of Entrepreneurship, Strategy, Organization and Leadership at Jönköping International Business School. She is affiliated with the inter-disciplinary Center of Family Enterprise and Ownership. She is a researcher and member of the European Leadership Council of the global research project STEP (Successful Transgenerational Entrepreneurship Practices). She is standing visiting professor at the University of the Western Cape, Cape Town, South Africa and at Witten Herdecke University, Witten, Germany. She is project manager for an international research project between Sweden and South Africa about family businesses and private ownership/black empowerment. The focus of her research interest is primarily micro processes in family businesses including different arenas of entrepreneurship and strategic leadership. She has published in international journals and edited books about emotions in strategic and entrepreneurial leadership as well as about immigrant, ethnic and social entrepreneurship. Prior to completing her PhD, she worked as a strategy and OD consultant and human resource manager in Sweden and the UK in businesses started by her.

Mr. Eslyn Isaacs

University of the Western Cape, Bellville, South Africa. He has been with UWC for the past 29 years, teaching, researching and consulting to small, medium and micro enterprises as well as students at under- and post graduate. His teaching focuses on Management, Marketing, Services Marketing, Corporate Governance and Entrepreneurship. His area of research to-date has been primarily on small, medium and micro enterprises (SMMEs) and family business. I hold an M. Com from the University of the Western Cape.

Dr. Kobus Visser
University of the Western Cape, South Africa

Dr. Caroline Wigren
Jönköping International Business School, Sweden

Dr. Daniel Oruoch
KCA University, Kenya

Renson Muchiri
KCA University, Kenya

Prof. Tim Coelli
Is a Professor of Economics in the Centre for Efficiency and Productivity Analysis, School of Economics

Prof. Prasada Rao
Is a Professor of Economics in the Centre for Efficiency and Productivity Analysis, School of Economics.

Dr. Ricardo Lozano
Dr. Ricardo Lozano is an Assistant Professor with the Educational Sciences Department at Yeditepe University in Istanbul where he teaches courses in Education and International Economic Development, Comparative Education, Educational Leadership and Planning, and Educational Management with an emphasis on Organizational Behavior. Ricardo is a graduate of Texas A&M University with a Ph.D. in Education Administration with an Academic Emphasis on International Economic Development, and a graduate of Concordia University, Texas with a M.Ed. in Curriculum Development and Instruction. Ricardo's main research interests are in the areas of education and international economic development, and comparative/international education.

Introduction

In short, social entrepreneurship is an approach to recognizing a social problem and using entrepreneurial principles to organize, create and manage a venture to achieve social change. Furthermore, microfinance is an approach of providing banking and other financial resources to low-income clients who otherwise would not have access to such financial resources. While social entrepreneurship and microfinance are not new phenomenon, these approaches to utilizing entrepreneurial and business principles to achieve social change has increased in popularity and usage across the world in recent years. As we live in an increasingly hyper-competitive and interconnected globalized world, social entrepreneurship and microfinance practices are increasingly being taught in top universities and being utilized more and more to drive social change and to give a hand-up to those in need around the globe.

This edited collection will help you answer the following questions:

- What is social entrepreneurship and what are its benefits and limitations?
- How might we best approach social entrepreneurship in the age of globalization?
- What is microfinance and what are its benefits and limitations?
- How can we best teach social entrepreneurship and microfinance principles in the university setting?
- What are some examples of social entrepreneurship and microfinance programs that have been implemented in various regions around the world?

Overview of the Format of the Book

This edited collection provides a comprehensive introduction to social entrepreneurship and microfinance and explores the impacts for the modern global economic landscape, presenting a wide range of cross-disciplinary research in an organized, clear, and accessible manner. It will be informative to social science academics and instructors, while also instructing social entrepreneurship practitioners of all types seeking to utilize sound entrepreneurial and business principles to achieve social change in an increasingly interconnected and competitive global economy.

This book is divided into four parts: (1) Overview of Social Entrepreneurship, (2) Overview of Microfinance, (3) Social Entrepreneurship and Microfinance Education, and (4) Cases in Social Entrepreneurship and Microfinance. Each part starts with a brief overview, outlining the overall theme of the section and specific chapters that it contains.

Chapters 1-5 make up Part 1 of the book, which provides an overview of social entrepreneurship. Chapter 1 makes the case for social-enterprise. Chapter 2 explores the benefits of social enterprise. Chapter 3 looks at the role of the social-entrepreneur. Chapter 4 looks at social enterprise in crisis situations. Chapter 5 looks at globalization and social entrepreneurship.

Chapters 6-9 make up Part 2 of the book, which provides an overview of microfinance. Chapter 6 explores the benefits of microfinance. Chapter 7 looks at sustainable microfinance. Chapter 8 explores stakeholders' perspectives on the effectiveness of microfinance. Chapter 9 looks at microfinance as a means for alleviating poverty around the world.

Chapters 10-12 make up Part 3 of the book, which focuses on social entrepreneurship and microfinance education. Chapter 10 looks at the university's role in promoting "new" entrepreneurship. Chapter 11 looks at educating the social conscious entrepreneur. Chapter 12 looks at educators as social entrepreneurs.

Part 4 of the book is made up of four cases, each looking at issues surrounding social entrepreneurship and microfinance. Chapter 13 explores the role of social entrepreneurship in South Africa. Chapter 14 looks entrepreneurial intentions in Kenya. Chapter 15 looks at microfinance in Vietnam. Chapter 16 looks at educational centers and microfinance in India.

Part 1: An Overview of Social Entrepreneurship

Chapters 1-5 make up Part 1 of the book, which provides an overview of social entrepreneurship. Chapter 1 makes the case for social-enterprise. Chapter 2 explores the benefits of social enterprise. Chapter 3 looks at the role of the social-entrepreneur. Chapter 4 looks at social enterprise in crisis situations. Chapter 5 looks at globalization and social entrepreneurship.

Chapter 1: The Case for Social Enterprise

Social Business: Enterprising at the Bottom of the Top of the Pyramid

Martin Brueckner, Sally Paulin, Jenna Burleson-Davis, and Samir Chatterjee

Abstract: The bottom of the pyramid (BoP) approach popularised Prahalad (2004) as well as other writers such as Hart (2005) and London (2007), calls for the engagement of business with the bottom segment of the global income pyramid, and has attracted considerable attention and debate. The BoP lens is applied chiefly to communities experiencing 'extreme poverty' in low income countries with little reference to the growing number of people living in 'relative poverty' in high income countries. For the purpose of stimulating academic debate this paper seeks to explore the role of the so-called fourth sector, a domain for hybrid business ventures of social (and, in the case of this paper, Indigenous) entrepreneurs, at what we refer to as 'the bottom at the top of the income pyramid' in Australia. Using examples of Indigenous and social entrepreneurship within disadvantaged communities, we seek to highlight the scope for fourth sector enterprises at the lower end of the income spectrum within developed countries. It is suggested that the business models found within the fourth sector offer promising, alternative approaches for addressing the economic as well as social and cultural needs of those living on the fringes of today's increasingly fragmented high-income societies.

Keywords: Social Enterprise, Indigenous Enterprise, Bottom of The Pyramid, Social Sustainability, NGOs, MNCs, For-Profit, Non-Profit

Introduction

In this chapter, we will outline our definition of 'the bottom at the top of the pyramid' in Australia, and discuss the rise of the so-called fourth sector. We will also explore the concepts of 'social and Indigenous entrepreneurship' to identify linkages and potential complementarities, using two brief examples. Our discussion focuses on the potential opportunities for fourth sector business ventures within the Australian Indigenous context.

We wish to emphasise here that chapter paper is presented with a view to stimulate discussion and academic debate on the role of social and Indigenous enterprise at the bottom of the income scale within high income countries. As such, the literature reviews presented below are aimed at providing an overview of the subject area only, and we lay no claim to an exhaustive treatment of what needs to be appreciated as a vast and growing body of literature.

Background

Poverty is one of today's most persistent social problems and one of the most pressing, yet unfulfilled, Millennium Development Goals (United Nations 2000). Despite recent improvements in absolute poverty levels (i.e., living on less than US$ 1.25 per day), the achievement of global poverty reduction targets set for 2015 remains in question (United Nations 2009) as global income disparities continue to widen (Calder 2008; Cheema 2005).

Today's poverty debate is focused chiefly on the over three billion people believed to be living in 'absolute' poverty in developing, low income countries (Chen & Ravallion 2008). These are the people Prahalad and Hart (2002) describe as living at the 'bottom of the world's income pyramid' (see Figure 1).

Annual Per Capita Income*	Tiers	Population in Millions
More Than $20,000	1	75–100
$1,500–$20,000	2 and 3	1,500–1,750
Less Than $1,500	4	4,000

Figure 1: The World's Income Pyramid - * based on purchasing power parity in US$
Source: UN World Development Report cited in Prahalad (2004)

In contrast, far less attention is focused in the BoP context on the 'relative poverty' experienced by those at the lower end of the income scale in developed and mature economies; what we describe as the bottom at the top of pyramid (see Figure 2) (Chatterjee in print). Even though, the economic 'problem' has been solved for the majority of the populations living in Tier 1 countries, a growing minority is found to be losing out on the promise of 'prosperity for the greatest number'. About 13 per cent of the population (Harding, Lloyd & Greenwell 2001), live in relative poverty in Australia, similar to the UK and the USA (Jenkins & Micklewright 2007). They lack access to socially perceived necessities (Pantazis, Gordon & Levitas 2006) and have reduced living standards compared with most other people. This socio-economic deprivation makes access to education, employment and income opportunities problematic, with flow-on consequences for health, cultural belonging and spirituality (Townsend 1987).

The BoP concept has triggered much debate and critique regarding the size of the fortunes to be found at the bottom of national income pyramids particularly with regard to the roles and responsibilities of multinational companies, NGOs and governments. There is also a litany of ethical, social and environmental concerns associated with the 'marriage' of the interests of commercial decision-makers and the so-called BoP 'markets' (e.g., Jenkins 2005; Jose 2006; Kandachar & Halme 2008; Karnani 2007; Landrum 2007; Walsh, Kress & Beyerchen 2005). At present, the theoretical debate is stalemated, and empirical evidence of socio-economic improvements in BoP markets remain mixed at best. We do not wish to add to this debate but instead seek to employ the BoP lens as a way of focusing attention on the issue of intra-country poverty in high income societies, using Australia as an exemplar case.

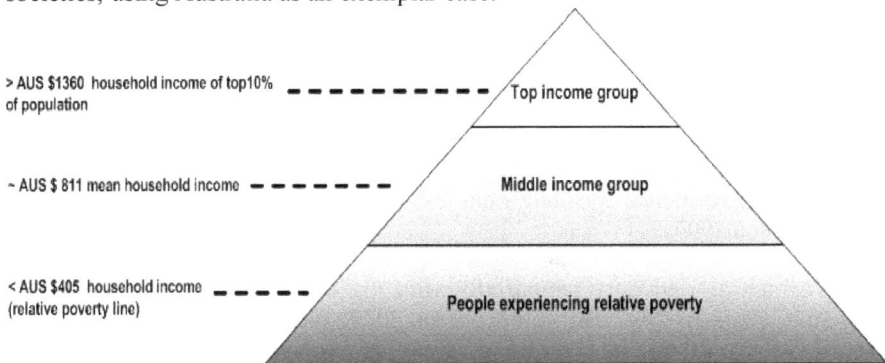

> AUS $1360 household income of top10% of population — Top income group

~ AUS $ 811 mean household income — Middle income group

< AUS $405 household income (relative poverty line) — People experiencing relative poverty

Figure 2: The Bottom at the Top of the Pyramid - Figures show weekly income per household. Household income is shown here as equivalised disposable income of a single person household, taking into account differences of size and composition of different households in Australia.
Sources: (Australian Bureau of Statistics 2009; Melbourne Institute of Applied Economic and Social Research 2009)

There are growing calls for hybrid, human-centred approaches for engagement with disadvantaged communities (Altman 2007; Kandachar & Halme 2008; Sabeti & Sector Network Concept Working Group 2009). Instead of the orthodox market-based conceptualisation of BoP, we offer an understanding of BoP as assisting communities in need of socio-economic improvements, social inclusion and cultural acceptance. While the lack of purchasing power is pivotal in explaining the hardship experienced by BoP communities, we contend that social belonging and recognition of socio-cultural and historical contexts are critical for effective engagement with disadvantaged, and, especially Indigenous communities (Schwab 1995). As Narayan (2000) suggests, the poor do not die due to lack of income but through lack of access to resources, which includes social and cultural identity as well as intact environmental systems and natural resources.

Social and Indigenous entrepreneurship have emerged in recent years as dynamic fields of academic inquiry and business practice, which – whilst remaining disparate disciplines – offer insights into alternative understandings and workings of business-society relations. It is these alternative business approaches that harbour the potential to alleviate disadvantage and offer pathways for the improvement of living standards and social cohesion, blending business acumen with a drive for innovation and a mission of social change. We argue in this paper that both Indigenous and social entrepreneurship focus on social over economic causes, driving community engagement and catering for, as well as, fostering a sense of collectivism.

The Bottom at the Top of the Pyramid: Australia's Growing Gap

The economic downturns and associated budget blowouts of the 1970s and 1980s led to Australia's wholesale adoption of economic rationalism by government (Carson & Kerr 1988; Pusey 1991; Weatherley 1994). The ensuing decades of neo-liberal economic reform under successive governments from both sides of politics (Castles 2001) have resulted in the thinning of the country's middle class (Pusey 2003) and growing income divides among Australian households (Meagher & Wilson 2008; Saunders 2003) owing to a dramatic redistribution of income and government spending from low income to high income earners (Jones 1996; Pierson 1994).

Income divisions were aggravated further by Australia's recent resources boom which slowed only temporarily with the onset of the global economic downturn (Denniss 2007; Stilwell & Jordan 2007; Western Australian Council of Social Service 2009). In contrast to Australia's boom years of the 1950s and 1960s, the economic boom in recent times resulted in pockets of concentrated and severe social disadvantage becoming entrenched across the country (Vinson, Rawsthorne & Cooper 2007). Overall, in the OECD comparison Australia compares poorly with other high incomes countries in light of widening gaps in income, wealth and opportunity between the rich and the poor (Leigh 2007; Organisation for Economic Cooperation and Development 2009a; UNICEF 2007). The experience of relative poverty in Australia is pronounced particularly amongst the country's youth (Boese & Scutella 2006; UNICEF 2007) and seniors (Organisation for Economic Cooperation and Development 2009b) as well as people with disabilities (The Physical Disability Council of Australia 2003), ethnic minorities (Dawkins, Gregg & Scutella 2002) and the country's Indigenous population.

Indigenous Australians rate as the most disadvantaged population segment in Australia (Foley 2003), with over 40 per cent living below the official poverty line (Hunter 2006) at income levels comparable to those of people in developing countries (Australian Medical Association 2008; Walter 2009). Past policies of dispossession and 'protection' led to the subjugation as well as social and economic exclusion of Indigenous people (Markus 1994). While the 1970s saw a policy shift toward self-determination and subsequently reconciliation,

Indigenous Australians still face socio-economic disadvantage and discrimination (Human Rights and Equal Opportunity Commission 2003).

While Indigenous people make up only 2.5 per cent of the country's population, they are overrepresented in the country's welfare statistics, facing much reduced life expectancy, higher incidences of mental and other health problems and high mortality rates. Comparably low high school completion rates and low household incomes mean that Indigenous Australians are about two to three times more likely to be impoverished than the rest of the population (see Australian Bureau of Statistics & Australian Institute of Health and Welfare 2008; Human Rights and Equal Opportunity Commission 2003; New South Wales Department of Education and Training & Charles Sturt University 2009). The political reforms of recent decades only served to widen the disparities between Indigenous and non-Indigenous Australians.

Against the background of life at the bottom of Australia's income pyramid we now explore the potential contribution of social and Indigenous enterprise to disadvantaged communities in Australia beyond socio-economic improvements as they relate to aspects such as empowerment, social cohesion and community well-being.

Social Enterprise: A Brief Overview

The last three decades witnessed a convergence of the three fundamental economic sectors in many countries around the world. These are the first sector (business or for-profit sector), the second sector (public or government sector) and the third sector (voluntary or non-profit sector). Economic downturns, budget blowouts and globalisation pressures have diminished the ability (and willingness) of governments to deliver effective social services (Kettl 2000). In response, governments in the UK and Australia are increasingly promoting social enterprise as a vehicle for the protection of the public good through business solutions (e.g., FaHCSIA 2009; Office of the Third Sector 2009). Meanwhile, third sector organisations, acting as welfare related service providers for governments, are assuming a stronger market orientation using enterprising to fund their programmes (Gray, Healy & Crofts 2003; Kerlin 2006; Nicholls 2006). Similarly, business has started to respond to growing stakeholder demands for 'triple bottom line' management (after Elkington 1994), and terms such as 'corporate governance', 'corporate social responsibility' and 'corporate citizenship' are now widely found (Blyth 2005; Pedersen 2006).

This convergence has led to a blurring of once clearly demarcated sectoral boundaries and given rise to a new fourth sector, which we view as the domain of a growing number of social enterprise models that fall outside the confines of the traditional sectors. Social entrepreneurship is a relatively new field of inquiry, debate and practice and as a discrete academic field still in its infancy (Borzaga & Defourny 2001; Bull 2008; Chell 2007; Dees 1996; Kerlin 2006; Rhodes & Donnelly-Cox 2008; Sud, van Sandt & Baugous 2009). Despite much interest in this area, social enterprise has remained a dispersed field owing to the varying definitions which co-evolved on both sides of the Atlantic.

Debates on social enterprise are frequently premised on the dichotomy between first sector (for-profit) and third sector (non-profit) and activities, each representing the respective endpoints of the spectrum of enterprising activities (Dees 1996, 2001). In recent years, social enterprise has emerged as a conceptual bridge between the goals of economic and social value (see Figure 3), effectively marrying the competing aims through the creation of 'blended value' or a 'dual value' (Alter 2007).

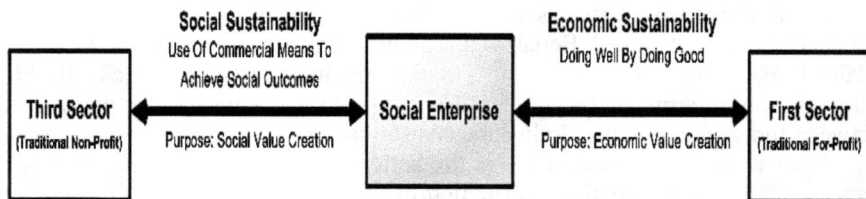

Figure 3: The Profit-Non-Profit Dichotomy
Source: based on Alter (2007: 14)

While some commentators see social enterprise as an effective way of reconciling conflict between economic and social causes (Evers 2001), others express concern about the dangers of associated tensions and trade-offs (Arthur et al. 2006). US social enterprise theorists and practitioners are more comfortable with the notion of revenue-generation than their international counterparts based on a tradition of fundraising by third sector organisations (Kerlin 2006). In contrast, Western Europeans limit the field of social enterprise to those organisations belonging to the third sector (Nyssens & Kerlin 2005). Their understanding of social enterprise includes the unique element of the social economy where social benefit is the main driving force (Kerlin 2006). In Australia, social enterprise practice is not new (Jones 2007) but as a field of academic inquiry still comparatively young (Gray, Healy & Crofts 2003). A recent study of social enterprises in Western Australia revealed a closer alignment with the US model (Davis 2009). It remains unanswered, however, which social enterprise tradition Australia as a whole will follow or whether the country will develop its own hybrid models as can be found in countries like Bangladesh, (e.g., Grameen Bank).

There is considerable debate as to whether social enterprise represents an area of sectoral overlap, a subset of one of the three existing sectors or a sector in its own right (see Figures 4 and 5). In other words, despite our earlier references to a fourth sector, agreement on its existence is by no means a given.

Social enterprises, when understood as a sector subset, largely fall within the domain of the third sector, highlighting that social over economic value creation is at the core of socio-entrepreneurial activity (Alter 2007; Westall & Chalkley 2007). However, despite the social orientation of the third sector, there is concern about the gradual subsuming of social enterprise by the first sector in the quest for greater efficiency as favoured by both business and the government (Arthur et al. 2006; Dart 2004; Dees 2001; Hardy 2004).

Supporters of a cross-sectoral understanding of social enterprise (see Figure 4) see it as a reflection of the multiple origins, drivers and contexts of the social enterprise tradition (Seanor, Bull & Ridley-Duff 2007). This approach highlights both the concurrent emergence of social enterprise within each sector and the convergence of the sectors, with social enterprise seen as the point of common overlap between them (Aiken 2006). The blurring of the sectoral lines (Dart 2004), however, makes delineation difficult in that socio-entrepreneurial activity of first and second sector organisations can be almost indistinct from third sector activities (Westall & Chalkley 2007).

Finally, social enterprise is seen by others as part of an emergent fourth sector (see Figure 5), driven by global concerns over income inequality, environmental degradation and social injustice (Feiss 2009). This new fourth sector allows hybrid entrepreneurs to set up new business models, which fall outside the traditional sectoral boundaries. These are the archetypal 'for-good' or 'for-benefit' organisations with an embedded social purpose and commitment to stakeholder responsibility (Sabeti & Sector Network Concept Working Group 2009).

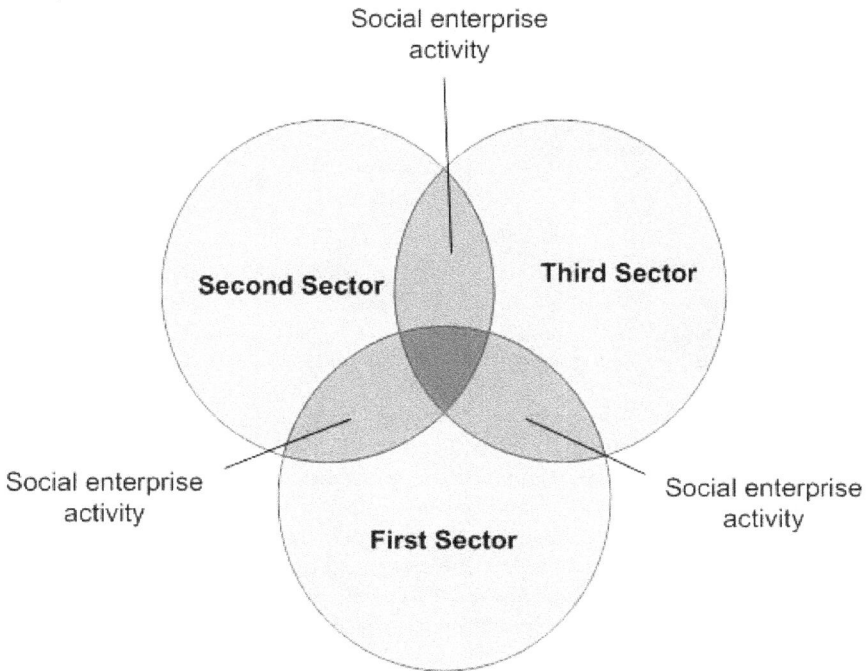

Figure 4: Cross-Sectoral Understanding of Social Enterprise
Source: based on Seanor, Bull & Ridley-Duff (2007: 5)

Examples of a these fourth sector ('for-good') organisations are shown in Figure 5, which also depicts the convergence of the traditional sectors and underlying drivers. While corporate social responsibility and ethical business conduct are shown as motivations for change within the first sector, a more pronounced market orientation is identified as the key driver within the second and third sectors for a shift toward social enterprise. The emerging fourth sector is shown to be made up of an array of organisational models, which borrow from, but fall outside, the traditional three sectors.

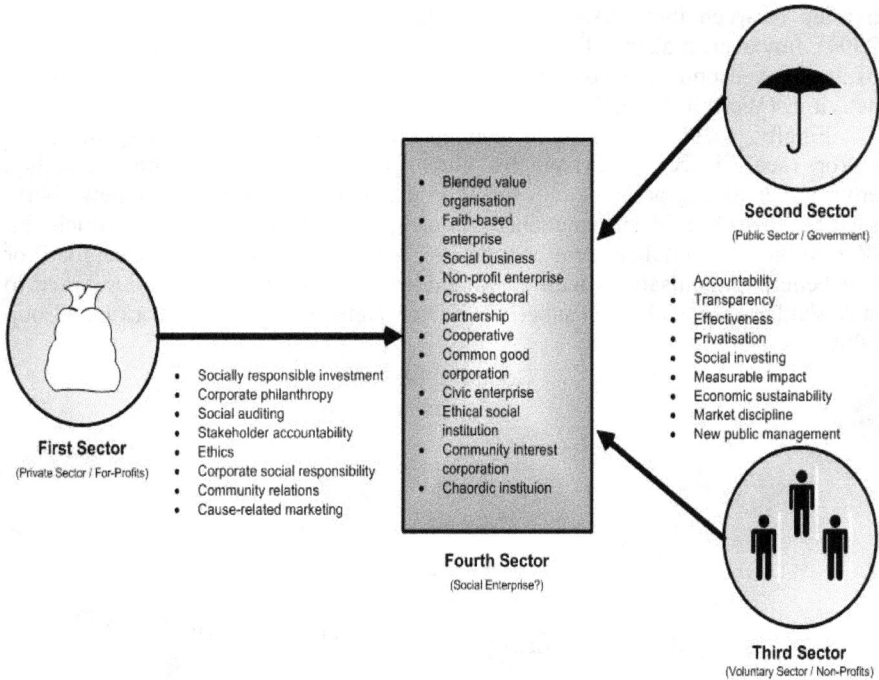

First Sector
(Private Sector / For-Profits)

- Socially responsible investment
- Corporate philanthropy
- Social auditing
- Stakeholder accountability
- Ethics
- Corporate social responsibility
- Community relations
- Cause-related marketing

- Blended value organisation
- Faith-based enterprise
- Social business
- Non-profit enterprise
- Cross-sectoral partnership
- Cooperative
- Common good corporation
- Civic enterprise
- Ethical social institution
- Community interest corporation
- Chaordic instituion

Fourth Sector
(Social Enterprise?)

Second Sector
(Public Sector / Government)

- Accountability
- Transparency
- Effectiveness
- Privatisation
- Social investing
- Measurable impact
- Economic sustainability
- Market discipline
- New public management

Third Sector
(Voluntary Sector / Non-Profits)

Figure 5: The Emerging Hybrid Models of the Fourth Sector
Source: based on Sabeti & Sector Network Concept Working Group (2009: 7-8)

Despite the obvious differences in typology, social enterprise traditions have three aspects in common: sociality or the pursuit of social objectives as a core function; market orientation, using business principles to organise their activities; and innovation, which is key to entrepreneurialism (after Nicholls & Cho 2006). These dimensions are also reflected in the concept of Indigenous entrepreneurship, which similar to the concepts of entrepreneurship (Dana 1996) and social entrepreneurship (Borzaga & Defourny 2001) lacks definitional clarity (Paredo & Anderson 2006), compounded by difficulties in defining indigeneity (Frederick 2008).

Marginality theory (e.g., Merton 1975), as argued by Frederick (2008), suggests enterprising activities to be more common among disadvantaged communities who seek to overcome socio-economic exclusion. Accordingly, Indigenous people might be considered more likely to start up a business venture in light of their experience of exclusion and discrimination (Hindle & Moroz 2009). On the face of it, this theory does not hold in the Australian context as systemic Indigenous disadvantage and cultural traditions has not translated into the strong uptake of Indigenous business ventures. At the same time, Indigenous Australians face a formidable list of barriers for setting up enterprising activities, which include geographic, cultural and economic disadvantage as well as political and structural hurdles (see Cape York 2005; European Commission 2003; Impax SIA Consulting 2001). Thus, the absence of large numbers of Indigenous businesses in Australia may need to be seen as a function of systemic disadvantage as opposed to a lack of entrepreneurial drive.

While Indigenous entrepreneurship may simply be understood as entrepreneurial activities carried out by Indigenous people (Dana & Anderson 2006), it is our contention that community based Indigenous entrepreneurship in Australia is well aligned with the key tenets of social entrepreneurship with social objectives at its core ; the delivery of benefits to Indigenous communities (Lindsay 2005). These benefits go beyond important socio-economic improvements. Enterprising activities are also seen as a means of liberation and self-determination and a vehicle for social inclusion and repositioning (Foley 2003). Indeed, the meta-analysis of Indigenous enterprise by Hindle & Moroz (2009) suggests the redress of relative disadvantage to be the dominant agenda for Indigenous entrepreneurs in Australia. They define Indigenous entrepreneurship as "venture creation or the pursuit of economic opportunity or both for the purpose of diminishing Indigenous disadvantage through culturally viable and community acceptable wealth creation." The generation of profits and income are vital in this regard for they lead to financial autonomy. Yet, they only form one of many other building blocks of Indigenous enterprise, which ensure what Hindle and Moroz (2009) call 'cultural viability' and 'community acceptability'. In this context, Moylan (2008) describes five interdependent building blocks of Indigenous enterprises, which include:

- culture;
- family;
- motivations, goals and priorities;
- decision-making; and
- commercial considerations.

While Indigenous entrepreneurship does not exclude individual wealth creation, due to its foregrounding of social, community-focused aspects we consider it well aligned with social entrepreneurship. Also, Indigenous business models found in Australia's remote Indigenous communities (Altman 2007), where customary practices are blended with commercial activities, mirror the character of the hybrid organisations ascribed to the fourth sector. It is against this background that we explore below two examples of Indigenous community focused social enterprises in Australia.

Social Business in Action: Local Experiences

The ventures of social and Indigenous entrepreneurs can take many organisational forms ranging from large publicly traded multinational companies to small local civil society institutions. The Social Enterprise World Forum held in Melbourne in 2009, which showcased successful social enterprises in the region, confirmed that the purpose and processes of social enterprise have a wide variation in their meaning to people. Nonetheless, in spite of these differences, as suggested by

Rangan, Leonard and McDonald (2008), the universal measure of social enterprise performance appears to be their 'social impact'; how well businesses mitigate the problem identified in their mission. We have cited two examples of successful case studies within the broad spectrum of Indigenous social enterprise below.

Prescribing solutions for social and economic difficulties faced by Indigenous communities through enterprise creation is a complex process, and there is no 'one size fits all' template that can be implemented due to differences in local conditions and community expectations. The first example refers to the Fred Hollows Foundation-Jawoyn Association Nyirranggulung Nutrition Project, undertaken in 2000-2003 in the Katherine East Region of the North Territory, which represents a case of working effectively within a local context (Sullivan et al. 2005). The Fred Hollows Foundation (FHF) signed a memorandum of understanding with the communities of Wugularr, Barunga, Manyallaluk and Bulman to assist them to promote healthy eating and redesign their stores to complement this. While the FHF employed nutritionists and partnered with a major supermarket retailer who provided a store consultant, the project outcomes were to ensure ownership and control of the enterprise remained with the communities. Sullivan et al (2005) carried out an evaluation of the FHF partnership project and for the purposes of this paper, we will refer to their comments on the community store project.

Nutrition in isolated Indigenous communities is generally poor and limited by the availability of fresh and healthy food choices and lack of education as to what comprises a healthy diet. Community members rely on their local 'store' for everyday items, supplemented by shopping trips to major towns to access a larger variety of goods and services. In many communities, stores are leased by individuals and thus lack connections to increased buying power and the ability to carry and store a wide range of fresh food. The Stores Consultant (an experienced supermarket manager) worked with the Wugularr community store committee to improve practices in the store with regard to layout, training, financial accountability and promotion and proper storage of a variety of healthy food stuffs including on the job training of the store manager and other employees in the Woolworths Supermarket in Katherine. This training and store development worked alongside the nutrition program by revamping the 'fast food' takeaway menus to more healthy choices and assisting the Women's Centre to provide meals for school children and the aged (Sullivan et al. 2005).

The Store Consultant worked with the community on an ongoing basis to implement the changes at the store and to support the community's appointed store manager. The success of this project depended on the ability of the experts to convey knowledge and information to the community members and, importantly, to listen to and understand the desires of the community. Some problems were encountered with regard to employee turnover, understanding of financial practices and trying to implement too much too soon. It was also apparent that a strong store committee needed to be representative of the community as a whole and that for the store and the wider project to succeed, the community needed to understand the financial and health implications for their community. The FHF successfully addressed this by introducing the Money $tory which presents financial information in a manner which does not rely on literacy and numeracy and "enables people with limited formal education to make financial decisions about their organisations, based on current accounting data. The program was developed by Hugh Lovsey of Little Fish/Pangaea" (Sullivan et al. 2005).

Sullivan et al. (2005) provide a comprehensive evaluation of this store program and list some of the issues identified with working with Indigenous communities including the readiness of individuals to be involved; availability of educational opportunities to develop appropriate skills; cross cultural awareness on the part of outsiders to ensure that the community supports programs and takes ownership. Indigenous community relationships are complex and not easily understood by European 'experts', with much respect given to Elders who must be included in all projects at the beginning stages and who may then devolve responsibility to other community members (Day 2009). The program was successful in many respects but successful transference of the store concept to partner communities proved more difficult due to issues raised when entering an Indigenous community and implementing new ideas.

The second example is a case from east Arnhem Land where ongoing entrepreneurial activities appear to bear the hallmarks of social enterprise. While the case is subject to further inquiry, preliminary insights suggest that local communities have been successful in harnessing local skills and capacity to carry out community-orientated ventures. The case reported here describes a successful housing construction project carried out by Gumatj community members, who represent one of the 13 Yolngu clans in the region (for a detailed description see Pearson & Helms 2010). The project entailed the construction of a five room bunkhouse at the Garrathiya cattle station located 100 km south of Nhulunbuy. The project is noteworthy since it was commenced and completed against the backdrop of the controversial former Howard government's 2007 Intervention in the Northern Territories of Australia, which - inter alia - sought to improve Indigenous housing and saw large sums of federal government money spent without successfully addressing the acute housing shortage (Mercer 2009; Toohey 2009).

The local housing project was a community-based venture (after Peredo & Chrisman 2006) embedded in existing social structures and cultural connections with the country. The local arrangements represent an amalgam of customary and commercial activities and mirror what Altman (2007) describes as hybrid economies in Australia's remote communities. Construction timber was harvested locally, sourced from the savannah forest on community-owned land using a mobile timber mill. Participants worked on their own ancestral lands with other community members, with the opportunity and flexibility to go hunting and fishing, while gaining valuable job skills and cultural benefits. At the core of the venture was the goal to build accommodation for five community members who worked at the Garrathiya cattle station, who until then had been living in 30-year old sea containers. In contrast, economic rewards, while a factor, were found to be a peripheral aspect of the project (Pearson & Helms 2010).

The project was largely funded by the Gumatj Corporation through the receipt of mining royalties and enjoyed outside support garnered by community leaders. Established industry links to Forestry Tasmania ensured appropriate training of community members and instruction in the timber production processes. Construction drawings and milled timber lists were provided by the Architectural School of the University of Tasmania. Links to and support from the three levels of government (Federal, State, Local) ensured logistical support and reductions in red tape as well as government subsidies.

The bunk house was completed in 2009 at a cost of less than AUS$200 000. The construction of comparable accommodation in the East Arnhem Land region is usually undertaken by non-Indigenous, non-local companies, using resources and building materials sourced from further afield. Therefore, the construction cost of a similar accommodation would usually be in the order of AUS$800 000. Overall, the housing project was not only completed more quickly and at a lower cost compared to conventional projects, it also served the purpose of creating community involvement, skill transfer as well as direct and indirect economic benefits accrued in a culturally sensitive manner (Pearson & Helms 2010).

Discussion

The examples above illustrate the various forms social enterprises can take. While partnerships with corporations can be effective in addressing community needs, they are dependent on partner organisations such as FHF to provide acceptance, penetration and, most importantly, deliver positive social impacts. In the absence of such partnerships, the involvement of corporations with poor and disadvantaged communities harbours the risk of being culturally insensitive and potentially exploitative and of companies being unable to gain access to communities in need. In addition, corporate engagements with disadvantaged communities in countries like Australia often form part of contractual arrangements (e.g., mining lease agreements) or are usually philanthropic and strategic in nature with companies seeking reputational and other commercial benefits (Centre for Corporate Public Affairs 2007). Concerns about problems such as these fuel the BoP debate today (e.g., Karnani 2007).

Similarly, government-led programmes are often problematic for they seek to 'mainstream' or 'normalise' disadvantaged communities through skill and employment initiatives which foster what Altman (2007: 1) refers to as the "orthodox engagement with the market either through sale of labour or through operation of commercial business", this being conventional for-profit ventures. Programmes such as these promulgate a free market ethic, which is prone to miss the mark of acceptability with communities who lack a sufficient economic base and/or have strong cultural attachments. In the Indigenous context these attachments often translate into strong community orientation and sense of collectivism which are in stark contrast to the individualistic, market orientation found within the dominant western culture (Altman 2000; Schwab 1995). Aspects of control and contextual fit are thus vital. In this regard both cases have illustrated how the respective ventures were able to generate local acceptance but also maintain local control whilst helping build local capacity and triggering community engagement.

The FHF initiative showed how careful facilitation enabled communities to have ultimate responsibility for owning and making the community stores work. The Gumatj housing project illustrated how through the combination of community internal initiative and outside assistance community members could participate in the local community on their terms and in ways that were compatible with their attachment to land and culture. Interestingly, the Gumatj housing project proved to be more efficient, to borrow a western market-orientated term, concerning project completion and more cost effective when compared to conventional non-Indigenous-run housing projects. In addition, the project led to both direct and indirect community benefits, which conventional skill and employment programmes tend not to achieve. Also motivationally, community-orientated programmes provide a stronger sense of ownership, control and belonging in contrast to initiatives that target individuals.

Projects such as community stores or community housing provide participants with the skills in demand within the formal economy. Arguably, conventional 'mainstreaming' programmes seek to accomplish similar outcomes, yet in the belief that the free market will reward the efforts of those who take responsibility for their economic future. The difference is, and this is why we argue in favour of hybrid, fourth sector approaches to dealing with relative poverty and disadvantage, that socio-entrepreneurial ventures, especially those that are community driven, can be mindful of contexts such as culture, history and local settings. We thus deem them more likely to offer targeted and more suitable opportunities for disadvantaged people to become involved in mainstream market activities. This is not to suggest that the ongoing, or even increased, involvement of the traditional sectors is not required. Nor are we suggesting that fourth sector models will prove to be financially viable or socially acceptable by default. In fact, the examples cited earlier still need to prove their long-term effectiveness. What fourth sector ventures model, however, is a different way of engaging with communities in need, which in turn may offer insights to actors operating within the traditional sectors. The seeming social effectiveness of these ventures is what sets them apart from conventional development-focused initiatives which typically foreground factors such as employability and income generation, assuming that social benefits will follow. Fourth sector models, in our estimation, reverse this formula by placing emphasis on social and community benefits which will translate into socio-economic improvements. While there are obvious unanswered questions concerning the transferability of such hybrid models as well as their economic footing and longevity, we hope to have illustrated the potential the fourth sector harbours within as well as outside the BoP context.

Earlier parts of this paper described the extent and drivers of relative poverty and disadvantage experienced by segments of Australian society. It was made plain that considerable scope exists for social and Indigenous enterprise in light of the growing needs of disadvantaged communities in this country. While we do suggest that relative poverty in Australia is comparable with the extreme poverty experienced in developing counties, we consider current trends in inequality and growing disadvantage a matter of concern and area in need of attention. In this regard, the exemplar cases illustrated how social enterprising can result in positive social impacts, underscoring the argument for the potential of fourth sector ventures. At present, however, 'for-benefit' organisations face institutional barriers, which potentially prevent their establishment and growth.

Neoliberal policy prescriptions, which have dominated Australian politics in recent decades, continue to favour an individualistic and pro-growth approach when dealing with disadvantage. This policy approach finds expression in rural and remote Australia where people who lack economic opportunity are called upon to relocate to places where such opportunities can be found (Altman 2007). This form of labour migration is currently being reintroduced in the Northern Territories, with a view to relocate communities living in remote so-called 'outstations' to regional centres to enhance their chances of employment and socio-economic improvements. It is policy approaches such as these that leave little room for alternative models to be tested in remote Australia and disallow the creation and coexistence of community-based hybrid economies. Also, Australia's taxation system merely distinguishes between first sector and third sector organisations, excluding alternative models which for example would allow for limited profit distribution as can be observed in parts of Europe (Kerlin 2006). Yet, with the taxation of third sector organisations in Australia currently under review (Third Sector 2009), it is hoped for that changes in taxation law will enable the establishment, growth and maturation of fourth sector ventures.

Conclusion

Overall, we hope to have provided stimulation for debate on the role and future of Indigenous and social enterprises within the BoP context and offered insights into their potential in addressing increasing levels of relative poverty in high income countries. As the fields of social and Indigenous entrepreneurship are still relatively young, they make fertile ground for academic work and discussion.

In particular, we see merit in the empirical investigation of the social and cultural efficacy of social and Indigenous enterprises and the degree to which they can act as drivers of social and inclusion and cultural acceptance. Empirical testing is also required of the economic base of fourth sector ventures coupled with an exploration of alternative uses for royalty schemes and government subsidies in support of fourth sector activities. Initiatives such as these should also be coupled with an examination of any structural barriers for the uptake of fourth sector business ventures (e.g., taxation systems) so as to facilitate their emergence and growth.

Finally, we consider there to be scope for cross-fertilisation between 'traditional' BoP-based research focusing on extreme poverty and work in the area of relative disadvantage. While we do not wish to suggest that attention be shifted away from those with arguably the strongest need for attention, complementarities and overlaps between research in the areas of extreme and relative disadvantage may well exist. In this regard, we see scope for social enterprise experiences to be transferrable and lessons learnt from BoP communities to be of relevance for disadvantaged communities in countries like Australia. For example, the concept of micro-credit, as modelled by Grameen

Bank in Bangladesh, is now widely applied across the world in both developing and developed countries.

Overall, our attempt here was to instigate discussion and debate on what we consider concepts and ideas that challenge as well as enrich our understanding of commerce and development as means of addressing relative poverty and disadvantage. Much needed empirical work in the area will hopefully enable us in future to test whether our inclinations were well-founded and whether these concepts have wider applications.

References

Aiken, M 2006, 'Towards market or state? Tensions and opportunities in the evolutionary path of three UK social enterprises', in M Nyssens (ed.), Social enterprise: At the crossroads of market, public policies and civil society Routledge, New York, pp. 259-71.

Alter, K 2007, Social enterprise typology, Virtue Ventures, Washington, DC.

Altman, JC 2000, The economic status of Indigenous Australians (CAEPR Discussion Paper No. 193), Centre for Aboriginal Economic Policy Research - The Australian National University, Canberra.

Altman, JC 2007, Alleviating poverty in remote Indigenous Australia: The role of the hybrid economy. Topical Issue No. 10/2007, Centre for Aboriginal Economic Policy Research, ANU, Canberra.

Arthur, L, Scott Cato, M, Smith, R & Keenan, T 2006, 'Where is the social in social enterprise?', in 4th Annual Social Enterprise Research Conference, London, 4th-5th July.

Australian Bureau of Statistics 2003, Revised household income distribution statistics [Cat.No. 1350.0], ABS, Canberra.

Australian Bureau of Statistics 2009, Household income and income distribution, Australia , 2007-08 [Cat.No. 6523.0], ABS, Canberra.

Australian Bureau of Statistics & Australian Institute of Health and Welfare 2008, The health and welfare of Australia's Aboriginal and Torres Strait Islander peoples, ABS & AIHW, Canberra.

Australian Medical Association 2008, Australian Medical Association report card series. Aboriginal and Torres Strait Islander health: Ending the cycle of vulnerability, AMA, Barton, ACT.

Blyth, A 2005, 'Business behaving responsibly', Director, vol. 59, no. 1, p. 30.

Boese, M & Scutella, R 2006, The brotherhood's social barometer. Challenges facing Australian youth, Brotherhood of St Laurence, Fitzroy, Vic.

Borzaga, C & Defourny, J (eds.) 2001, The emergence of social enterprise, Routledge, London.

Bull, M 2008, 'Challenging tensions: critical, theoretical and empirical perspectives on social enterprise', International Journal of Entrepreneurial Behaviour & Research, vol. 14, no. 5, pp. 268-75.

Calder, J 2008, 'Mobilizing human energy', in G Gardner & T Prugh (eds), State of the world 2008, Worldwatch Institute, Washington, DC, pp. 169-80.

Cape York 2005, Cape York Indigenous employment strategy: "Local jobs for local people", Kleinhardt-FGI Pty Ltd: Business Mapping Solutions Pty Ltd.

Carson, E & Kerr, H 1988, 'Social welfare Down Under', Critical Social Policy, vol. 8, no. 23, pp. 70-82.

Castles , FG 2001, 'A farewell to Australia's welfare state', International Journal of Health Services vol. 31, no. 3, pp. 537-44.

Centre for Corporate Public Affairs 2007, Corporate community investment in Australia, CCPA, Melbourne.

Chatterjee, S in print, 'Multinational firm strategy and global poverty alleviation: Frameworks and possibilities for building shared commitment', Journal of Human Values.

Cheema, GS 2005, Building democratic institutions: Governance reform in developing countries, Kumarian Press, Bloomfield, CT.

Chell, E 2007, 'Social enterprise and entrepreneurship. Towards a convergent theory of the entrepreneurial process ', International Small Business Journal vol. 25, no. 1, pp. 5-26.

Chen, S & Ravallion, M 2008, The developing world is poorer than we thought, but no less successful in the fight against poverty, World Bank, New York.

Dana, L 1996, 'Self-employment in the Canadian sub-arctic: An exploratory study', Canadian Journal of Administrative Sciences, vol. 13, no. 1, pp. 65-81.

Dana, L & Anderson, R (eds.) 2006, International handbook of indigenous entrepreneurship, Edward Elgar, Cheltenham, UK.

Dart, R 2004, 'The legitimacy of social enterprise', Nonprofit Management and Leadership, vol. 14, no. 4, pp. 411-24.

Davis, J 2009, An overview of current conceptions of social enterprise in Western Australia, Business Dissertation, Curtin University of Technology.

Dawkins, P, Gregg, P & Scutella, R 2002, 'The Australian Economic Review', 35, vol. 2, no. 133–154.

Day, J 2009, Perth, March 5.

Dees, JG 1996, The social enterprise spectrum: From philanthropy to commerce, Harvard Business School Press, Cambridge, MA.

Dees, JG 2001, The meaning of social entrepreneurship, Center for the Advancement of Social Entrepreneurship - Duke University, Durham, NC.

Denniss, R 2007, The boom for whom? Who benefits from the WA resources boom? , The Greens - Office of Senator Rachel Siewert, Perth.

Elkington, J 1994, 'Towards the sustainable corporation: Win-win-win business strategies for sustainable development', California Management Review, vol. 36, no. 2, pp. 90-100.

European Commission 2003, Building the information society in Europe: A pathway approach to employment interventions for disadvantaged groups, Itech Research, Dublin.

Evers, A 2001, 'The significance of social capital in multiple goal and resource structure of social enterprises', in C Borzaga & J Defourny (eds), The emergence of social enterprise, Routledge, London, pp. 296-311.

FaHCSIA 2009, A National Compact with the Third Sector. Retrieved 5th November, from http://www.fahcsia.gov.au/sa/communities/progserv/nationalcompact/Pages/default.aspx

Feiss, C 2009, 'Social enterprise - the fledgling fourth sector', Financial Times [on-line], 15th June.

Foley, D 2003, 'An examination of Indigenous Australian entrepreneurs', Journal of Developmental Entrepreneurship, vol. 8, no. 2, pp. 133-51.

Frederick, HH 2008, 'Introduction to special issue on indigenous entrepreneurs', Journal of Enterprising Communities, vol. 2, no. 3, pp. 185-91.

Gray, M, Healy, K & Crofts, P 2003, 'Social enterprise: is it the business of social work?', Australian Social Work, vol. 56, no. 2, pp. 141-53.

Harding, A, Lloyd, R & Greenwell, H 2001, Financial Disadvantage in Australia – 1990 to 2000, The Smith Family, Sydney.

Hardy, R 2004, 'Social enterprise the new economic engine', Business Strategy Review, vol. 15, no. 4, pp. 39-43.

Hart, SL 2005 Capitalism at the crossroads, Wharton School Publishing, Upper Saddle River.

Hindle, K & Moroz, P 2009, 'Indigenous entrepreneurship as a research field: Developing a definitional framework from the emerging canon', International Entrepreneurship and Management Journal. Availabale online: http://dx.doi.org/10.1007/s11365-009-0111-x.

Human Rights and Equal Opportunity Commission 2003, Social justice report, Human Rights and Equal Opportunity Commission, Canberra.

Hunter, B (ed.) 2006, Assessing the evidence on Indigenous socioeconomic outcomes: A focus on the 2002 NATSISS, ANU E Press, Canberra.

Impax SIA Consulting 2001, Submission to the Joint Standing Committee on Foreign Affairs, Defence and Trade, trade Sub-Committee Enquiry. Enterprising Australia – Planning, preparing and profiting from trade and investment, Impax SIA Consulting, Brisbane, Queensland.

Jenkins, R 2005, 'Globalization, corporate social responsibility and poverty', International Affairs, vol. 81, no. 3, pp. 525-40.

Jenkins, SP & Micklewright, J 2007, Inequality and poverty re-examined, Oxford University Press, Oxford.

Jones, MA 1996, The Australian welfare state, Allen & Unwin, Crows Nest, NSW.

Jones, MA 2007, 'Unpacking social enterprise. A discussion paper', Public forum with a focus on youth, enterprise and Indigenous affairs, 14th August, Sydney.

Jose, PD 2006, 'Rethinking the BoP: A critical examination of current BoP models', in Workshop at the Centre for Business Relationships, Accountability, Sustainability and Society (BRASS), Cardiff University, 3rd April.

Kandachar, P & Halme, M (eds.) 2008, Sustainability challenges and solutions at the base of the pyramid: Business, technology and the poor, Greenleaf Publishing, Sheffield.

Karnani, A 2007, 'The mirage of marketing to the bottom of the pyramid. How the private sector can help alleviate poverty', California Management Review, vol. 49, no. 4, pp. 90-111.

Kerlin, JA 2006, 'Social enterprise in the United States and Europe: Understanding and learning from the differences', Voluntas, vol. 17, pp. 247-63.

Kettl, DF 2000, 'The transformation of governance: Globalization, devolution, and the role of government ', Public Administration Review, vol. 60, no. 6, pp. 488-97.

Landrum, NE 2007, 'Advancing the 'base of the pyramid' debate', Strategic Management Review, vol. 1, no. 1, pp. 1-12.

Leigh, A 2007, The distribution of top incomes in Australia, The Australian National University, Canberra.

Lindsay, NJ 2005, 'Toward a cultural model of indigenous entrepreneurial attitude', Academy of Marketing Science Review, vol. 5. Available: http://www.amsreview.org/articles/lindsay05-2005.pdf.

London, T 2007, A base-of-the-pyramid perspective on poverty alleviation (Growing inclusive markets working paper series), United Nations Development Program, Washington, DC.

Markus, A 1994, Australian race relations 1788-1993, Allen & Unwin, Sydney.

Meagher, G & Wilson, S 2008, 'Richer, but more unequal: Perceptions of inequality in Australia 1987-2005', The Journal of Australian Political Economy, vol. 61, no. June, pp. 220-43.

Melbourne Institute of Applied Economic and Social Research 2009, Poverty lines: Australia June Quarter 2009, University of Melbourne, Melbourne.

Mercer, P 2009, 'Delays hit Aboriginals homes plan', BBC News, 5th September. Retrieved 1st November, from http://news.bbc.co.uk/2/hi/asia-pacific/8239402.stm.

Merton, RK 1975, Social theory and social structure, Free Press of Glencoe, Glencoe, IL.

Moylan, L 2008, 'Aboriginal enterprise implications for government and industry', in Desert Knowledge Symposium, Alice Springs, NT, 3rd - 7th November.

Narayan, D 2000, Voices of the poor: Can anyone r us?, Oxford University Press & World Bank, Oxford, UK.

New South Wales Department of Education and Training & Charles Sturt University 2009, Social justice & human rights issues: A global perspective Retrieved 21st December, from http://www.hsc.csu.edu.au/ab_studies/rights/global/social_justice_global /sjwelcome.status.front.htm

Nicholls, A 2006, Social entrepreneurship: New models of sustainable social change, Oxford University Press, New York.

Nicholls, A & Cho, AH 2006, 'Social entrepreneurship: The structuration of a field', in A Nicholls (ed.), Social entrepreneurship. New models of sustainable social change, Oxford University Press, New York.

Nyssens, M & Kerlin, J 2005, Social enterprise in Europe, Unpublished paper.

Office of the Third Sector 2009, Office of the Third Sector supports government departments to explore social enterprise ideas. Retrieved 5th November, from http://www.cabinetoffice.gov.uk/third_sector.aspx

Organisation for Economic Cooperation and Development 2009a, 2009 OECD Factbook, OECD, Paris.

Organisation for Economic Cooperation and Development 2009b,

Pensions at a glance 2009. Retirement-income systems in OECD countries, OECD, Paris.

Pantazis, C, Gordon, D & Levitas, R 2006, Poverty and social exclusion in Britain: the millennium survey, The Policy Press, Bristol.

Paredo, AM & Anderson, RB 2006, 'Indigenous entrepreneurship research: Themes and variations', International Research in Business Disciplines, vol. 5, pp. 253-73.

Pearson, CAL & Helms, K 2010, 'Building social entrepreneurship in a remote Australian indigenous community: the East Arnhem land housing construction case', *Journal of Australian Indigenous Issues* vol. 13, no. 4, pp. 2-18.

Pedersen, ER 2006, 'Making corporate social responsibility operable: How companies translate stakeholder dialogue into practice', Business and Society Review, vol. 112, no. 2, pp. 137-63.

Peredo, AM & Chrisman, JJ 2006, 'Toward a theory of community-based enterprise', Academy of Management Journal, vol. 31, no. 2, pp. 309-28.

Pierson , P 1994, Dismantling the welfare state? Reagan, Thatcher and the politics of retrenchment, Cambridge University Press, Cambridge.

Prahalad, CK 2004, The fortune at the bottom of the pyramid, Wharton School Publishing, Upper Saddle River, NJ.

Prahalad, CK & Hart, SL 2002, 'The fortune at the bottom of the pyramid', Strategy + Business, vol. 26, pp. 1-15.

Pusey, M 1991, Economic rationalism in Canberra: a nation-building state changes its mind, Cambridge University Press, Cambridge.

Pusey, M 2003, The experience of middle Australia: the dark side of economic reform, Cambridge University Press, Cambridge.

Rangan, V, Leonard, H & McDonald, S 2008, The future of social enterprise. Harvard Business School Working Paper No. 08-103. Harvard Business School, Boston.

Rhodes, ML & Donnelly-Cox, G 2008, 'Social entrepreneurship as a performance landscape: The case of 'front line'', Emergence: Complexity and Organization, vol. 10, no. 3, pp. 35-50.

Sabeti, H & Sector Network Concept Working Group 2009, The emerging fourth sector, The Aspen Institute, Washington, DC.

Saunders, P 2003, Examining recent changes in income distribution in Australia (SPRC Discussion Paper No. 130), Social Policy Research Centre - University of New South Wales, Sydney.

Schwab, RG 1995, The calculus of reciprocity: principles and implications of Aboriginal sharing (CAEPR Discussion Paper No. 100), Centre for Aboriginal Economic Policy - The Australian National University, Canberra.

Seanor, P, Bull, M & Ridley-Duff, R 2007, 'Mapping social enterprise: Do social enterprise actors draw straight lines or circles?', in 4th Annual Social Enterprise Research Conference, London, 4th-5th July.

Senate Standing Committee on Community Affairs 2004, A hand up not a hand out: Renewing the fight against poverty (Report on poverty and financial hardship) Commonwealth of Australia, Canberra.

Stilwell, F & Jordan, K 2007, Who gets what? Analysing economic inequality in Australia, Cambridge University Press, New York.

Sud, M, van Sandt, CV & Baugous, AM 2009, 'Social entrepreneurship: The role of institutions', Journal of Business Ethics, vol. 85, no. Supplement pp. 201-16.

Sullivan, K, Colyer, C, Johnston, L, McCarthy, L & Willis, J 2005, Evaluation of the Nyirranggulang East Katherine nutrition project, The Fred Hollows Foundation, Rosebery, NSW.

The Physical Disability Council of Australia 2003, Senate Inquiry into poverty in Australia. A response from The Physical Disability Council of Australia Ltd, The Physical Disability Council of Australia Ltd, Northgate, Qld.

Third Sector 2009, Productivity Commission to review the contribution of NFPs. Retrieved 30th December, from http://thirdsectormagazine.com.au/news/productivity_commission_to_re view_the_contribution_of_nfps/00298/

Toohey, P 2009, 'Roadblock on remote housing as progress stables on Indigenous response. ', The Australian, 4th July Retrieved 7th November, from http://www.theaustralian.news.com.au/story/0,25730613-2702,00.html.

Townsend, P 1987, 'Deprivation', Journal of Social Policy, vol. 16, pp. 125-46.

UNICEF 2007, Child poverty in perspective: An overview of child well-being in rich countries. A comprehensive assessment of the lives and well-being of children and adolescents in the economically advanced nations, UNICEF Innocenti Research Centre, Florence.

United Nations 2000, United Nations millennium declaration, UN, New York.

United Nations 2009, The millennium development goals report, United Nations Department of Economic and Social Affairs, New York.

Vinson, T, Rawsthorne, M & Cooper, B 2007, Dropping off the edge: the distribution of disadvantage in Australia, Jesuit Social Services, Richmond, Vic.

Walsh, J, Kress, J & Beyerchen, K 2005, 'Book review essay: Promises and perils at the bottom of the pyramid / The fortune at the bottom of the pyramid: Eradicating poverty through profits', Administrative Science Quarterly, vol. 50, no. 3, pp. 473-82.

Walter, M 2009, 'An economy of poverty? Power and the domain of Aboriginality', International Journal of Critical Indigenous Studies, vol. 2, no. 1, pp. 2-14.

Weatherley, R 1994, 'From entitlement to contract: Reshaping the welfare state in Australia', Journal of Sociology & Social Welfare, vol. 21, no. 3, pp. 153-73.

Westall, A & Chalkley, D 2007, Social enterprise futures, The Smith Institute, London.

Western Australian Council of Social Service 2009, The boom is busted for 400,000 of us, WACOSS, Perth.

Chapter 2: Benefits of Social Enterprise

The Added Value of Social Enterprise

Brigita Baltaca

Abstract: Social enterprises are positioned between the traditional private and public sectors. Although there is no universally accepted definition of a social enterprise, their distinguishing characteristics are their social purpose combined with the entrepreneurial spirit of the private sector. Social enterprises devote their activities and reinvest their surpluses to achieving a wider social or community objective either for their members' or a wider interest. The development of these organisations driven by an entrepreneurial spirit, but focused on social aims, is a trend that can be observed in countries with different levels of economic development. With the current global economic slow-down, it is very important to assist individuals to become involved in entrepreneurial activities to generate additional income in order to maintain an acceptable standard of living. This paper focuses on savings and credit unions as a specific form of social enterprises emphasising their participatory nature, which involves the persons affected by the activity, limited profit distribution and additional aim to benefit the community. The results and findings of the paper show that the development of savings and credit unions has proven to be essential in Latvia because it also serves as a vehicle for democracy and participation in the local community for thousands of people who have become socially passive through the breakdown of the old system and establishment of the new in the whole country.

Keywords: Social Economy, Social Entrepreneurship, Credit Unions

Social Economy and Social Entrepreneurship

During the last twenty years the economies of Central and Eastern Europe have lived through repeated cycles of decline and growth, beginning with recession in the early transition years, followed by several years of growth to varying degrees and then the current economic slowdown, stemming from the global financial crisis of 2008. In the face of a so rapidly changing environment, different groups of society have been affected in various ways and it has proven to be very challenging to sustain a balanced society where all groups of society are satisfied with their well-being. Under such circumstances it is very important to assist individuals to become involved in civic and entrepreneurial activities that are aimed at establishing and maintaining an acceptable standard of living. Social enterprises, being organisations of the social economy, have proved to be an effective way to foster the civic and economic activities of individuals. Social economy organisations are positioned between the traditional private and public sectors and they offer potential to communities in delivering services which are not provided by neither the private and market sectors nor the public sector.

The social economy usually develops because of a need to find new and innovative solutions to issues (whether they be socially, economically, or environmentally based) and to satisfy the needs of members and users which have been ignored or inadequately fulfilled by the private or public sectors. In less developed countries, the social economy is more widespread and devoted to facing the main problems of these countries – for example, the creation of jobs for those groups of people excluded from the labour market (Perrini 2006, 43).

The importance of the social economy was formally recognised by the European Union in its 1994 White Paper on Growth, Competitiveness, and Employment (Commission of the European Communities 1993, 126). The White Paper described the third sector as a potentially important contributor to the growth of employment and as a means to ensure that additional jobs are most effectively made available to those in a disadvantaged position within the labour market. As the social economy operates where the market has failed to respond to the needs of citizens, both for the provision of services and for employment, the social economy is an effective way to respond to specific local needs and to involve those otherwise excluded from mainstream economic activity. Social economy organisations are characterised by their aims and methods: a different way of doing business, which combines and associates the economic and social dimensions.

The social economy has also become known as the 'Third Sector'. Stephen P. Osborne (Osborne 2008, 16-39), according to the European tradition, views the third sector as the set of organisations whose mission is to benefit either their members or a large collective, rather than to generate profits for investors. In such a perspective the social impact of social enterprises (which are generally organisations of the not-for-profit or cooperative type) on the community is not only a consequence or a side-effect of their economic activity, but their motivation in itself. By using solutions to achieve not-for-profit aims, it is generally believed that social entrepreneurship has a distinct and valuable role to play in helping create a strong, sustainable, prosperous, and inclusive society. According to Mark Lyons (Lyons 2001, 5-33) the 'third sector' consists of private organisations that are formed and sustained by groups of people (members) acting voluntarily and without seeking personal profit to provide benefits for themselves or for others; that are democratically controlled, and; where any material benefit gained by a member is proportionate to their use of the organisation.

Although there is no universally accepted definition of a social enterprise, their distinguishing characteristics are their social purpose combined with the entrepreneurial spirit of the private sector. J. Gregory Dees (Dees 2001, 1-61) highlights two key characteristics that make social enterprises different from any other kind of business:

- Social enterprises have a social objective. The primary objective of a social enterprise is to maintain and improve social conditions in a way that goes beyond financial benefits created for the organisation's funders, managers, employees, or customers.
- Social enterprises blend social and commercial methods. In addition to using their ability to tap into the goodwill of some of their stakeholders, they look for creative ways for generating revenue, like businesses. Where businesses are completely commercial, social enterprises are a hybrid of commercial and philanthropic methods.

Professor Dr. Muhammad Yunus (Yunus, Weber 2007, 66), founder of the Grameen microfinance institution in Bangladesh and joint 2006 Noble Peace Prize winner, defines what social entrepreneurship is and what it is not. It boils down to the following requirements:

- Social objectives: it needs to have positive social objectives (help comes from the altruistic social services that the business provides to the poor); e.g. health, education, poverty, environment, or climate urgency;
- Community ownership: it needs to be owned by the poor or disadvantaged (dividends and financial growth return to the poor where their fiscal participation is helping to bring them out of poverty); e.g. women, young people, or the long-term unemployed;
- No profit distribution: investors may not, after having had their investments paid back, take profits out of the enterprise.

The definition of social enterprises as provided within the Study on Practices and Policies in the Social Enterprise Sector in Europe (Austrian Institute for SME Research 2007, 11-47) includes the following criteria, where the first four relate to the economic and entrepreneurial dimension and the following five encapsulate the social dimension:

- A continuous activity producing goods and/or selling services. In contrast to some not-for-profit organisations with advocacy activities or in charge of redistribution of money, the provision of goods and services is a main reason for the existence of the social enterprise.

- A high degree of autonomy. Social enterprises are often (co-)financed, but never managed by public authorities. This autonomy is also apparent in the right of 'voice' and 'exit'.
- A significant level of economic risk. The founders of a social enterprise assume the major part of the economic risk, with financial viability dependent on the efforts of members and workers.
- A minimum amount of paid work. Social enterprises can combine monetary and non-monetary resources, voluntary and paid workers, not only operating with volunteers.
- An explicit aim to benefit the community. Social enterprises have social aims. This aim to serve the community or a specific group of people constitutes an essential characteristic of the organisation.
- An initiative launched by a group of citizens. Social enterprises are the result of collective dynamics involving people that share certain needs or aims.
- Decision-making power not based on capital ownership. In general, the principle of 'one member, one vote' is applied in the decision-making process and decision-making power is not linked to an individual's invested capital.
- A participatory nature which involves the persons affected by the activity. Social enterprises are characterised by the participation of customers (users), workers, and a stakeholder orientation.
- Limited profit distribution. In contrast to traditional not-for-profit organisations, surpluses may be distributed to a limited extent, thus avoiding a profit-maximising behaviour.

Thus social enterprises can be described as organisations that devote their activities and reinvest their surpluses to achieving a wider social or community objective either for their members' or a wider interest. The development of these organisations driven by an entrepreneurial spirit, but focused on social aims, is a trend that can be observed in countries with different levels of economic development.

Cooperatives have been recognised as one of the most widespread actors in the social economy (UNDP 2008, 16). A cooperative is an autonomous association of people united voluntarily to meet their common economic, social, and cultural needs and aspirations through a jointly-owned and democratically-controlled enterprise. The cooperative movement brings together over 800 million people around the world (UN 2009).

Although cooperatives are not the only way to build social capital, they are clearly one means for doing so by the ongoing involvement of employees, members, or clients – a process that does not rely directly on governments. There are two kinds of comparative advantage to cooperatives: general ones derived from the nature of cooperatives as member-owned businesses, and particular ones derived from specific types of cooperative (Birchall, Ketilson 2009, 12).

Savings and Credit Unions

Savings and credit cooperatives, also recognised as savings and credit unions, share the dual roles of being both a direct participant in the social economy, as a specific form of social enterprise, and also as an important facilitator for other social economy actors. As a means of harnessing local capital for local use, savings and credit cooperatives are the segment of the financial services sector best placed to bridge the gap between mainstream financial service providers and the social economy. Savings and credit unions were formed in many countries as a response to the difficulty entrepreneurs and farmers often had in dealing with large financial institutions. By pooling their limited capital, individuals who did not have the necessary resources to undertake a venture, were able to start a small retail business, buy some simple power tools, or upgrade some property for their business. The principle of small amounts of capital judiciously applied at the right time and the right place, has been shown to work throughout the globe. By the end of 2011 there were over 196 million credit union members, that were united in some 51,013 credit unions spread across 100 countries, including over 2,300 credit unions operating in 12 European countries, uniting nearly nine million members (WOCCU 2011).

Being a financial cooperative, credit unions follow very strict operating principles defined by the World Council of Credit Unions:

- Open and Voluntary Membership. Membership in a credit union is voluntary and open to all within the defined common bond of association that can make use of its services and are willing to accept the corresponding responsibilities.
- Democratic Control. Credit union members enjoy equal rights to vote (one member, one vote) and participate in decisions affecting their credit union, without regard to the amount of savings or deposits or the volume of business. The credit union is autonomous, within the framework of law and regulation, recognising the credit union as a cooperative enterprise serving and controlled by its members. Credit union elected offices are voluntary in nature and incumbents should not receive a salary.
- Service to Members. Credit union services are directed to improve the economic and social well-being of all members.
- Distribution to Members. To encourage thrift through savings and thus to provide loans and other services, a fair rate of interest is paid on savings and deposits, within the capacity of the credit union.
- Building Financial Stability. A prime concern of the credit union is to build its financial strength, including adequate capital reserves and operating internal controls that will ensure continued service to membership
- On-going Education. Credit unions actively promote the education of their members, officers, and employees, along with the public in general, in the economic, social, democratic, and mutual self-help principles of credit unions. The promotion of thrift and wise use of credit, as well as

education on the rights and responsibilities of members, are essential to the dual social and economic character of credit unions in serving member needs.

- Cooperation Among Cooperatives. In keeping with their philosophy and the pooling practices of cooperatives, credit unions within their capability actively cooperate with other credit unions, cooperatives, and their associations at local, national, and international levels in order to best serve the interests of their members and their communities.

- Social Responsibility. Continuing the ideals and beliefs of cooperative pioneers, credit unions seek to bring about human and social development. Their vision of social justice extends both to the individual members and to the larger community in which they work and reside. The credit union ideal is to extend service to all who need and can use it. Every person is either a member or a potential member and appropriately part of the credit union sphere of interest and concern. Decisions should be taken with full regard for the interest of the broader community within which the credit union and its members reside

As described by the World Council of Credit Unions, when compared to other financial institutions, a savings and credit union is unique because it follows a philosophy of self-help, member control, and economic democracy. Savings and credit unions generate local pools of capital that wouldn't otherwise exist. The source of development capital and its ownership and control are all at the local level. Credit unions are funded through member shares and deposits and therefore are not dependent upon the capital markets for funding. Figure 1 demonstrates the self-sufficiency of credit unions.

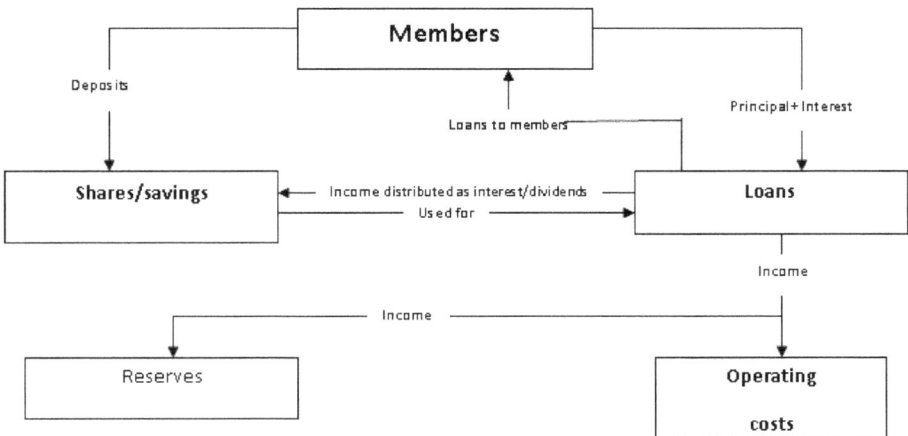

Figure 1: Self-sufficiency of a credit union
Source: Dennis Schroeder, 1989

The development of cooperative savings and credit organisations is essential in countries in transition because it also serves as a vehicle for democracy and participation in their local community for thousands of people who have become socially passive under previous systems. According to the Report at the International Labour Conference in 2001, in several transition economies of Central and Eastern Europe, savings and credit unions have had an enormous upsurge since 1992. In December 1996 there were 224 of these in Poland, comprising 150,000 members with US$69 million in savings. Latvia's first savings and credit unions started in early 1995 and had 1,400 members with US$ 245,000 of savings by early 1997.

The cooperative advantage of savings and credit unions was well proved during the recent global financial crisis. The nature of the credit union markets means that they were less exposed to the internationally traded financial instruments generally accepted as the root cause of the crisis. As credit unions are not driven by profits or shareholders interests, they were not compelled to force people into inappropriate loans (McDougall 2008). The type of ownership and methods of capitalisation are two of the key factors that have created the disparity in the financial position of credit unions and banks to the advantage of savings and credit cooperatives or credit unions (Coombes 2008).

Savings and Credit Unions: Latvia's Case

Although Latvia has been a member of European Union since 2004, a process of socioeconomic segregation is ongoing in society. For example, the Gini index reflecting polarisation of material welfare shows how unequally income is distributed within the country. The Gini value of 0 represents income being distributed absolutely equally; in contrast, the value of 1 demonstrates there is marginal inequality, meaning that all income have been received by a few members of the society. The constant increase of the Gini index in Latvia proves that inequality in income distribution is ongoing and the gap between the wealthy and the poor is increasing.

Civic participation in Latvia is also very low, with about 62% of society not having been involved in any non-governmental organisation (LU Akadēmiskais apgāds 2005, 156). Due to a lack of experience and entrepreneurial courage, resulting in a generally risk-averse population, it is very problematic for the great part of society to take advantage of the opportunities provided by the market economy. Furthermore, a high level of mistrust in commercial enterprises, banks in particular, leads people to try to manage their financial problems with their own efforts or ask for assistance from their relatives. Since regaining independence in 1991, Latvia has struggled to free itself from state ownership and the previous centralised support system in all sectors of the economy. The former financial and crediting system did not meet the needs of the general public. It was necessary to have a type of financial institution able to meet the interests of people with small incomes and savings deposits, thus providing practical support to the population of Latvia to fill their need for effective personal financial services, as well as providing access to finance for entrepreneurial economic activities. The development of credit unions was considered as one of the most prospective possibilities to solve these problems. An additional benefit of cooperative savings and credit organisations in Latvia is the creation of a vehicle for democracy and community participation. Credit unions actively promote the education of their members and employees, alongside with the general public, in economic, social, democratic, and principles. As member-owned not-for-profit cooperative financial institutions, operated by members democratically, credit unions have proved to be "agents of change" in a society on its way to become a mature civic society. Credit unions therefore have a key role to play in the regional development of Latvia.

Latvia has encountered significant economic turmoil in the last 20 years. Enterprises have experienced a significant decrease in their equity, making them very vulnerable to the current economic context. Indeed, very few cooperative forms have survived this economic transition period, but financial cooperatives since 1995 have increased in number, starting from one in 1995 to 34 in 2009, and extended their membership from an initial 29 to more than 25,000 by the end of 2009 (see Figure 2).

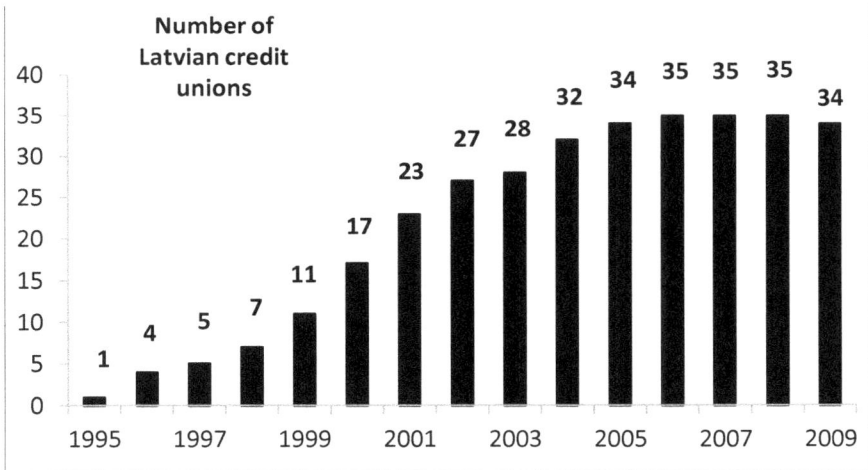

Figure 2. Number of Credit Unions in Latvia, 1995-2009
Source: Developed by the author, based on information from Financial and Capital Market Commission, Latvia

The Latvian savings and credit union movement has put much effort into promoting its members' civic activities. The Association of Cooperative Credit Unions of Latvia (LKKSS, www.lkkss.lv), founded in 1997 with the main aim to advocate for a savings and credit union national development policy and protect and represent their interests. It has established an excellent relationship with senior government officials and politicians. LKKSS has organised conferences on topics that are critical for the future of the network's expansion in Latvia. LKKSS has used every opportunity to present the features of an advanced cooperative banking system. LKKSS has achieved notable success in the legal area with the adoption of a legal strategy, technical work, and effective lobbying and liaison that resulted in a new Law on Credit Unions implemented in January 2002.

Members of a credit union need to share a "common bond". The Law on Credit Unions of the Republic of Latvia sets the following three principles for the common bond of credit union members:

1.   according to the territorial principle;
2.   according to the employment principle;
3.   according to the principle of mutual interests.

Latvian credit unions, after the regaining of independence, have proven themselves as good financial partners to their members. According LKKSS, the main features of the current credit union network in Latvia are the following:

- Two main groups of credit unions - Community and Trade Union credit unions
- Low loan delinquency ratio
- Good image within communities
- Leaders – elected officials from credit union members
- Support from community deputies
- The best marketing principle of "each member brings a new member"
- Easy loan granting process
- Close link between members.

By supporting credit union development, trade unions have taken the initiative to protect the social guarantees of employees. The promotion of such 'self-help' efforts of citizens to organise affordable credit services is even more essential in the rural areas of Latvia, where people have become socially passive, even depressed. Credit unions have raised people's self-confidence and belief in their own abilities. The Latvian credit union network follows the geographical and demographical peculiarities of the state. This means the credit union network can be divided into two main groups – credit unions in Riga and those in rural areas. Riga credit unions are based on trade union principles and their membership is based on trade union organisations. In rural areas credit unions are mostly connected with communities or groups of communities. In Riga the most popular group of loans is for consumption. In rural areas credit union members mostly borrow for both consumption and entrepreneurial needs, thus playing an important role also as a microfinancing institution supporting community economic activity.

As shown in Figure 3, the key activity of a credit union operation is the mobilisation of member deposits. By the end of December 2009, Latvian credit unions had custody of a total of LVL6.5 million[1] of members' savings, having grown by 9.8% from the previous year. The growth in savings and loans demonstrates the success Latvian credit unions have had in building community trust as reliable financial institutions.

Twenty-seven savings and credit unions are operating outside Riga, the capital of Latvia. Twenty-two of them, or 62,86% of total number of savings and

---

[1] Exchange rate, according to the Bank of Latvia 1 LVL = EUR 0.702804

credit unions, are community based as they have been organised according to the territorial principle.

Rural savings and credit unions foster participation of their members in the local economy not only by pooling their financial resources but also by investing their time and skills, thus creating additional value for the community. At the end of 2009, the author conducted a survey of 22 of 27 Latvian rural savings and credit unions to collect relevant data for analysis focusing on the role of credit unions in fostering the economic, social, and civil inclusion of their members in community activities. Sixty percent of the surveyed savings and credit unions have been operating between six to ten years; 40% have been serving their members from one to six years. Additional statistical data is based on the information received from managers of the respective organisations and 100 respondents-members.

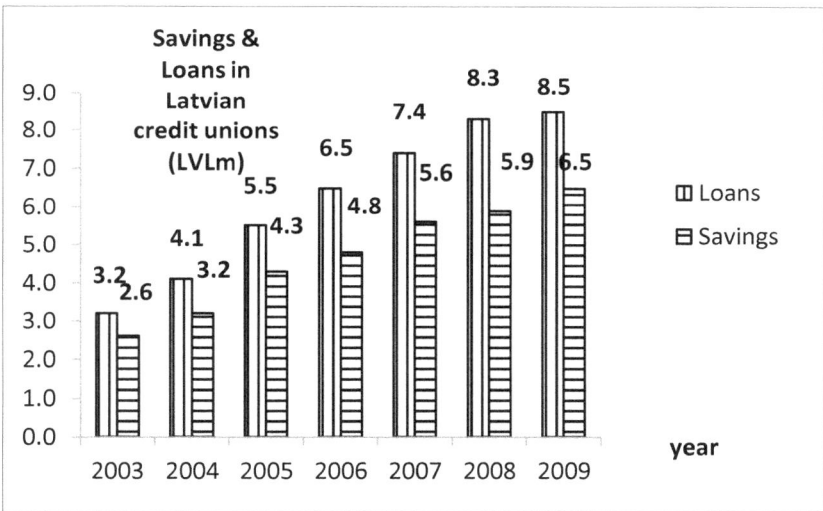

Figure 3. Total Loans and Savings in Savings and Credit Unions (Latvia 2003-2009)
Source: Developed by the author, based on information from Financial and Capital Market Commission, Latvia

As shown in table 1, over half of the membership consists of the so-called "marginal groups" of the society. Marginal or sensitive groups of people include young people who find it difficult to obtain employment because of lack of experience as well as those of pre-retirement age, that is people older that 55, as well as senior people over 65.

Table 1. Credit Union Member Distribution by Age

Age group (years)	% of total membership
18 - 30	19
31- 50	42
51 - 65	25
65 <	14

Figure 4 shows that the resources of community credit unions available for lending mostly consists of members' savings (42%) and shares (22%). In the event of high demand for microloans, credit unions borrow from commercial banks - in the surveyed credit unions such borrowings totaled 28% of all resources.

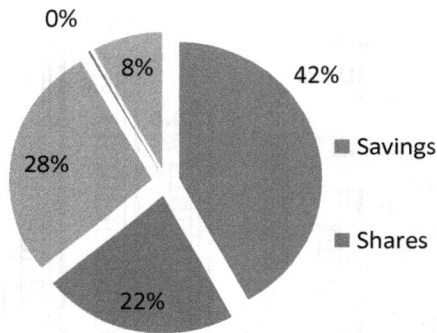

Figure 4: Credit Union Capital for Lending in Community Credit Unions

Savings and credit unions are globally recognized microfinance institutions which help people to access financial services. Microloans are provided by credit unions to their members, including those who are financially excluded and rely on low or no regular income. Such loans offer an important means to encourage entrepreneurship through self-employment and microenterprises, in particular among women, and minorities. This instrument favors not only competitiveness and entrepreneurship, but also social inclusion (EU 2007). Therefore microcredit can become an efficient tool in the realization of Lisbon strategy for growth and jobs and the promotion of social inclusion that has become very important with the enlargement of European Union.

The average amount of credit provided by credit unions in European Union (EU) member states is far below the threshold used by EU institutions to define microcredit (EU definition: >€25,000.) According to the information provided by the European Network of Credit Unions website (http://www.creditunion network.eu/ eu_and_cus), the average credit union loan in Poland is €1,000; in the Republic of Ireland, €8,150; in the UK, £1,000; and in Romania, €700. Loans are used by members for various reasons, including consumer purposes, starting a small business, growing an existing small business, or financing a university education or other studies.

The experience of Latvia has proven that community savings and credit unions, through providing microcredit, are fostering economic activity within their community of operation.

To promote microcrediting in Latvia, the government on 2 December 2008, issued the order of Cabinet of Ministers Nr. 752 On the Programme for Crediting Small and Medium Entities. Raising the rate of employment and increasing the living standards of Latvians were mentioned as one of the goals of the program. The program is being implemented through the state-owned Mortgage and Land Bank of Latvia (LHZB). As many people are often very hesitant to cooperate with banks to solve issues related to access to finance, due to their lack of experience and knowledge as well as remote location, LHZB has involved community savings and credit unions in issuing microloans. According to date provided by LKKSS, LHZB has issued loans to 11 credit unions totalling LVL560,000 for further lending to members for entrepreneurial activities. The loans range from LVL795 for purchase of fruit tree saplings and LVL950, issued for a period of one and a half years, for drilling water bores for cattle, to LVL700 for the period of five years for a business start-up.

Data from the website of Latvian Finance and Capital Market Commission (http://www.fktk.lv/en/statistics/credit_unions) - the institution supervising the activities of all participants in the Latvia financial market, shows that savings and credit unions are safe partners for providing microlending, as the capital adequacy ratio of savings and credit unions by the end of 2009 was 21.1% - significantly exceeding the minimum required ratio of 10%. At end of 2009, 66.2% of credit unions' loan portfolio was assessed as standard loans; 30.1% as close-watch; and 3.7% as the total sum of substandard, doubtful, and lost loans. Special loan loss provisions at the end of December made up 5.1% of the total loan portfolio.

Conclusions

There is an emerging interest in European countries in social enterprises that encourage the participation of individuals in social entrepreneurship activities. Social economy organisations and enterprises offer the potential for communities to deliver services which are not provided by either the private or the public sector. Social economy organisations and enterprises are characterised by their aims and methods: a different way of doing business which combine and associate the economic and social dimensions.

The development of cooperative savings and credit organizations has proven to be essential in Latvia because it also serves as a vehicle for democracy and participation in the local community for thousands of people who have become socially passive through the breakdown of the old system and establishment of the new in the whole country. Credit unions actively promote education of their members and employees alongside with the general public, in economic, social, and democratic principles. As member-owned, not-for-profit, cooperative financial institutions, operated by members democratically, credit unions have proved to be "agents of change" in a society on its way to become a civic society. Community credit unions being actively involved also in microcrediting have a key role to play in the regional development of Latvia

References

Coombes, Andrea. 2008. Given Turmoil at Banks, Time May Be Right to Try a Credit Union. Market Watch, accessed March 31, 2010, http://www.foxbusiness.com/story/markets/industries/finance/

EU 2007. A European Initiative for the Development of Micro-credit in support of growth and employment, COM (2007) 708, accessed May 28, 2010, http://eur-lex.europa.eu/LexUriServ/LexUriServ.do?uri=OJ:C:2009:077:0023:01: EN:HTML

FKTK.Credit union statistics, accessed May 25, 2010, http://www.fktk.lv/en/statistics/credit_unions

J. Gregory Dees, J., Emerson, J. Economy, P. 2001. Enterprising nonprofits: a toolkit for social entrepreneurs. John Wiley and Sons, 9

Johnston Birchall, Lou Hammond Ketilson. 2009. Resilience of the cooperative business model in times of crisis. International Labour Office, Sustainable Enterprise Programme. - Geneva: ILO, 12

Lindquist, Evert A., Restakis, J. 2001. The co-op alternative: civil society and the future of public services. Institute of Public Administration of Canada, 23

LU Akadēmiskais apgāds. 2005. Cik demokrātiska ir Latvija: demokrātijas audits (How democratic is Latvia: audit of democracy), 156

Mark Lyons. 2001. Third sector: the contribution of nonprofit and cooperative enterprise in Australia; Allen & Unwin, Australia, 5-33

McDougall, P. 2008, September 12. Credit Unions Take On Big Banks, accessed Jaunuary 20, 2010, www.thestreet.com

Microfinance in Europe. European Microfinance network, accessed February 28, 2010, http://www.european-microfinance.org/europe-microfinance_en.php

Perrini, F. 2006. The new social entrepreneurship: what awaits social entrepreneurial ventures? Edward Elgar Publishing, 43

Promotion of cooperatives. Report V (1), International Labour Office Geneva, 2001. Accessed April 10, 2010, http://www.ilo.org

Schroeder Dennis. 1989. Savings Mobilisation. World Council of Credit Unions, Inc. Kendal/Hunt Publishing Company, 16

Statistical Report, World Council of Credit Unions, Inc, accessed April 15, 2012, www.woccu.org

Stephen P. Osborne. 2008. The third sector in Europe: prospects and challenges. Routledge, 16-23

Study on Practices and Policies in the Social Enterprise Sector in Europe. Final Report, Vienna, June 2007, accessed April 29, 2010 http://ec.europa.eu/enterprise/policies/sme/files/craft/social_economy/do c/report_study_kmu_social_entreprises_fin_en.pdf

The Law on Credit Unions of the Republic of Latvia. (Krājaizdevu sabiedrību likums LR likums) accessed on April 15, 2010 http://www.likumi.lv/doc.php?id=711

UNDP. 2008. Social Enterprise: A new model for poverty reduction and employment generation. UNDP Regional Bureau for Europe and the Commonwealth of Independent States, 16

Yunus, M., Weber, K. 2007. Creating a World without Poverty - Social Business and the Future of Capitalism. Public Affairs, 66

Chapter 3: The Civic Entrepreneur

From Scarcity to Abundance: Organisational Sustainability and the Role of the Civic Entrepreneur

Sam Wells and Stephanie Betz

Abstract: This paper examines the challenges confronting corporate change leaders, faced with the task of reconceiving established organisations in response to an emerging 'sustainability' paradigm, and of convincing change followers to engage with the concrete, organisational expression of that new paradigm. Successful adaptation requires change leaders, first, to achieve their own conceptual shift – a 'reconception' of the purpose, priorities and strategies of the institution. They must then be able to convince their change followers to embrace the concrete institutional changes that reflect the shift. In this context, the paper proposes that the 'pilot' programme, often utilised by change agents, may serve to bridge the conceptual thinking gap between leader and follower, by providing a concrete experience of the envisioned destination. We explore some of the changes in mental models that need to be made if organisational thinking is to take the important step from fragmentation and 'scarcity', to integration and 'abundance'. We describe the important role of commercial enterprise, which is naturally integrative, in grappling with some of these critical issues. Finally, we propose a special role for the 'civic entrepreneur', who shares with the corporate world a capacity and respect for integrative enterprise, but is not constrained by inherited institutional rigidities. Civic entrepreneurs pursue the creation of 'common' or community wealth – value created over and above the cost of financial, social and natural capital. In doing so, they become a resource for the corporate change leader. By 'piloting' new models of integration and abundance, civic entrepreneurs can provide conceptual inspiration to corporate change leaders. But they can also present corporate change followers, vicariously, with a concrete experience of 'sustainability' – examples of enterprise-based sustainability in practice.

Keywords: Organisational Sustainability, Civic Entrepreneurship, Paradigm Shift, Pilot

Prologue

It could be argued that the core institutions in any age pursue 'sustainability'; however they may conceive that term. Whether those institutions are religious, educational, political or commercial, they seek to preserve and nourish – to sustain – the principles, or values, or priorities that are seen to lie at the heart of contemporary civilisation. From time to time, there is a fundamental shift in how sustainability is understood. Established institutions shaped around one notion of sustainability, if they are to retain their relevance and their leadership role, must find ways to give expression to the new paradigm, within their existing institutional framework.

We are used to the idea of being flexible in pursuit of a fixed objective. In these cases of paradigm shift, however, the means may be institutionally entrenched, but they must somehow be reconceived and brought to bear in pursuit of ends that are fundamentally changed. The success or failure of institutions to reconfigure themselves in this way is the stuff of world histories.

The twelfth century in what we now call Europe saw some fundamental shifts in contemporary spirituality – one expression of the so-called 'twelfth-century renaissance'. These new religious impulses within the Christian church reflected a desire to cultivate a richer interior life, a more personal, 'authentic' spirituality, based on a 'return' to a simple existence, not distracted by material concerns.

Bernard, abbot of Clairvaux and spiritual leader of the reforming Cistercian monastic order, fulminated against the materialism of the traditional Benedictine monasteries, especially the wealth, the grandeur and the elaborate liturgy of the great abbey of Cluny, situated near Mâcon, in modern-day Burgundy (for example, Scott James 1953, 255). Bernard was forging new links between monastic spirituality and the society in which it was imbedded, and creating new 'markets' for monasticism – a kind of 'spiritual entrepreneurship'. Cluny's abbot, Peter the Venerable, was loyal to the traditions he had inherited at Cluny, but was also sympathetic to the new spirituality (Constable 1975, 137). He strove to preserve what he saw as some essential features of Cluniac monastic life, including much of the liturgy, while reshaping its policies and practices to accommodate the desire for a simpler, more direct relationship with the Divine (Folz 1975).

Peter admired Bernard and the Cistercians,[1] and drew inspiration from their practice of founding new monasteries in wild, remote, unsettled places, free from the more worldly economic and political distractions of the Benedictine

---

[1] Indeed, outside the polemical debate on the merits of their two orders, it is clear that mutual respect, even admiration, marked the relationship between Peter and Bernard (Leclercq 1949, 68-87).

establishments. In his reforming Statutes, Peter set aside part of the new abbey church (the biggest in Europe before St Peter's Basilica was completed in Rome in the seventeenth century), where individual monks could retreat from the formal, regimented communal life and make their personal devotions, 'as if in the desert, far from the sight of men'.[2] Peter was expressing the same impulse that drove the Cistercians into the wilderness, but he gave it a form that made sense in his own institutional context (Constable 1975, 120).

And in a letter to Pope Innocent II, defending Cluny and his own governance from Bernard's unrelenting attacks, Peter makes an observation on the institutional context that resonates down the centuries: "… it is easier to build anew, to make a fresh start, than it is to reform or repair that which already exists" (Constable 1967, vol 1, 43).[3]

Peter was dealing not only with an artefactual attachment to the status quo – an entrenched monastic culture, reflected in the customs, practices, rules and rhythms of daily life at Cluny – but also with a conceptual challenge. Standing in the midst of the inherited institution, where thinking was so powerfully shaped by the habits (so to speak) and assumptions of Cluny's way of life, how was it possible even to conceive of changes that would give expression to new ways of thinking and feeling, within the context of the old 'paradigm'? How does a change leader, first, envisage a way forward that integrates a new perspective on the monastic purpose, without dismantling the long-established institutional vehicles for pursuing a monastic vocation? Second, how does the change leader convince the change followers to make that journey on the ground, to give concrete expression to the conceptual insight?

Peter was never going to be able to replicate at Cluny the daily life of the Cistercians, or of the still more eremitical Carthusians, with whom he was on even closer terms (Leclercq 1946, 97) – the reform orders could not provide the blueprint for a reinvented Cluny. But as a change leader he could draw on their examples in two ways.

First, he could find his own conceptual inspiration by observing the new orders in action. Here were ways of integrating the new spirituality with monastic life – they may not have been completely transferable to the Cluniac context, but they opened the mind to new ways of seeing and thinking. They gave him insights into how he could adapt his inherited institutional framework to the demands of a new understanding of what was required for salvation…or sustainability.

Second, the successful implementation of these new models of monasticism provided Peter's change followers with something concrete to observe and consider and evaluate – just as concrete as their own daily experience. It enabled them to venture, vicariously, from the safety of their customary experience and to consider real alternatives, which might otherwise have languished in the less compelling world of their imaginations.

---

[2] *…velut in heremo, ab hominum remoti conspectibus* (Charvin 1965, 'Causa' to Statut 53, p. 34; Constable 1975, 133).

[3] *… in negotio religionis facilius possunt noua fundari quam uetera reparari…* (Peter goes on to cite an observation by Pope Gregory the Great that it seems harder for men and institutions to think on new things than on old – this clearly frames the challenge in cognitive terms).

This chapter examines the challenges confronting corporate change leaders, faced with the tasks of reconceiving established organisations in response to a changing 'sustainability' paradigm, and of convincing change followers to engage with the concrete, organisational expression of that new paradigm. The reforming orders provided Peter the Venerable with a source of conceptual inspiration and concrete illustration. In the same way, the activities of civic entrepreneurs, unfettered by the institutional rigidities of corporate culture, but joined to the corporate world by a shared commitment to enterprise, can inspire change leaders and provide less visionary change followers with real examples of the new 'sustainability'.

Fragmentation of Sustainability Knowledge

> We've made tremendous progress in science for 300 years, since the days of Isaac Newton and the scientific revolution, by chopping problems up into smaller and smaller bits and analysing the tiniest parts … but the time has come to move back up. I mean how [do] we understand the behaviour of a whole economy? How do we understand the resilience and stability of ecosystems? Or global warming? These are problems with a similar character in that you can't understand them by looking at the little bits. And this is a daunting challenge – going up turns out to be much harder than going down. Synthesis and holism is much more scientifically subtle than analysis and reductionism.

Steve Strogatz, Professor of Applied
Mathematics, Cornell University[4]

The notion of sustainability, as the term has come to be used over the last 15 years or so, reflects a very wide range of interests and aspirations. They all have their origins in a general awareness that the 'ecology' of human existence on earth is not healthy. Past that shared awareness, however, it is difficult to identify a single thread that runs through the myriad studies exploring the problems and solutions associated with the 'ecological' dilemma – in all its expressions – or that brings to them a sense of disciplinary (or inter-disciplinary) integrity and unity of purpose.

It was in the nature of the dilemma that every facet of human ecology should come to be considered a legitimate field of study, under the banner of sustainability. The result was an explosion of knowledge, a huge amount of work undertaken on relatively narrow fronts by social and physical scientists, academics in all disciplines, consultants, practitioners – explosive not only in its speed and scope, but also in its fragmentation.[5] These discreet packets of new expertise and understanding came to be seen as 'add-ons' to various spheres of

---

[4] On *The Science Show*, "The New Science of Networks", written and produced by Annamaria Talas and presented by Simon Nasht, Saturday 8 January 2005 on Australian Broadcasting Corporation (ABC) Radio National.
[5] We acknowledge here the research assistance of Julia Inverarity in grappling with the literature.

human activity, ways of addressing some particular manifestation of the sustainability challenge. It has been an essentially reactive process – we are making a mess of this or that activity, so what are the things that we should stop doing or do differently?

Nowhere has this been more apparent than in regard to corporations. The early 'sustainability' focus on corporations was prompted by a perception that they were, wittingly or unwittingly, doing harm that needed to be put right (Dunphy, D, Griffiths, A and Benn, S 2007, 8-10). They were seen by some, not as potential vehicles for beneficial change, or potential models of a new human ecology, so much as errant institutions whose ways needed to be mended by the piecemeal application of new knowledge to this or that activity, or whose ways were, perhaps, beyond mending (Bakan 2004). Where the mending was begun, it occurred problem by problem, issue by issue, in a fragmented 'greening' of corporate activity. This reflected the old paradigm of Newtonian 'reductionism' more than the emerging science of complex systems and networks, in which the whole is recognised as greater than the sum of its parts, and the integration and interdependency of those parts lie at the heart of any 'solution'.

Only quite recently, commentators have begun to explore models of enterprise and of corporate thinking in which the corporation, itself, is seen as a vehicle – perhaps the vehicle – for humankind's response to the pressing global issues of sustainability – a potential white knight, rather than a raper and pillager (for example, Dunphy et al 2007; Hart 2007). Perhaps the next major step towards practical sustainability will involve "going up" to a new level of synthesis and integration that cannot be achieved simply by adding the numerous, but fragmented, pieces of expert knowledge together. Rather than being seen as an essentially self-contained, but destructive force at large in the world, we are beginning to explore the corporation's potential to nourish the complex systems or 'ecologies' in which it is imbedded.

A New Way of Seeing Things—The Role of Vision

In what follows, these issues of synthesis and integration will be explored as they apply to the study of how established corporate institutions attempt to preserve their relevance and leadership, in the face of a major shift emerging in the meaning attached by our civilization to 'sustainability'. A clear distinction should be made between two branches of that study: a) what businesses should do, and b) what businesses could do. Our concern is with the latter only, and the distinction is very important.

A great deal has been written about the obligations – legal and moral – on corporations to behave in a particular way, and about the best way of ensuring that they meet those obligations. The notion of 'sustainability' itself has often become associated, by virtue of the reactive nature of the thinking and work done under its banner, with a sense of maintaining an acceptable status quo, preventing any decline, preserving what we have. When used in this way, 'sustainability' tends to reflect and cement a paradigm of 'scarcity,[6] in which we are always trying to hold the line, prevent entropy, corral, protect, conserve, make the most of what's left. It reinforces a sense of limited integration.

One can sympathise with those who seek to prevent the damage caused by corporate neglect or vandalism, but a glance at what we know about individual motivation suggests that debate about regulation or obligation is not a sound basis for the next major step towards sustainability. Kohn's (1993) landmark article on incentives spelled out what so much research before and since has confirmed: Sticks and carrots, punishment and rewards, are all controlling, not liberating – they are two sides of the same coin. These so-called "extrinsic motivators", while perhaps achieving temporary and superficial compliance, actually undermine the foundations of longer-term, sustainable behaviour – they undermine intrinsic motivation and creativity.

In short, and in regard to corporations, by putting in place a floor – a minimum acceptable standard – we also imply a ceiling. By focusing on what is required, we constrain the thinking on what is possible (Ostrom E., Burger J., Field C.B, Norgaard R.B. and Policansky D. 1999) The important questions are not about whether organisations can be induced to 'do the right thing', but about what the world looks like when we go beyond what is merely acceptable, and how the best possible outcome can be pursued by those who want to pursue it. In other words, the next big step towards organisational sustainability is only likely to be conceived and achieved by those who seek it – you cannot legislate for vision, for conceptual insight, for innovation, or for enterprise. "It is a very grave mistake to think that the enjoyment of seeing and searching can be promoted by means of coercion and a sense of duty" (Albert Einstein, in Schilpp 1949, 17).

Donella Meadows describes the first, critical and often-neglected step in meeting the real challenge of 'seeing and searching' for organisational sustainability – the creation of a coherent and compelling vision towards which all our policy and implementation must be directed. It should be a vision of abundance, not scarcity, capturing "what we really want, not what we'll settle for":

> The best goal most of us who work toward sustainability offer is the avoidance of catastrophe. We promise survival and not much more. That is a failure of vision.
>
> Even if information, models, and implementation could be perfect in every way, how far can they guide us, if we know what direction we want to move away from but not what direction we want to go toward? There may be motivation in escaping doom, but there is even more in creating a better world. And it is pitifully inadequate to describe the exciting possibilities of sustainability in terms of mere survival…(Meadows 1994, 2)

---

[6] Covey (1990, 119-120) coined "abundance mentality" and "scarcity mentality" in relation to individuals and how they approach their relationships. We suggest that the principles have wider application wherever complex systems are in play – an abundance mentality is the basis of synergistic thinking and creative interdependence.

In 1962, Thomas Kuhn introduced us to the notion of paradigm and paradigm shift in the world of scientific research. Kuhn's piercing insights, however much they may still invite scholarly debate, have generally proved to be as prophetic as they were historically acute. Two of his observations on the process of paradigm change are particularly relevant to our discussion.

First, he described the response of those immersed in the current paradigm to evidence that appears to challenge that paradigm; generally the response to apparent crisis is to keep assuming that the paradigm fundamentals are sound, but that they need expanding, refining, 'completing' in some way (Kuhn 1970, 77-78). In other words, the first response to crisis tends to be change at the margins in a way that effectively reinforces the status quo. We can see this beautifully illustrated in many of the current political responses to the threat of climate change, which favour 'solutions' that cause the least possible disruption to the socio-political frameworks that precipitated the crisis. At the level of corporations, it is reflected in the 'greening' of organisations in a way that reacts to environmental crisis, but makes no fundamental shift in strategic vision (Hart 1997).

Second, Kuhn observed that a change in scientific paradigm is not inspired by a comparison of the current paradigm to incompatible evidence presented by nature. Such apparent weaknesses in the fabric of orthodoxy can cause discomfort, even an increasing preparedness to explore the fallibility of the existing theoretical framework, but they will not force a paradigm shift. That shift, when it comes, will not be a shift away from the existing paradigm, so much as a shift towards a new and fundamentally different paradigm (Kuhn 1970, 77-110). The rejection of a long-standing framework requires a new vision, a new way of seeing things, which more adequately encompasses the emerging realities as we come to understand them.

And Kuhn alerts us to an intriguing feature of the new paradigm – it does not, cannot, simply build on what has come before; it must be based on assumptions and perspectives that are incompatible with the old view. In fact it renders the fading paradigm not merely incomplete, but flawed. It could be argued that just such a shift is required in the final stage of an organisation's journey from scarcity to abundance.

The Transformation of "Corporations"

"You can never solve a problem on the level on which it was created." Einstein captures the sustainability challenge for organisations. The solutions lie in a higher level of synthesis, which does not shrink from the uncertain and unpredictable nature of complex systems, but which emerges from a willingness to 'dance' with complexity and, in so doing, to bring a positive vision "lovingly into being" (Meadows 2001, 59).

Students of corporate sustainability, who seek insights into a more integrated vision of possibilities for the world of organisation, have reason to be grateful – and to express gratitude –for the work of Dexter Dunphy and his colleagues (Dunphy et al 2007). Here is a willingness to seek solutions at a more holistic and subtle level than that at which the problems present (Dunphy et al 2007, 218).

And this powerful thinking is presented, also, as a foundation for practical action: "The time to debate abstract theories is past; what we need now is to imbed our theories in action and to engage in dialogue around working models." (Dunphy et al 2007, 4). By focusing on corporations, in pursuit of sustainability, Dunphy et al are mindful of the power of larger corporations, for good and ill:

> "Corporations …control most of the resources of our global society; if we are to have effective leadership of the sustainability movement, then much of the movement must come from the corporate sector." (Dunphy et al 2007, 218).

The challenge is to work out how we can help these organisations along the path to becoming 'sustaining corporations', and it is logical that Dunphy and his colleagues should take the perspective of corporate 'change agents' or 'change leaders' at various levels, in various roles, inside and outside the organisation. They track the corporation through a phased evolution, from resistance, to non-responsiveness, to compliance, to sustainable efficiency, to strategic proactivity, and, ultimately, to the 'sustaining organisation' – the change agent must develop the skills and resources to play a part in "unfolding the 'implicate order'" (Dunphy et al 2007, 322).

We have highlighted this work of Dunphy et al. on corporate sustainability, for three reasons. First, it stands out as a particularly insightful and bold (and compelling) conception of the 'sustaining' organisation and its cultivation. Second, it argues the case for a special role for commercial enterprise, in the broadest sense of the word, in leading the practical pursuit of sustainability – this is a theme we will build on.

Finally, in the context of organisational change, Dunphy et al. touch on one particular change component – the role of the 'pilot' (Dunphy et al 2007, 255-56) – that should be explored further if we are to do justice to the value of enterprise, in particular entrepreneurial enterprise, in underpinning the pursuit of sustainability. We propose here an extension of the thinking reflected in Dunphy et al., as a "dwarf standing on the shoulders of a giant" – perhaps it may still be possible to see a little further.[7]

Special Contribution of Commercial Enterprise

Large corporations certainly do have substantial resources that can be brought to bear on the complex challenges of sustainability, as Dunphy et al. suggest. But commercial enterprises of all shapes and sizes exhibit other qualities that enable them to make a special contribution.

---

[7] In the early 12th Century, the Chancellor of the Cathedral School of Chartres, Bernard of Chartres, said that compared to the newly re-discovered authors of classical Greece and Rome the contemporary scholar was "like a dwarf, standing on the shoulders of a giant". The best account is in Southern 1975, 194.

We have characterised the central challenge in taking the next step towards sustainability as achieving a new level of synthesis or integration. Enterprise is naturally integrative. Enterprises act as 'open systems' (Katz and Kahn 1969), pulling together a vast array of interconnected and interdependent components, in order to convert resources into goods and services that create wealth. The best of them manage to "balance everything" – "It's not a case of A or B but A and B...and C and D and so on" (Hubbard et al 2002, 266). There is an unwillingness to compromise, to seek the lowest common denominator – "...a highly visionary company doesn't want to blend the yin and yang into a gray, indistinguishable circle...it aims to be distinctly yin and distinctly yang – both at the same time, all the time" (Collins and Porras 1994, 44-5). When we begin to question the assumption that shareholders are the only stakeholders whose interests can legitimately be reflected in the activities of the corporation (Handy 2002; Driver 2006; Starik 1995), then this genius for integration in the best enterprises emerges as an important consideration in modelling sustainability.

Corporations can be thought of as communities in their own right (Handy 1997, 179-204). As such they can become practical models of sustainable living, not just for other organisations, but also for the wider communities in which they operate and, indeed, for 'the community' generally. Their special capacity for integration and wealth creation can be directed to the creation of sustainable "common wealth". Hart and Milstein (2003) begin to explore the possibilities presented by this capacity for value creation. The connection is made even more powerfully in the special case of enterprise operating at the "base of the pyramid" in the poorest communities (Prahalad 2002, 2005; Hart 2007; Hart and Prahalad 2002; Hart and Christensen 2002) – an example to which we will return.

So corporations have an important role to play in building a sustainable world, not just because they are resource rich and powerful, but also because, as enterprises, they are naturally integrative and have the capacity to establish themselves as models of sustainable community. In order to bring this capacity for integration and wealth creation to the service of sustainability, established businesses must travel the path of organisational change mapped out by Dunphy et al. But change leaders are dealing with the entrenched values and assumptions of corporate cultures – and corporate 'orthodoxies' – that are extraordinarily resilient, and resistant to managed, incremental change, let alone to a paradigm shift.[8] Dunphy et al (2007, 321) emphasise the critical role of change leaders in shaping corporate culture, but the unspoken assumptions that are the foundations of culture are a product of time – they are often values that have stood the test of time (Schein 1990, 16). – and any superficial change at the level of cultural artefacts will quickly rebound if not accompanied by "deep change" (Dunphy et al 2007, 264, citing Quinn, R 1996 Deep Change: Discovering the Leader Within, Jossey-Bass, San Francisco, p.3), which can, in time, transform the underlying assumptions or "mental models" (Senge 1993, 174). It is difficult for change makers even to conceive this way forward themselves, let alone to carry their

---

[8] Buchanan et al. (2003) canvass the complexities of organisational change and the challenges of sustaining it. Beer and Nohria (2000, 133) put it simply: "The brutal fact is that about 70% of all change initiatives fail".

unwieldy organisations with them down the path to a new vision of sustainability – it's like wading through molasses.

Value of 'Pilots' in Facilitating Change

Dunphy et al (2007, 255) recommend piloting new practices and innovations. They see this as a means of testing and refining, "rather like debugging a software program before its widespread adoption". Pilot programmes also allow us to "test the appropriateness of the tools, and redesign techniques and forms of participation…".

We would propose that pilots have a value beyond that signalled by Dunphy et al – that their value is often as great to change followers as it is to change leaders.

Change leaders often become frustrated. Although the need for change, and the picture of what things will look like after the change, is very clear to them, it often happens that many of the potential followers somehow do not 'get it', no matter how often or passionately the word picture is painted for them. It could be argued that a significant part of this gap between change leader and follower can be attributed to differences in conceptual thinking capability.[9]

Conceptual thinking involves the ability to recognise patterns, to think beyond linear analysis to a point that can only be reached by a conceptual 'leap' but that, once reached, seems logical in hindsight.[10] Greenleaf (1983, 66) contrasts "conceptual" and "operational" talent – "Leadership, in the sense of going out ahead to show the way, is more conceptual than operating". Simply by virtue of the way they think – conceptually – change leaders can sometimes separate themselves from their followers.

Change leaders can 'see' the great merits in moving from organisational state A to state B, and they can happily make that journey – the conceptual leap – in their heads. Many of their followers, whose thinking is shaped by the more prevalent analytical, linear, 'logical' mode, will struggle to make sense of the conceptual journey to state B – that is, they will struggle to make the journey in their heads. The journey's destination, which the leader espouses in such passionate terms, can only be real to them if they can touch and taste and hear and see and smell it. Once they have had that concrete experience of state B, they can look back to state A and make sense of the journey in retrospect. This is not a matter of good or bad thinking or more or less intelligence, but a different mode of thinking – a difference that must be recognised by the change leader.

Enter the pilot programme. Assuming it is well designed and conducted (and correctly conceived!), the pilot provides a concrete experience of the end point to a group of change followers. It allows them to make sense of the journey in

---

[9] Spencer and Spencer (1993, 70-71) provide an excellent framework for understanding the nature and organisational applications of conceptual thinking capability.

[10] Edward de Bono, in his public seminars, has made famous the ant on a tree leaf: The chances of the ant climbing from earth up the trunk to that particular leaf may be one in ten thousand – from the starting point on the trunk, it requires a conceptual or creative leap to 'see' the ant on that leaf. But once on that leaf, the chances of the ant coming back to earth via the trunk are 1:1 – it's the same pathway, but logical in hindsight.

retrospect and to embrace its merits. Furthermore, the journey they have travelled and their approval of its destination have been witnessed, and shared vicariously, by their peers, to whom they can communicate their experience in a way that may be more compelling than the visionary pronouncements of the leader. Looking back from their experience of the destination, the conceptual leap becomes a logical step.

At the same time as it provides concrete experience of the journey for change followers, the pilot also provides conceptual stimulation to other change leaders – here is a new way of approaching things, new linkages and patterns to think about. Change leaders and change followers feed off the pilot in different ways, opening a new vision of possibilities for change leaders, and making the change journey real for change followers.

The same principles that underpin this value of pilots within established organisations have application in the wider community of enterprise. In the "phase model" of corporate sustainability proposed by Dunphy et al (2007, 13-17), the final phase – the Sustaining Corporation – represents the "third wave" of sustainability, a transformation that "sees society moving into a new paradigm where complexity and interconnectedness are central...." (Dunphy et al 2007, 197). It is still difficult to identify a corporation that represents all that is encompassed in the notion of the sustaining organisation, so Dunphy et al cite a number of organisations (typically smaller, private, one could say 'entrepreneurial') whose activities or aspirations in some part reflect transformation to the third wave.

> None of these organizations yet meets the ideal, but collectively they help us create an image of how a fully committed organization would operate. The future is emerging around us, if we have eyes to see it, as innovative companies explore sustainability practices in a range of operations. The analogy is to constructing a jigsaw puzzle – we assemble one piece from one organization, another piece from another organization, until we have an overall image of the organization of the future which is modelling sustainability in its own operations and supporting the wider sustainability movement. (Dunphy et al 2007, 196).

Dunphy et al provide a tool kit for change agents, operating within the cultural and conceptual constraints of a particular corporation. The resilience of corporate 'orthodoxy' and the entrenched values and assumptions that shape the culture of corporations – the old paradigm – make it difficult to lead organisational change, so Dunphy et al recommend drawing on the examples of sustaining activity in other organisations, a series of organisational 'pilots' that can, individually, open our eyes to the possibilities and at the same time, collectively, make them real.

But there is a special kind of 'enterprise piloting', operating outside the boundaries of corporates, large and small, which can give concrete expression to new, integrated models of sustainable enterprise. The enterprise activities of civic entrepreneurs, operating in the community at large, can inspire corporate change leaders with a 'library' of practical examples, and also help their 'followers' (which may include the Senior Executive Committee, or the Board of Directors) to make sense of the change journey to a new sustainability paradigm.

The Civic Entrepreneur in Action

Entrepreneurs are wealth seekers and wealth creators. They see the 'big picture', the underlying patterns and linkages that others miss – they understand, value and leverage the interdependence and interconnectedness of the components in their economy. They are innovators (Drucker 1999), risk takers (Stewart, Wayne and Roth 2004), or at least have an optimistic view of 'risk' (Palich and Bagby 1995) and visionaries (Greenberger and Sexton 1988, 4). In particular, they have an abundance mentality. Their ability to integrate, to make the connections between things that other people have not connected, impel them to embrace the "genius of the AND" (Collins and Porras 1994, 44). They refuse to be constrained in their thinking and action by fighting for 'their share' of a finite cake. Their recipe has more in common with Norman Lindsay's "Magic Pudding" (1918), which regenerates as it is consumed and can be whatever kind of pudding the owner desires, slice by slice – constraints and limitations stimulate them to higher levels of creativity (Mackay et al 2005, 26-27).

Civic entrepreneurs bring all these qualities to the table, but the pursuit of personal wealth is complemented by, or subsumed in, the desire to create sustainable 'common wealth' with and for the community in which they operate. There are many variations on the theme of civic entrepreneurship. Banuri and Najam (2002) focus on the role of 'civil society' and 'civil will' in nurturing sustainable development within developing nations, in ways that are beyond the reach of policy makers and market forces. Henton, Melville and Walesh (2002) focus on civic entrepreneurs as the vehicles for economic development in urban communities. Sayani (2003, 13) describes a model of "integrated" social entrepreneurship, in which "economic activities are designed to lead to positive social outcomes and profitable economic activities create social benefits and horizontal, vertical, forward, or backward economic linkages". MacKay, Scheerer and Takada (2005, iv) coin the description "community sustainability entrepreneur (CSE)", which is less wieldy than 'civic entrepreneur', but may be more complete. CSE's "have the creativity and drive that motivate new possibilities, informed by an assessment of local needs and assets, and they operate through market mechanisms bounded by a socio-ecological sustainability framework" (MacKay et al 2005, 66).

Whatever the community context, and whatever we may call these individuals whose vision, creativity and drive help to build sustainable community, this brand of entrepreneur does not seek to exploit one component of the complex system in which they operate, but looks to understand, nourish and elevate the performance of the whole system. Enterprise is not seen as a vehicle for extracting wealth from the community, but for generating new capital to underpin new community enterprise and wealth. Environmental and social 'wealth' and 'capital' are not add-ons, but are indistinguishable from their economic counterparts – integration extends across 'currencies'. The civic entrepreneur's abundance mentality cultivates the collaboration required between businesses, government (especially local government), educators, non-government agencies, and community groups and members in order to support this level of integration (Austin, Stevenson and Wei-Skillern 2006, 13; MacKay et al 2005, 59). There is no need to protect the 'turf', or the profile, or the commercial interests, or the special mission of this or that collaborative partner. There is enough for everyone – enough independence, kudos, profit, fulfilment. More than enough – an abundance...because the 'incompressibility' of complex systems ensures that there are no boundaries (Richardson, Cilliers and Lissack 2000).

Civic entrepreneurs have an eye out for the 'little guy' – they understand the special opportunities that exist when operating at, or near, the 'base of the pyramid' (Prahalad and Hart 2002; Hart and Christensen 2002; "Bridging the Gap: Sustainable Environment" 2004). They also understand, at least intuitively, that in the non-linear, 'emergent' world of the complex system, small causes can have very large effects (MacKay et al 2005, 59-60; Meadows 2001; Seel 1999).

The following sketch of civic entrepreneurship in action draws on a project currently being designed, in conjunction with a wide range of stakeholders. Its value in the context of this discussion is not so much in whether or not it 'works' – there are many examples of community being reinvigorated by this kind of approach – but in how it provides a conceptual pathway, linking enterprise and sustainability.

This framework recognises that the interactions and feedback loops in the complex system of 'community' can generate a powerful, self-reinforcing downward spiral. So too, if we approach with humility and a willingness to 'dance with the system' (Meadows 2001) – to work with the emergent, self-organising possibilities – the spiral can be reversed, without the fracturing of social capital (Spoehr, Wilson, Barnett, Toth and Watson-Tran 2007), or the application of massive government spending, both of which are so often features of well-meaning attempts to impose 'prosperity' on depressed communities.

The project aims to provide a long-depressed suburban community with the opportunity to reinvent and reinvigorate itself by creating common wealth at all levels. As facilitator of this community revival, the civic entrepreneur operates on two fundamental principles. First, that the generation of common wealth must be undertaken by a community, not for it (Sirolli 1999) – this sounds simple enough, but it requires genuine respect for the community and trust in the capacity of its members to take responsibility for their own individual and collective destinies. Second, that the economic, social and environmental benefits created by civic entrepreneurship only become 'real' when they are imbedded in the community – when the community itself becomes both the vehicle and the guardian of common wealth (Shuman 1994). This demands what we might call a 'quadruple bottom line'; economic benefit, social benefit, environmental benefit and sustainable community (cf. Stead et al 2002, especially 64).

A Vision of Possibilities[11]

Imagine, then, 2000 new homes to replace this community's dilapidated, depressing, public and private rental housing. They are built in commercial partnership between the builder/developer and the community's central economic vehicle – perhaps a limited liability company that encourages individual and corporate investment but is controlled by the community. The new homes are simply and inexpensively constructed, with a strong emphasis on natural materials and low imbedded energy. They are also beautiful (not ornate) and make a positive ecological contribution – for example, whenever the solar or wind energy they generate collectively is greater than net consumption, the excess is sold back to the grid. The housing development is designed to reinforce the health of the community – support for extended family, integration of living, working and playing, and the breaking down of boundaries between 'living' space and agricultural/horticultural enterprise. (The latter can be safely achieved on the basis of commitment to the booming organic produce market, which eliminates the residential dangers of chemical 'overspray'.)

The buying power generated by such a large building volume secures a financing deal that pegs mortgage payments at no greater than public housing rents. Finance may be provided by the new community bank, or a community joint venture with an existing bank or credit union.[12]

The involvement of the principle builder in this project is subject to a non-negotiable proviso – apart from expert building and trades supervisors, the houses are to be built by their new owners – members of the community – employed by the builder under 'traineeships', in collaboration with the local colleges for vocational and technical education. So these members of the community acquire new homes, employment during the duration of the housing project, new skills to support subsequent employment or self-employment and, most importantly, a sense of 'ownership' that goes well beyond the finance package. Indeed, every community initiative is underpinned by learning – vocational education, tertiary studies or skill training (Alvord 2002, 11), and every collaboration with private enterprise is conditional on its support for community education and training.

So many new homes require a lot of new trees to be planted. Sufficiently numerous, in fact, to support the creation of a community nursery, owned partly

---

[11] We owe much of what follows to the vision and generosity of Steve Thomas, civic entrepreneur *par excellence*. Working with Steve is an adventure in abundance! Various elements in this model are echoed in the explosion of work on sustainable community development, worldwide. The following institutions are representative – the key for the civic entrepreneur, of course, is in the breadth and depth of integration:

Sustainable Communities Network (http://www.sustainable.org/economy/commecon.html);
Tompkins Tomkins Institute for Human Values and Technology
(http://www.randburg.com/ca/tompkins.html);
Institute for Community Economics (http://www.nhtinc.org/ice.php);
Community Business Scotland Network (http://www.cbs-network.org.uk/).

[12] The cooperative bank, or credit union, can become the engine room of common wealth, as evidenced by the remarkable story of the Mondragon cooperative in the Basque territories of Spain (Gilman, 1983). Whilst the Mondragon credit union remained a commercial enterprise, its core mission was not profitability, but to ensure that no new businesses, spawned under the umbrella of the community cooperative, failed.

by the community investment company (CIC) and partly by its new, local managers.

This business has the additional task of supplying trees for the new golf course (funded by corporate investment, the CIC and individual community members, who have access to very affordable 'units' of ownership). Each hole in the golf course is designed and, eventually, built by its own group of local citizens, acting under the training and guidance of a professional golf course developer – they may not have immediate access to the most complex machinery, but they pick up lots of other skills in design, project management and landscaping along the way.

Golf courses require a great deal of water, a prospect that can no longer be taken for granted. This course is watered by the community's collective stormwater, gathered in an elongated 'lake', filtered of excess nutrients and other pollutants through extensive reed beds, stored in underground aquifers and recovered as required for the golf course and other community green spaces.

The lake becomes a practice space for rowing crews from the local high schools. Historically it would have been laughable for them even to contemplate competing against the private colleges – but in the hands of the civic entrepreneur, nothing is unimaginable, no symbol of abundant community is beyond reach.

The nursery mentioned above is just one of a range of community-controlled and -managed businesses, supplying a local market for basic goods and services – groceries, fresh foodstuffs, hardware, motor fuels, videos/DVD's etc. These would typically be provided by 'chains', which may provide local employment, but which extract wealth from the community for the benefit of external shareholders.

Other businesses are built on particular strengths of the community (Alvord, Brown and Letts 2002, 10). Widespread graffiti, so often decried as the expression of an incorrigibly delinquent youth, becomes the basis of a design competition. The winning designs will launch an up-market range of organic clothing for street-savvy young people, with all the associated learning and enterprise opportunities for the community – design, manufacture, marketing, selling, managing, exporting, franchising, etc.

In the same way, this community's history of producing rock music stars, and a myriad of young people aspiring to rock stardom, is celebrated through the disciplines of enterprise. Performance is one thing, but the best performers need to be heard in concert and recorded; venues to be organised, events managed and marketed; sound studios to be designed, built, wired, operated; recordings to be designed, manufactured, marketed, sold. All of this on the foundation of continuous learning. If you want to play in a band, you cannot just 'rock up' with guitar in hand – you have to be a good guitarist, and that might require formal tuition, no less than the electrician who wires your studio must serve (or be serving) an apprenticeship.

And so the endless fabric of community interconnections and synergies is woven. Every need is an opportunity for collaborative enterprise. Every new enterprise is a springboard for generating more common wealth. Social capital that has been generated by the community under stress is now leveraged to build a network of interdependencies. A spiralling sense of abundance brings the conceptual insight and creativity of the entrepreneur to the service of sustainable community.

Piloting Sustainability for Corporations

These mechanisms for building sustainable community are not transferable, as they stand, to the corporate context, any more than Peter the Venerable could replicate, exactly, the simple isolation of the reform orders in the complex institutional world of Cluniac custom. Their value to the corporate world is in opening conceptual windows, building a vision of possibilities, and providing concrete demonstrations of the richness that emerges when enterprise embraces sustainability. In short, their value is in helping to shape that paradigm of wholeness and interdependence – flagged by the new science of networks and complex systems – which the corporate world must embrace if it is to fulfill its promise as the vehicle of global sustainability. The enterprise frameworks conceived and pursued in order to nourish sustainable community can act as 'piloting' for larger organisations, where change leaders are looking for conceptual models and concrete expressions of a new level of integration – the sustaining corporation.

If large corporations, with all the resources at their disposal, are to lead the next step towards a new paradigm, they must provide their change leaders with a vision of possibilities, and their change followers, at all levels, with live demonstrations, and the vicarious experience, of 'third wave' sustainability. Models of visionary 'abundance' must present themselves as alternatives to that reactive 'scarcity' which effectively reinforces the old corporate paradigm by prompting change only at its margins.

This is the world of the civic entrepreneur. Such individuals are a rare and precious resource.

Their thinking and their work should be made familiar to corporations and corporate change agents – Peter the Venerable would have approved.

References

Alford, SH, Brown, D and Letts, CW. 2002. *Social Entrepreneurship and Social transformation: An Exploratory Study*. Working Paper No. 15, Hauser Center for Nonprofit Organisations.

Austin, J, Stevenson, H and Wei-Skillern, J. 2006. "Social and Commercial Entrepreneurship: Same, Different, or Both?" *Entrepreneurship Theory and Practice*, January:1-22.

'Bridging the Gap: Sustainable Environment'. 2004. *UN Global Compact Academic Conference, Summary of proceedings*. September. Retrieved 7th January 2005 from http://www.wharton.universia.net/index.cfm?fa =viewArticle&id=888&language=english &specialId=79

Bakan, J. 2004. *The Corporation*. Canada:Penguin.

Beer, M and Nohria, N. 2000. 'Cracking the code of change'. *Harvard Business Review* May-June: 133-141

Brooke, C. 1969. *The Twelfth Century Renaissance.* London: Thames & Hudson.

Buchanan, DA, Ketley, D, Gollop, R, Jones, JL, Lamont, SS, Neath, A and Whitby, E. 2003. "No going back: a review of the literature on sustaining organisational change", *NHS Modernisation Agency, Research into Practice Report No. 7, November.*

Charvin, G, ed. 1965. *Statuts, Chapitres Generaux et Visites de l'Ordre de Cluny,* Vol 1, Paris: Boccard.

Collins, J and Porras J. 1994. *Built to Last: Successful Habits of Visionary Companies,* New York: Harper Collins.

Constable, G, ed. 1967. *The Letters of Peter the Venerable.* 2 vols. Cambridge, Mass: Harvard University Press.

Constable, G. 1975. "The Monastic Policy of Peter the Venerable", in *Pierre Abélard, Pierre le Vénérable: Les courantes philosophique, littéraires et artistique en occident au milieu du XIIe Siècle,* 119-142. Paris: Editions du Centre Nationale de la Recherche Scientifique.

Covey, S. 1990. *The 7 Habits of Highly Effective People.* New York: Simon and Schuster.

Driver, M. 2006. "Beyond the Stalemate of Economics versus Ethics: Corporate Social Responsibility and the Discourse of the Organizational Self". *Journal of Business Ethics* 66 (4): 337–356.

Drucker, P. 1999. *Innovation and Entrepreneurship: practice and principles* (2nd rev. edn). Oxford: Butterworth-Heinemann.

Dunphy, D, Griffiths, A and Benn, S. 2007. *Organizational Change for Corporate Sustainability: A guide for leaders and change agents of the future* (2nd edn). Routledge.

Folz, R. 1975. "Pierre le Vénérable et la liturgie", in *Pierre Abélard, Pierre le Vénérable: Les courantes philosophique, littéraires et artistique en occident au milieu du XIIe Siècle.* Paris: Editions du Centre Nationale de la Recherche Scientifique:143-163.

Gilman, R. 1983."Mondragón: The Remarkable Achievement". *Economics In An Intelligent Universe (IC#2)*(Spring): 44.

Greenberger, DB and Sexton DL. 1988. "'An Interactive Model of New Venture Creation", *Journal of Small Business Management* 26(3):1-7.

Greenleaf, RC. 1983. *Servant Leadership.* Mahwah: Paulist Press.

Handy, C. 1997. *The Hungry Spirit.* London: Hutchinson.

Handy, C. 2002. "What's a Business For?" *Harvard Business Review* December: 49-55.

Hart, SL. 2007 *Capitalism at the Crossroads* (2nd edn). New Jersey: Wharton School Publishing.

Hart, SL and Christensen, C. 2002. "The great leap: driving innovation from the base of the pyramid". *Sloan Management Review* 44: 51-56.

Hart, SL. 1997. "'Beyond Greening: Strategies for a Sustainable World". *Harvard Business Review* January-February: 66-76.

Hart, SL and Milstein, MB. 2003. "Creating Sustainable Value" *Academy of Management Executive* 17: 56-67.

Henton, D, Melville, JG and Walesh, K. 1997. *Grassroots Leaders for a New Economy: How Civic Entrepreneurs Are Building Prosperous Communities.* San Francisco: Jossey-Bass.

Hubbard, G, Samuel, D, Heap, S and Cocks, G. 2002. *The First XI: Winning Organisations in Australia.* Milton: John Wiley & Sons.

Katz, D and Kahn, RL. 1969. "Common Characteristics of Open Systems". In *Systems Thinking,* edited by Emery, FE. New York: Penguin.

Kohn, A. 1993. "Why Incentive Plans Cannot Work". *Harvard Business Review* September-October: 54-63.

Korhonen, J. 2004. "Industrial ecology in the strategic sustainable development model: strategic applications of industrial ecology". *Journal of Cleaner Production* 12:809-823.

Kuhn, T. 1970. *The Structure of Scientific Revolutions* (2nd edn). Chicago, London: University of Chicago Press.

Leclercq, J.1946. *Pierre le Vénérable.* Abbaye S.Wandrille.

Lindsay, N. 1918. *The magic pudding: being the adventures of Bunyip Bluegum and his friends Bill Barnacle and Sam Sawnoff.* Sydney: Angus & Robertson.

MacKay, L, Scheerer, A, Takada, T. 2005. *Entrepreneurs as Change Agents to Move Communities Towards Sustainability.* Thesis submitted for completion of Masters of Strategic Leadership towards Sustainability, Blekinge Institute of Technology, Karlskrona, Sweden

Meadows, D. 1994. "Envisioning a Sustainable World". Paper presented at the Third Biennial Meeting of the International Society for Ecological Economics, San Jose, Costa Rica.

Meadows, D. 2001 "Dancing with Systems". *Whole Earth* Winter: 58-63

Newton, T and Harte, G. 1997. "Green business: Technicist kitsch?". *Journal of Management Studies* 4: 75-98.

Ostrom, E, Burger, J, Field, CB, Norgaard, RB and Policansky, D. 1999. "Revisiting the Commons: Local Lessons, Global Challenges". *Science* 284 (5412):.278

Palich, LE and Bagby DR. 1995."Using cognitive theory to explain entrepreneurial risk-taking: Challenging conventional wisdom". *Journal of Business Venturing* 10(6): 425-438

Prahalad, CK. 2005. *The Fortune at the Bottom of the Pyramid: Eradicating poverty through profits.* Wharton School Publishing.

Prahalad, CK and Hart, SL. 2002. "The Fortune at the Bottom of the Pyramid". *strategy + business* 26 January: 54-67.

Richardson, K, Cilliers, P,and Lissack, M. 2000. "Complexity Science: A 'Grey' Science for the 'Stuff in Between'". Paper presented at the 1st International Conference on Systems Thinking in Management, Deakin University, Geelong, Australia.

Schein, E. 1990. "Organizational Culture". *American Psychologist* February: 109-119.

Schilpp, P. 1949. *Albert Einstein: Philosopher-Scientist.* Evanston, IL: Library of Living Philosophers

Scott James, B. trans. 1953. *The Letters of St Bernard of Clairvaux.* London: Burnes Oates.

Seel, R. 1999. "Complexity & Organisation Development: An Introduction". Accessed 29/01/07. http://www.new-paradigm.co.uk/complex-od.htm.

Sirolli, E. 1999. *Ripples from the Zambezi: Passion, Entrepreneurship and the Rebirth of Local Communities.* Gabriola Island: New Society Publishers.

Shuman, M. 1994.*Towards a Global Village: International Community Development Initiatives.* London Pluto Press.

Southern, RW. 1975. First published 1953. *The Making of the Middle Ages.* London: Hutchinson.

Spencer, LM and Spencer, SM. 1993. *Competence at Work: Models for Superior Performance.* USA: Wiley.

Spoehr, J, Wilson, L, Barnett, K, Toth, T and Watson-Tran, A. 2007. *Measuring Social Inclusion and Exclusion In Northern Adelaide: A report for the Department of Health.* Australian Institute for Social Research, The University of Adelaide

Starik, M. 1995. "Should Trees Have Managerial Standing? Toward Stakeholder Status for Non-Human Nature". *Journal of Business Ethics* 14(3): 207-17.

Stead, WE, Stead, JG and Shemwell, D J. 2002. "Community sustainability comes to the Southern Appalachian region of the USA: the case of Johnson County, Tennessee". In *Research in Corporate Sustainability* edited by Sharma, S, and Starik, M, 61-84. Cheltenham, UK; Northampton, USA: Edward Elgar Publishing.

Stewart Jr, Wayne H and Roth, PL. 2004. " Risk propensity differences between entrepreneurs and managers: a meta-analytic review". *Journal of Applied Psychology* 89(1): 3-13.

Chapter 4: Social Entrepreneurship in Crisis Situations

Roni Kaufman, Amos Avgar, and Julia Mirsky

Abstract: Adoption of global economy principles might lead to social disaster situations as happened in Former Soviet Union (FSU) in the late 1980-ies. In light of the scale of this crisis following the collapse of the social and medical safety net during the fall of communism, and the absence of a local welfare model - the role of the outside entrepreneur as a change agent became critical. There was an urgent need to develop support systems for vulnerable groups such as the elderly and the disabled. The paper deals with social entrepreneurship in a crisis situation and studies the actions that led to the establishment of an innovative network of social service community centers in FSU. In line with contemporary approaches, we adopt a multidimensional perspective and describe and discuss three levels of factors and the interplay between them: a) the social-cultural environment within which the innovation developed, b) characteristics of the organization that provided the framework, drive, and opportunity for the entrepreneur and its field group representatives c) processes and activities that shaped the development of the end product.

Keywords: Social Entrepreneurship, Disaster Situations, Community Development, Former Soviet Union

Introduction

The term 'entrepreneur' suggests shifting economic resources from lower to higher productivity and yield. Early literature claims that the primary function of entrepreneurs is to start new profit-seeking business ventures (Mort et al., 2003). Similar to business ventures whose goal is to create superior value for customers, the primary purpose of the social entrepreneur is to create superior value for clients. Social entrepreneurship leads to the establishment of new social organizations, programs, and services and to continued innovation in existing ones (Dees, 1998). Social entrepreneurship differs from business entrepreneurship in that its social mission is explicit and central (Dees, 1998). This feature is often viewed as a key dimension in the conceptualization of social entrepreneurship[1].

Traditional literature on entrepreneurship focused on individual characteristics of the entrepreneur (Klein & House, 1995; Mort et al., 2003). It argued that to understand entrepreneurship, one must examine the predisposition, abilities, and orientation qualities of the entrepreneur, including intuitive abilities, psychological characteristics (i.e., motivating values, attitudes, and needs), innovative behavior, managerial and organizational capability, propensity to take risks, and leadership qualities[2].

In recent literature, the focus has shifted from analyzing the characteristics of the entrepreneur to examining the organizational and social environment in which the entrepreneur operates. The individual and personal traits of the entrepreneur are now viewed within the social and organizational context (Waldman et al., 2001). Letts et al. (1997) explained, "Social entrepreneurs do not act alone; they develop and then act within an organizational context." Therefore, Mort et al. (2003) suggested that entrepreneurship be viewed as the behavioral characteristics of an organization (e.g., risk tolerance, pro-activeness, innovativeness), whereby the traits of an individual entrepreneur may be perceived as reflections of the organizational environment within which the entrepreneur operates. Greenfieled and Strickon (1981) suggested that in order to reveal the reasons for the success of new innovations, the activities of the social entrepreneur need to be studied in the field.

This article deals with social entrepreneurship in a crisis situation and the actions that led to the establishment of *Hesed*—an innovative social service delivery system. Consistent with contemporary approaches, we adopt a multidimensional perspective to understand the factors that enabled the success of this large-scale social innovation venture. We examine three levels of factors and the interplay between them: (a) the social-cultural environment within which the innovation developed, (b) characteristics of the organization that provided the framework, drive, and opportunity for the entrepreneur and field representatives, and (c) processes and activities that shaped the development of the end product. The article is based on analysis of countless documents and reports, and numerous interviews with persons involved in the enterprise.

The Social Context of the Entrepreneurship

Understanding the prevailing environmental factors during the development of an innovation is critical to understanding the successful implementation of the innovation (Van De Van, 1993). Two sets of factors are relevant to the present

---

[1] This is a revised version of a former publication by two of the authors published in: Mirsky, J., Kaufman, R. & Avgar, A. (Eds.) (2006). Social Disaster as an Opportunity. Langham, M: University Press of America.

[2] Roni Kaufman and Julia Mirsky are senior lecturers at the Spitzer Department of Social Work, Ben-Gurion University of the Negev; Amos Avgar is Chief Operating Officer, Tag International Developmentram

context: the socioeconomic, health, political, and demographic conditions of the general population in the FSU; and those applying specifically to the Jewish population. These conditions and the resulting needs of the Jewish population created the impetus to innovation as well as the conditions necessary for its implementation and acceptance.

Following the disintegration of the Soviet Union, all state and municipal social and health services virtually collapsed. The chaotic conditions that prevailed can be described as a post-disaster situation (Field & Twigg, 2000). Life expectancy dropped to 59 years for males, and pensions (the sole financial resource of the elderly) were insufficient to acquire basic necessities such as food, medicine, and home services. Savings were wiped out by hyperinflation.

While the Jewish community was adversely affected by these general conditions there were additional processes unique to the Jewish population. The age structure of the Jewish community in FSU was an inverted pyramid due to migration and a low birth rate. During the decades of Soviet regime Jews were deprived of their national identity and prevented from congregating on the basis of faith. As a result there was no Jewish community as such and virtually no social support systems. Due to increased emigration and internal migration, the strength of the Jewish family was undermined and many Jews, especially the elderly, suffered severe social isolation. Their physical needs (for food, housing, health services, medicine, etc.) were acute, and so were their social needs for companionship, sense of affiliation or belonging and for spiritual life.

The unique conditions in the post-Soviet environment in which these complex needs were to be addressed paradoxically benefited the intervention. During the Communist era, civil society was nonexistent. Thus, when governmental services disintegrated, there were no models for the establishment of non-governmental civic organizations to fill the gap. The JDC (American Jewish Joint Distribution Committee), an international NGO, was one of the first to introduce the NGO model in the sphere of welfare services. The JDC maintained a sustainable competitive advantage in welfare services due to its record and experience. In the period following the disintegration of the Soviet Union, social services were virtually unregulated, with little governmental support or supervision. Therefore, there was very little governmental intervention in the work of the JDC during its early years of operation, and it was possible to innovate with little or no outside interference. In addition, the tremendous gap in services made the Jewish community receptive to outside intervention and to the introduction of novel programs and approaches. Lacking in leadership, the Jewish community expected and was willing to accept outside leadership.

Characteristics of the Entrepreneurial Organization

Social entrepreneurship develops and operates within the context of an organization (Mort et al., 2003). Therefore, it is important to examine the JDC as an organization and evaluate how its characteristics shaped the basic parameters of the innovation.

The JDC is the overseas arm of the American Jewish community and was established in 1914. According to Winnet (1976), "It has evolved from a simple relief agency to a multi-service agency – changing as needs dictated." The organizational characteristics, culture, and principles (described below) of the JDC provide a fertile framework for social entrepreneurship.

Flexibility typifies the JDC. Working under conditions of uncertainty, the structure of the JDC has been flexible to allow it to adapt to changing needs and conditions. Flexibility is reflected in both the headquarters and the field (Winnet, 1976). The JDC is a *non-political organization* (Winnet, 1976). Working in highly politicized and changing political environments, the JDC has always kept a non-political approach to achieve its social humanitarian mission. The main mode of intervention is to strengthen local communities, especially the capacity and scope of the voluntary sector, thereby promoting self-sufficiency. JDC's *comprehensive approach in program delivery* is important in confronting social needs in an integrative manner. *A community building approach* is a major strategic avenue of the JDC. As opposed to directly providing services, the JDC uses community building intervention strategies. The JDC assumes responsibility and provides direct services when necessary, but a built-in phasing-out process gradually transfers responsibility to local partners. Thus, the JDC is able to act in a flexible manner and move quickly to new areas and programs as conditions dictate (Avgar, 1991). The JDC's *tailor-made programs* are sensitive to local needs and conditions. "Canned programs" are avoided. *Decentralization* is an important operating principle of the JDC. The decision-making structure delegates discretion and professional judgment to the field staff. The JDC accepts that the field staff are the experts on local conditions and thus best suited to propose programs and make operational decisions. The budgetary process grants a high degree of freedom to the field staff, also reflecting the decentralized nature of the organization.

The organization of the JDC is characterized by a high tolerance for risk-taking and "trial and error". Due to the uncertainty and ambiguity under which the JDC operates and the need to continuously innovate, field staff are encouraged to take risks and experiment.

Together, the above characteristics demonstrate the entrepreneurial nature of the JDC. The JDC continuously responds to changing needs, shifting emphasis and strategy as conditions change by introducing innovative social programs. In addition to its core, welfare-related activities, the JDC has been involved in educational programs, leadership development, promotion of Jewish life, and community and organizational development.

Processes and Activities that Shaped the Development of the Innovation

The Field Entrepreneur

In 1988, the JDC embarked on a massive intervention program in the FSU, drawing manpower from experienced JDC staff. Its mission was threefold: (a) to provide welfare assistance to the neediest segment of the Jewish population, (b) to establish and strengthen viable local Jewish infrastructure, and (c) to reconnect FSU Jews to the Jewish people.

The *Hesed* model was developed by a field team of experts that was led by an urban planner (Weiner, 2003). Professional literature addresses a number of characteristics when analyzing the role of the entrepreneur: experience, tolerance for ambiguity and risk-taking, commitment to social values, flexibility, and innovativeness (Mort et al., 2003). The leader of the team had rich experience in responding to disaster and his research in Post-Disaster Development was most applicable for confronting the crisis at hand. This research conceptualized disaster as an opportunity for community development and provided conceptual guidelines for the welfare intervention model in the FSU (Avgar, 1978). His experience included disaster relief efforts in refugee camps of southern Lebanon and the Kurdish refugee camp in eastern Turkey. He also served as Director of Policy and Planning for Israel's Project Renewal (urban redevelopment), a national rehabilitation venture aimed at empowering local communities to take control of their life. In addition to experience, this entrepreneur possessed important leadership qualities: charisma, and team-building abilities.

The conceptual framework and organizational principles of *Hesed* were unfamiliar to local communities in the FSU. In order to implement the model, a buy-in on the part of local activists was necessary. A former activist and present Director of *Hesed* Abraham in St. Petersburg, recalls, "He (the entrepreneur) was able to convince everybody of the advantages of the model. With his enthusiasm, he sold his vision of our team and the newly created service" (Kolton, personal communication. April 22, 2002). He successfully marketed the *Hesed* model also to the JDC executive staff and his colleagues in the FSU department, who approved the plan.

Entrepreneurial Characteristics of Innovation

The outcome of the entrepreneurship discussed herein was a network of multifunctional community service centers—the *Hesed* centers. The centers were established in Jewish communities throughout the FSU, beginning in 1993 with establishment of the first center in St. Petersburg. From its inception, *Hesed* was intended to become, if successful, a model for other service organizations in the FSU (Avgar, 1993). Following the successful implementation of *Hesed* Abraham, the model was accepted and adopted in additional cities. While the basic operating principles and conceptual framework were maintained, each *Hesed* was tailored to the specific needs and conditions of its respective community and established as an independent NGO. From its inception, the *Hesed* model operated as an entrepreneurial organization characterized by a community building orientation, comprehensive services, and flexibility.

Community-building orientation. Rather than providing direct services, the *Hesed* model aimed to develop a local entity that would address the needs of the population, empower the local community and serve as a lever for its development and capacity building. At the same time, *Hesed* was designed to cooperate with and mobilize other community organizations as levers for promoting welfare.

Comprehensive services. *Hesed* was conceived as a comprehensive service intervention model for confronting the physical, social, and spiritual needs of the Jewish population in the FSU. As such, it provided an ideological and conceptual framework and incorporated a host of in-house and outreach services (home care, loan of medical equipment, winter relief, food programs, social clubs, day centers, social visits, cultural and art programs, libraries, etc.). As a multi-service agency, it was designed to address the needs of its clients in a comprehensive manner, by examining and confronting the total needs of clients in an integrated way rather than addressing specific needs in a discrete fashion.

Flexible structure. The professional and organizational structure of *Hesed* was flexible, conducive to including and developing new services and allowing a different variety of services in different locations. Food programs were continually modified as conditions changed; social programs for clients and volunteers were added as necessary; specialized services were developed for at-risk populations such as the hearing impaired and visually impaired. New populations such as children and single mothers were targeted in a systematic fashion.

Local entrepreneurial team. The *Hesed* model was disseminated throughout the FSU by the "commando *Hesed*" (Weiner, 2003), experienced *Hesed* Abraham staff who traveled to other communities and trained local professionals to assume leadership positions in newly-created *Hesed* centers. The use of local professionals as the disseminators of the innovation increased the receptivity of communities to the model and prevented a sense of imposition by an outside foreign organization. It also saved funds which would otherwise have been spent to import more expensive manpower from abroad.

Training. Simultaneously with the establishment of *Hesed* Abraham, JDC created the Rosenwald Institute for Community and Welfare Workers. In the absence of training programs in social work and welfare in the FSU (Iarskaya-Smirnova, 1999), the Institute trained a cadre of professionals, paraprofessionals, volunteers, and lay leaders for existing and future *Hesed* centers. It concentrated on administration, social and community work, service skills, and leadership development with Jewish values and traditions cutting across all areas. The Institute provided not only professional training for skills required to operate the *Hesed* centers but also, and perhaps as important, a vehicle for the socialization of new professional staff and volunteers. The basic values and ideological orientation of *Hesed* guided the work of the Institute. The Institute provided an opportunity for continuous exchange of information regarding practices between *Hesed* centers. With the geographic expansion and increased labor force of the *Hesed* movement, eight regional institutes were established throughout the FSU.

The *Hesed* model created an opportunity to restructure the social reality in a situation of chaos and ambiguity. Sharir (2001) noted that "the entrepreneur is able to identify and create structures where others perceive only chaos." For the entrepreneur, the situation of the Jewish community in the FSU was "a planner's paradise"—while seemingly nothing was possible, everything was possible.

Discussion

It is often argued that an innovation and the cultural/ organizational environment into which it is introduced must be highly compatible. The innovation described in this article demonstrates, however, that organizational 'mutations' can occur. The cultural characteristics of *Hesed* were totally alien to the FSU environment. How did such an unfamiliar mode of operation take root? The present case study suggests that the most critical factor that enabled the introduction of the innovation was the organization that brought it forth. The JDC had a compelling mystique in the FSU and was conceived as a powerful agency with unlimited capabilities. The trust of the Jewish community in the JDC in its initial stage of operation enabled the creation of a social structure based on trust, as well as the carry-over of this trust to interpersonal relationships within *Hesed* centers.

A large-scale revival of religious life was taking place throughout the FSU. Churches that had been converted to warehouses and synagogues that were transformed to boxing clubs reopened. *Hesed* provided a vehicle for the Jewish population to reconnect with Jewish life, a need that had generally been unarticulated. The wide acceptance of the ideological principles of *Hesed*—not only its services—can be explained by the fact that it met virtually human basic needs.

It can be argued that for an innovation to take root, the entrepreneur must have an in-depth understanding of the scope of the needs and the organizational, legal and financial aspects of the environment in which he is to operate. However, in the present case, neither the organization nor the entrepreneurial team completely understood the environment. In particular, they were unfamiliar with the pitfalls, obstacles, and constraints that would be met in the process. Although a survey of needs and a planning process were conducted prior to establishment of *Hesed*, the complex and rapidly changing reality in the FSU could not have been fully anticipated. The innovation was successful because the JDC has always worked under conditions of uncertainty and is willing to take risks. The entrepreneurial team had earlier experience with uncertain conditions and received full backing from the JDC to take risks. The flexible resources and the opportunity to develop a small-scale model minimized the risk and enabled the team to tolerate an approach that demanded a leap of faith.

Most members of the entrepreneurial team were professionals from the FSU who lived their adult life in Israel. They were completely bicultural when they returned to work in the FSU. Other team members were multicultural. The innovation was tailor-made to local conditions according to Western, Israeli, Soviet, and Jewish principles. The intimate knowledge of most team members of several cultures allowed them to present new concepts in a manner acceptable to the local community.

Social crises often require structural changes. Typically, the response to such crises addresses immediate needs, and the crisis is seldom seen as an opportunity for development. However, short-term tactics and immediate relief measures do not foster long-term development. The *Hesed* experience represents an alternative strategy and illustrates the critical role played by outside entrepreneurs – organizations and professionals – in leading the intervention process and integrating immediate relief with long-term reconstruction.

Entrepreneurs are organizations and people who, often habitually, create and innovate something of value around perceived opportunity (Bolton & Thomson, 2000). Social entrepreneurs identify a need and related opportunities, imagine and envision, recruit and motivate, build essential networks, secure resources, overcome obstacles and challenges, handle risks, and introduce systems for controlling the venture (Leadbeater, 1997; Thompson, 2002).

The present case study demonstrates the complex role of social entrepreneurship in a crisis situation. Social entrepreneurship began by diagnosing the situation, identifying potential key players, and mobilizing them. It continued by designing tailor-made models to meet the needs of the community and adjusting them to the cultural context in which they operated. In this respect, the social entrepreneurs acted as agents of change in that they applied and adjusted new ideas and technologies to a new situation. Finally, the entrepreneurship includes continuously monitoring and adjusting the intervention model. The most critical decisions are related to using the crisis as an opportunity and taking advantage of new directions and developments created in its aftermath.

The success of the *Hesed* community service network is related to a number of factors: the entrepreneurial nature of the intervening organization, the JDC; the professional background and abilities of the field-entrepreneur and his team; the fit between the innovation and the environmental conditions and special needs of the target population; and the entrepreneurial qualities of the innovative model, the *Hesed* model, that enabled replication and diffusion.

Hesed demonstrates how a context of social disaster may call for the intervention of outside NGO organizations with entrepreneurial characteristics, together with the development of local NGOs with entrepreneurial qualities.

References

Avgar, A., (1978). Post-disaster development: Implications for public policy. Ph.D. Dissertation, Cornell University, Ithaca, NY.

Avgar, A. (1991) - JJDC-JAFI July 28, 1991p 11-12.

Avgar, A. (1993) – JDDC, June 5, 1993, .5.

Bolton, W. K., & Thompson, J. L. (2000) Entrepreneurs: Talent, temperament, technique. Oxford: Butterworth & Heineman.

Dees, J. G. (1998). "The meaning of social entrepreneurship. Enterprising nonprofits." Harvard Business Review, 76, 55-67.

Greenfield, S. & Strickon, A. (1981). "A new paradigm: Study of entrepreneurship and social change." Economic Development and Cultural Change, 29(3), 467-499.

Field, M. G. & Twigg, J. L., (2000). "Introduction." In M. G. Field & J. L. Twigg (eds.), Russia's torn safety nets: Health and social welfare during the transition (pp. 1-10), London: Macmillan.

Iarskaya-Smirnova, E. (1999). "Social work in Russia: Professional identity, culture and the state." In B. Lesnik (ed.), International perspectives in social work: Social work and the state (pp. 31-44), Brighton: Pavilion Publishing.

Klein, J. K. & House, R. J. (1995). "On fire: Charismatic leadership and levels of analysis." Leadership Quarterly, 6, 183-198.

Kolton, L. (April 22, 2002). Personal communication.

Leadbeater, C. (1997). The rise of the social entrepreneur. London: Demos.

Letts, S. V., Ryan, W., & Grossman, A. (1997). "Virtuous capital: What foundations can learn from venture capitalists." Harvard Business Review, 75(2), 36-44.

Mort, G. S., Weerawardena, J., & Carnegie, K. (2003). "Social entrepreneurship: Towards conceptualization." International Journal of Non-Profit and Voluntary Sector Marketing, 8(1), 76-88.

Paneyakh, E. & Uryupina, K (1989). Organizational structure forming under conditions of transitional economies. St. Petersburg: Institute of Communal Welfare Workers.

Sharir, M . (2001). Gauging the success of social ventures initiated by individual social entrepreneurs. Ph.D. Dissertation , Ben-Gurion University, Israel.

Thompson, J. L. (2002). "The world of social entrepreneur." International Journal of Public Sector Management, 15(4/5), 412-431.

Van De Van, A. H. (1993). "The development of an infrastructure for entrepreneurship." Journal of Business Venturing, 8, 221-230.

Waldman, D. A., Ramirez, G. G., House, R., & Puranam, P. (2001). "Does leadership matter? CEO leadership attributes and profitability under conditions of perceived environmental uncertainty." Academy of Management Journal, 44(3), 134-143.

Weiner, A. (2003). Renewal: Reconnecting Soviet Jewry to the Jewish People. A decade of American Jewish Joint Distribution Committee (JDC) activities in the former Soviet Union, 1988-1998. Lanham, MD: University Press of America.

Winnet, N. (1976). Compassion in action: A continuing task. A study of the American Jewish Joint Distribution Committee. New York: JJDC.

Chapter 5: Globalization and Social Entrepreneurship

Appreciating Social Entrepreneurship in the Context of a Globalized Landscape

Joanne Neal

Abstract: The net sociological and economic impacts of globalization are as yet undetermined. But one of the positive outcomes has been in the field of social entrepreneurship. Intentionally pursuing the ethical before the profitable, social entrepreneurs are dynamic, creative individuals with a passion for improving the world. Their success stories are many as they work tirelessly for sustainable improvement for populations that are often marginalized, poverty stricken, and/or simply forgotten.

Keywords: Social Entrepreneurs, Social Entrepreneurship

Introduction

Globalization is a reality of our current multinational economy and of our worldwide culture. The research literature on the topic of globalization is plentiful, with some authors citing it as a positive phenomenon and others condemning it as a negative trend. While there have been many instances of corporate financial success linked to globalization, there have also been many documented episodes of human and environmental exploitation associated with the processes of globalization. The challenge for the entrepreneur operating within a globalized economy is to consider issues of sustainability, social justice, and human rights alongside issues of profit. This is where the work of the social entrepreneur becomes particularly relevant.

Understanding Social Entrepreneurship

> Few will have the greatness to bend history itself; but each of us can work to change a small portion of events and with the total of all those acts will be written the history of this generation (Robert F. Kennedy).

Social entrepreneurship has proven to be a largely positive outcome of globalization. Social enterprise is a dimension of entrepreneurial activity focused on generating social value and sustainable social change. Monetary profit is considered to be of secondary importance and viewed more as a tool for creating additional social value and change rather than being an end unto itself. Although social enterprise has many commonalities with more classically defined entrepreneurial activity, it offers an alternative agenda that is closely bound to social and cultural contexts. As globalization has accelerated in speed and scope over the past twenty years, socially entrepreneurial activity has had a parallel growth.

William Drayton of the Ashoka foundation is credited with having coined the phrase *social entrepreneurship* in the early 1980s. He views the primary objective of social entrepreneurship as systemic change.

> The job of the social entrepreneur is to recognize when a part of society is not working and to solve the problem by changing the system, spreading solutions, and persuading entire societies to take new leaps. Social entrepreneurs are not content just to give a fish or to teach how to fish. They will not rest until they have revolutionized the fishing industry. Identifying and solving large-scale social problems requires social entrepreneurs because only entrepreneurs have the committed vision and inexhaustible determination to persist until they have transformed an entire system (Drayton, 2002, 123).

In a later work, Drayton furthers this description with a list of defining attributes of the social entrepreneur.

> What qualities define an effective social entrepreneur? First, the person must be creative in both goal setting and problem solving. Second – and this is the toughest screen – is entrepreneurial quality. This is not leadership, or the ability to administer, or the ability to get things done. The driving force here is the fact that such a person is emotionally, deeply committed to making change throughout the whole of society. Once one understands that this commitment itself is the driving force, then everything else follows. The final quality essential to success as a social entrepreneur is ethical fiber. People will not make significant changes in their lives if they do not trust the person asking them to do so (2005, 3).

J. Gregory Dees echoes Drayton's perspective, citing five critical attributes of social entrepreneurship:

> a mission to create and sustain social value, as change agents in the social sector, the relentless pursuit of new opportunities to serve that mission, a commitment to a process of continuous innovation, adaptation, and learning, the readiness to act boldly without being limited by resources currently at hand, and heightened accountability to the constituencies served and for the outcomes created (Dees, 1998, 4).

In bringing additional clarity to this definition, Dees wrote in 2003:

> Far too many people still think of social entrepreneurship in terms of nonprofits generating earned income. This is a dangerously narrow view. It shifts attention away from the ultimate goal of any self-respecting social entrepreneur, namely social impact, and focuses it on one particular method of generating resources. Earned income is only a means to a social end, and it is not always the best means (1).

Simms and Robinson (2009, p.9 in International perspectives on social entrepreneurship as edited by Mair, Robinson, and Hockets) contend that the social entrepreneur identity is composed both of the activist and the entrepreneur identities which can effectively function in both the for-profit and nonprofit organizational structures. This theme of dual identity is also echoed in an earlier work of Robinson et al.

> The concept of social entrepreneurship is, in practice, recognized as encompassing a wide range of activities: enterprising individuals devoted to making a difference; social purposes business ventures dedicated to adding for-profit motivations to the nonprofit sector; new types of philanthropists supporting venture capital-like 'investment' portfolios; and nonprofit organizations that are reinventing themselves by drawing on lessons learned from the business world (2006, 1).

Paul Light (2008) notes that socially entrepreneurial activity operates in degrees rather that as an "either/or" construct. The following table illustrates Light's point.

According to Light, the separations between high, moderate, and lower levels of social enterprise are determined by the amount of time and energy that a given individual or organization dedicates to innovative efforts geared towards solving intractable or challenging social problems.

The common themes that appear to be emerging from these descriptions of social entrepreneurship include: a focus on solving significant and complex social problems, the creation of social value, sustainable and systemic change, the ability to be a visionary, creativity and innovativeness, deep commitment, and an ethical approach that fosters credibility. But this still does not seem to sufficiently capture social entrepreneurship at the conceptual level. To this end, the work of Sullivan Mort, Weerawardena and Carnegie (2003) is extremely helpful.

Table 1: A Continuum of Socially Entrepreneurial Activity

Level	Definition
Highly socially entrepreneurial	The organization shows clear and consistence evidence (80-100 percent of its energy) that it seeks to create social change through innovative and pattern breaking methods and ideas. Nearly all of the organization is focused on addressing significant social problems through its programs, processes, or applications.
Moderately socially entrepreneurial	The organization shows moderate evidence (20-80 percent of its energy) of an effort to pursue pattern breaking change. These moderately entrepreneurial organizations tend to have a single department or section of the organization that is pursuing pattern-breaking change, while the rest of the organization focuses on service-delivery or other standard organizational activities.
Not-too socially entrepreneurial	The organization shows the least evidence (less than 20 percent of its energy) of an effort to create social change. While the organization does provide needed services to society, it is more focused on effective service delivery than on developing innovative programs.

Source: Light, P. 2008. The Search for Social Entrepreneurship. p.153. Washington, DC: The Brookings Institution Press.

In summarizing the research literature, Sullivan Mort et al draw on more than twenty definitions of social entrepreneurship. They concluded that, as a theoretical construct moving towards operationalization, it was much more complex and dynamic than the research literature to that point had described it. They define social entrepreneurship as:

> …a multidimensional construct involving the expression of entrepreneurially virtuous behavior to achieve the social mission, a coherent unity of purpose and action in the face of moral complexity, the ability to recognize social value-creating opportunities and key decision-making characteristics of innovativeness, proactiveness and risk-taking (76).

In a more detailed explanation of *entrepreneurially virtuous behavior,* the authors note the following:

> Social enterprises have a spiritual or virtue dimension very often missing from or only latent in commercial enterprises. Social entrepreneurs' attitudes and behaviors must involve a virtue dimension. It is this virtue dimension of vision of moral purpose that will aid in operationalizing the social mission, and differentiates the social entrepreneur from the commercial entrepreneur…Virtues are positive, morally good values

such as love, integrity, honesty and empathy, which must be acted upon to become genuine virtues (83).

Translated into graphic form, the conceptualization that Sullivan Mort et al put forth combines four facets of social entrepreneurship, situating *entrepreneurially virtuous* in interplay with the other three areas.

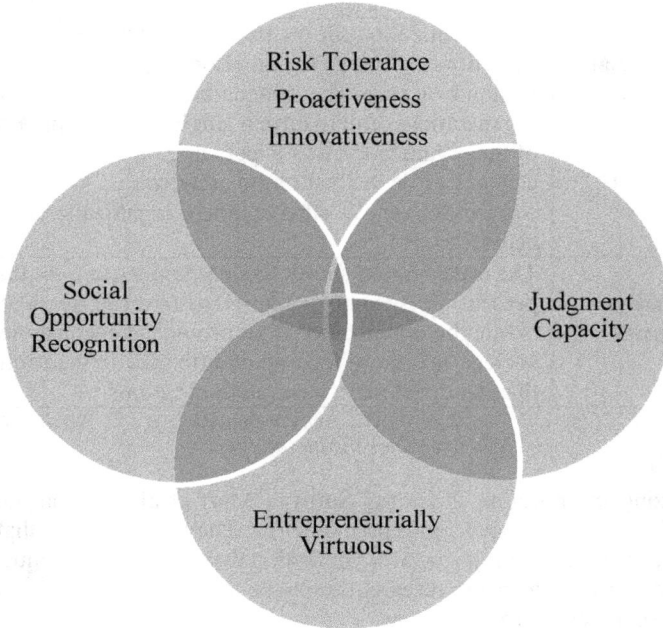

Figure 1: A Conceptualization of Social Entrepreneurship Based on the Work of Mort, Weerawardena and Carnegie (2002)
Source: Sullivan Mort, G., Weerawardena, J., Carnegie, K. 2003. Social Entrepreneurship: Towards Conceptualization. International Journal of Nonprofit and Voluntary Sector Marketing, Volume 8, Number 1, pp. 76-88. Henry Stewart Publications.

Going one step further in separating social entrepreneurship from a more traditional understanding of business entrepreneurship, we can draw on the work of Shaw and Carter (2007) as they offer the following comparison.

- Business entrepreneurship focuses on profits, while social entrepreneurship draws upon and builds community support.
- Business entrepreneurship engages market forces, while social entrepreneurship draws upon and builds community support.
- Business entrepreneurship involves financial risk, while social entrepreneurship depends on organizational and personal credibility
- Business entrepreneurship produces individual financial gain, while social entrepreneurship generates collective public good.

- Business and social entrepreneurship both involve creativity, but business entrepreneurship uses creativity to enter new markets, while social entrepreneurship uses creativity to solve intractable problems.

Synthesizing this perspective with the previously noted definitions, we can see the areas of distinction and commonality between a traditional approach to entrepreneurship and social entrepreneurship.

Table 2: Comparing Traditional Entrepreneurship & Social Entrepreneurship

Traditional Entrepreneurship	Areas of Commonality Between Traditional Entrepreneurship & Social Entrepreneurship	Social Entrepreneurship
Focus on creation of value, traditionally in terms of monetary profit	Ability to recognize and capitalize on opportunities; being a visionary	Focus on creation of social value
Involves financial risk	Taking risks	Depends on personal credibility through a consistently ethical approach
Produces individual financial gain	Importance of timing	Generates collective public good
Creativity to enter new markets	Creativity and innovation	Creativity to solve intractable and complex social problems

In summary, social enterprise is a specific form of entrepreneurship that has many similarities to but also some important distinctions from entrepreneurship as we have traditionally conceived it within a business/management context. But how do we separate social enterprise activity from corporate social responsibility?

Distinguishing Social Entrepreneurship From Corporate Social Responsibility

Some men see things as they are and say, "Why?' I dream of things that never were and say, "Why not?" (George Bernard Shaw).

Globalization has allowed businesses from developed nations to move their production to third world and lesser developed countries. Because labour standards and wages are often lower in lesser developed countries, this can translate into a higher profit margin for the business. It can also mean employment for workers in struggling parts of the planet. As well, regulations and restrictions regarding the use of natural resources may be less stringent in third world countries, allowing businesses to increase production at lower costs. But there can also be a down side to this.

United Nations Global Impact Principles

Human Rights
Principle 1: Businesses should support and respect global human rights.
Principle 2: Businesses should make sure they are not associated with any human rights abuses.

Labour Standards
Principle 3: Businesses should allow the freedom of association and recognize collective bargaining of their employees.
Principle 4: Businesses should eliminate all forms of forced and/or compulsory labour.
Principle 5: Businesses should abolish child labour.
Principle 6: Businesses should eliminate all forms of discrimination in the workplace.

Environment
Principle 7: Businesses should support a precautionary approach to global environmental challenges.
Principle 8: Businesses should undertake all initiatives that promote a higher level of environmental responsibility.
Principle 9: Businesses should encourage the development and dissemination of environmentally-friendly technologies.

Anticorruption
Principle 10: Businesses should stop all forms of corruption including extortion and bribery.

Figure 2: United Nations Global Impact Principles, 1999
Source: Stanwick, P., Stanwick, S. 2009. Understanding Business Ethics .p.195. Upper Saddle River, NJ: Pearson Prentice Hall.

Different countries throughout the world have different laws and cultural norms regarding the use of the natural environment and the Earth's resources, and regarding working conditions, wages, and labour standards. This means that what may be illegal in North America may be legal business practice in other parts of the world; particularly in developing or third world countries. It also means that what may not be culturally acceptable in North America may be culturally acceptable in other nations (e.g., wage discrimination based on gender). This opens the door for potential exploitation of the environment and of human beings. The essential question for the entrepreneur then becomes, *Even if this practice is legal in this country, is it ethical?*

Recognizing the growing impact and pace of globalization through the 1980s and 1990s, the United Nations compiled a series of principles in 1999 to encourage responsible business practices across the globe. While these standards cannot be legislated by the UN, the hope was that they would provide some structure and incentive for achieving positive outcomes of globalization. The principles are organized around the four key themes of human rights, labour standards, environment, and anticorruption.

These principles are also important because they lay the foundations for *corporate social responsibility*; a phenomenon that has gained momentum in the 21st century.

Daniel Diermeier (2007) notes that:

> Corporate social responsibility has been broadly defined as the ways in which a company's activities affect its stakeholders and fulfill its perceived obligations to society, including the environment. Some businesses are on the cutting edge of the movement to make corporations more socially responsible. Others are driven to join it by unfortunate disclosures or the consequences of missteps in regard to social responsibility. Nevertheless, most large companies grapple with a broad range of corporate social responsibility issues ranging from global poverty to renewable energy ...

> What is new is an emerging consensus that corporate social responsibility is no longer a luxury for a few prosperous companies but a necessary component of sound business practice. Companies are increasingly held accountable by standards other than maximizing shareholder value, and they need to develop strategies and policies to address these challenges (xii-2).

In her work, *Corporate Social Responsibility and Globalization – An Action Plan for Business,* Jacqueline Cramer describes corporate social responsibility as being compromised of three key elements or *pillars*: people, planet, and profit. Figure 3 explains this concept in greater detail.

Bhagwati (2007) examines the issue of how and why corporate social responsibility should be undertaken.

> It would appear, therefore, that the true, indeed only, compelling reason for corporations to assume social responsibility is that it is the right thing to do. For in doing so, they will **enhance** the social good that their economic activities promote when they invest in these developing countries, and for which there is now much evidence...

The edifice of corporate social responsibility, however, must rest on two foundations. One has to be altruism, which deals with what corporations **should** do. But the other must deal with regulation that defines what corporations **should not** do (191).

People relates to a range of subjects, including both internal and external social policies. This concerns not only the company's own part in the chain, but also the rest of the chain for which the company can take responsibility.

Internal social policy includes the nature of employment, labour/management relationships, health and safety, training and education, as well as diversity and opportunities. External social policy encompasses three main categories, each with several sub-categories, namely"

1.   Human rights issues, including strategy and management, nondiscrimination, freedom of association and collective bargaining, child labour, forced and compulsory labour, disciplinary practices, security practices and indigenous rights.
2.   Society, including community activities, bribery and corruption, financial contributions to political parties, competition and pricing.
3.   Product responsibility, including consumer health and safety, products and services, advertising and respect for personal privacy.

Planet relates to the environmental impact of the company's production activities: the use of scarce goods (such as energy, water and other raw materials) and the environmental impact in the product chain.

Profit stands for the company's contribution to economic prosperity in the broadest sense. Here, a distinction is made between direct and indirect economic impact. Direct impact involves the monetary flows between the organization and its key stakeholders and the impact which the organization has on the economic circumstances of those stakeholders.

The indirect impact is related to the spin-off from company activities in terms of innovation, the contribution of the sector to gross domestic product or national competitiveness and the local community's dependence on the company's activities.

Figure 3: The Three Pillars of Corporate Social Responsibility – People, Planet, and Profit
Source: Cramer, J. 2006. Corporate Social Responsibility and Globalization: An Action Plan for Business. p.15. Sheffield, UK: Greenleaf Publishing Ltd.

One would hope that businesses develop corporate social responsibility agendas for the altruistic reasons that Bhagwati has cited. Some companies have intentionally given corporate social responsibility initiatives a prominent place in their organizational cultures, working from a values based perspective. Others have been motivated to adopt such policies because being seen to be environmentally and socially responsible appeals to its customers. That is, some businesses have been sufficiently sensitive to trends in our broader societal culture to know that consumers are interested in patronizing companies that respond to concerns about the environment and about social justice. Consider the example of the coffee company that advertises the fact that it uses "fair trade coffee beans". They may be engaging in an act of social justice because it is the right thing to do, or they may be simply engaging in marketing practices that will increase their sales. Ultimately, the entrepreneur needs to reflect on his or her motives for crafting and implementing a corporate social responsibility agenda and thinking through where such a policy will figure in the organizational culture of the company.

There are themes that potentially run a parallel course between social enterprise and corporate social responsibility. But in the final analysis, it is having the desire to create social value and to bring about sustainable change – pursuits that are at the forefront of the social entrepreneur's agenda – that help to separate the two forms of entrepreneurial activity. Again, we are also drawn to Drayton's (2005) use of the term *ethical fiber* and the idea of *entrepreneurially virtuous behavior* (Sullivan Mort et al, 2003). While these are qualities that may be present in corporate social responsibility, they need not be so. However, for the social entrepreneur, they are vital.

Conclusion

Globalization is an undeniable reality of the worldwide economy and culture. It has created both opportunities and challenges for entrepreneurs. While the debate regarding the net effects of globalization (be it a positive or negative force) will likely not ever be definitively settled, social entrepreneurship as a constructive outcome of globalization has its own niche. Although it shares some common characteristics with traditional entrepreneurial activity and with corporate social responsibility, social entrepreneurship clearly has its own place on the globalized landscape.

References

Bhagwati, J. 2007. *In Defense of Globalization.* Oxford, UK: Oxford University Press.

Cramer, J. 2006. *Corporate Social Responsibility and Globalization: An Action Plan for Business.* Sheffield, UK: Greenleaf Publishing Ltd.

Dees, J. G. 1998. Enterprising Nonprofits. *Harvard Business Review 76* (January-February)*: 55-67.*

Dees, J.G. 2003. *Social Entrepreneurship is About Innovation and Impact, Not Income.* www.fuqua.duke.edu/centers/case/articles/1004/corner.htm.

Diermeier, D. 2007. *Global Corporate Citizenship.* Evanston, IL: Kellogg School of Management.

Drayton, W. 2002. The Citizen Sector: Becoming as Entrepreneurial and Competitive as Business. *California management review, 44:* 120-133.

Drayton, W. 2005. Everyone a Changemaker. *PeerReview 7* (Spring): 8-11.

Light, P. 2008. *The Search for Social Entrepreneurship.* Washington, DC: Brookings Institution Press.

Mair, J., Robinson, J., Hockets, K. 2006. *Social Entrepreneurship.* New York: Palgrave Macmillan.

Mair, J., Robinson, J., Hockets., K. (eds.) 2009. *International Perspectives on Social Entrepreneurship.* New York: Palgrave Macmillan.

Shaw, E., Carter, S. 2007. Social Entrepreneurship: Theoretical Antecedents and
    Empirical Analysis of Entrepreneurial Processes and Outcomes. *Journal
    of Management and Organization* 13: 331-344.
Stanwick, P., Stanwick, S. 2009. *Understanding Business Ethics*. Upper Saddle
    River, NJ: Pearson Prentice Hall.
Sullivan Mort, G., Weerawardena, J., Carnegie, K. (2003). Social
    Entrepreneurship: Towards Conceptualization. *International Journal of
    Nonprofit and Voluntary Sector Marketing*, Volume 8, Number 1, pp.
    76-88. Henry Stewart Publications.

Part 2: An Overview of Microfinance

Chapters 6-9 make up Part 2 of the book, which provides an overview of microfinance. Chapter 6 explores the benefits of microfinance. Chapter 7 looks at sustainable microfinance. Chapter 8 explores stakeholders' perspectiveness on the effectiveness of microfinance. Chapter 9 looks at microfinance as a means for alleviating poverty around the world.

Chapter 6: The Benefits of Microfinance

Microfinance: Providing Two Waves of Education

Jennifer Butler

Abstract: In September 2000, United Nations member states gathered for the United Nations Millennium Summit and agreed upon a set of eight development targets, which became known as the Millennium Development Goals. The Millennium Development Goals aim to eradicate extreme poverty and hunger, achieve universal primary education, promote gender equality, reduce child mortality, improve maternal health, combat HIV/AIDS, ensure environmental sustainability, and develop a global partnership for development by the year 2015. The year 2005 was declared the "International Year of Microcredit" by the United Nations and in 2006; Muhammad Yunus and Grameen Bank were awarded the Nobel Peace Prize "for their efforts to create economic and social development from below." The Nobel Committee claimed, "Lasting peace cannot be achieved unless large population groups find ways in which to break out of poverty. Micro-credit is one such means." As microfinancing is becoming more utilized as a development tool, it has become necessary to research the impact this strategy has on achieving the Millennium Development Goals. This paper looks to examine what microcredits are, how microcredits work, the two waves of benefits created by microcredit programs in the areas of women's empowerment and education for their children, along with the results of implementing this type of development strategy. Former Deputy Secretary-General of the United Nations, Mark Malloch Brown, was quoted saying, "Microfinance is much more than simply an income generation tool. By directly empowering poor people, particularly women, it has become one of the key driving mechanisms towards meeting the Millennium Development Goals, specifically the overarching target of halving extreme poverty and hunger by 2015."

Keywords: Microfinance, Millennium Development Goals, Poverty Alleviation, Sustainability, Education in Developing Countries

The hand that rocks the cradle rules the world. And in many cases that hand is uneducated, unemployed, and impoverished. Where does that leave the future of the world? In 2008, according to World Bank estimates, 1.4 billion people, many of them women and children, live on $1 a day. It is obvious aid is required. This paper looks at microfinance as aid with a future and shows that microfinance results in two waves of education with the ability to break the cycle of poverty.

In his 2010 State of the Union Address, President Barack Obama said, "In the 21st century, the best anti-poverty program around is a world-class education." But how can this education be paid for? In developing countries there are schools, but families are required to provide uniforms for the children and money for supplies. With budgets already stretched to breaking, education often appears superfluous even while world charitable donations heavily subsidize the family's cost of living. What if the two are linked? What if the money needed to raise the family from poverty linked to not only children's school attendance, but also adult education programs? The most successful microfinance models do exactly this, link funding to education.

Subsistence farming is a way of life for many of the developing poor. The most repetitious and menial of farm chores are usually allocated to the children of the family. These poverty areas are often plagued with a lack of natural resources, requiring diligent scouring of the land for necessary fuel and/or water. Planting or tending crops, animal care, gathering wood, and hauling water are likely to occupy the daylight hours of the children. These families would argue that the children cannot be spared for school. Yet a mother with an improving financial condition can afford to release at least some of the family's children for school. Her increased income allows her to buy a few more goods at the market, replacing the work of the students. These students carry the hopes and dreams of the family into the future.

> Women are indeed the linchpin of the region's development strategy. Economists who scrutinized East Asia's success noted a common pattern. These countries took young women who previously had contributed negligibly to gross national product (GNP) and injected them into the formal economy, hugely increasing the labor force. The basic formula was to ease repression, educate girls as well as boys, give the girls the freedom to move to the cities and take factory jobs, and then benefit from the demographic dividend as they delayed marriage and reduced childbearing. The women meanwhile financed the education of younger relatives, and saved enough of their pay to boost national savings rates. This pattern has been called "the girl effect." (Kristof & WuDunn 2009, xix)

"Evidence has mounted that helping women can be a successful poverty-fighting strategy anywhere in the world, not just in the booming economies of East Asia." (Kristof & WuDunn 2009, xix)

The "girl effect" is unique in that moving young women into the work force increases their formal or informal education and then increases the incident of formal education for their younger family members, thus resulting in two waves of educational benefit. "When women and girls earn income, they reinvest 90 percent of it into their families, as compared to only 30 to 40 percent for a man" (Borges 2007, 13).

Launching women into the work force can be as simple as providing a small loan to start a family business. This is microfinance. Grameen Bank offers a successful model for microfinance institutions. Though it is just one of many, it sports a 97 per cent loan recovery rate and has impacted almost 8 million families with 97 per cent of its loans going to women (Grameen Bank 2008).

Considering that 97 per cent of recipients are women it is important to note the impact this capital has on a family. "Women's empowerment helps raise economic productivity and reduce infant mortality. It contributes to improved health and nutrition. It increases the chances of education for the next generation" (United Nations Development Programme 2006). The women that receive microfinance capital are able to start small family businesses, participate in the economic framework of their communities, as well as send their children to school. "The role of education in poverty eradication, in close co-operation with other social sectors, is crucial. No country has succeeded if it has not educated its people. Not only is education important in reducing poverty, it is also the key to wealth creation" (United Nations Educational, Scientific, and Cultural Organization 2001). Linking capital to adult education gives the burgeoning entrepreneur opportunities to learn about business and community enterprise by participating in the system. "Wealth creation is a significant aspect in education programmes intended to contribute to poverty eradication. How can education assist learners to create wealth? Integration of school education within the economic activities of a community is one example" (United Nations Educational, Scientific, and Cultural Organization 2001). Economist Milton Friedman once said, "The poor continue to be poor not because they don't want to work but because they don't have access to capital." A microloan with organization educational support has been shown to break the poverty cycle.

Another notable microfinance institution, Pro Mujer, begins with starter loans of only $50 USD. Reporting a 99 per cent repayment success for 2007 indicates that women in developing countries are responsible and capable of learning to participate in the economic world (Pro Mujer 2010).

> Consider the costs of allowing half a country's human resources to go untapped. Women and girls cloistered in huts, uneducated, unemployed, and unable to contribute significantly to the world represent a vast seam of human gold that is never mined. The consequence of failing to educate girls is a capacity gap not only in billions of dollars of GNP but also in billions of IQ points. (Kristof & WuDunn 2009, 239)

"Nearly everyone who works in poor countries recognizes that women are the third world's greatest underutilized resource" (Kristof & WuDunn 2009, 238). "The question is not whether countries can afford this investment, but whether countries can afford not to educate more girls" (Summers as cited in Kristof & WuDunn 2009).

With $119.8 billion worldwide applied to aid in developing countries, what percentage of this would be better employed as microfinance loans? The total amount spent on humanitarian assistance by the twenty-two major donors that comprise the OECD Development Assistance Committee was approximately $119.8 billion in 2008 (Organisation for Economic Co-Operation and Development 2008). It is important to note that this $119.8 billion is given as aid with no pay back of funds, so when the aid is consumed, other sources have to be found. By contrast, microfinance loans are repaid, allowing the capital to be reinvested over and over.

A loan is granted and the money is used to launch a woman's career. The effect of this momentum is life changing.

> First, outside employment for wages can provide women with an income to which they have easier access, and it can also serve as a means of making a living on which women can rely, making them less vulnerable. Second, the social respect that is associated with being a 'bread winner' can improve women's status and standing in the family, and may influence the prevailing cultural traditions regarding who gets what in the division of joint benefits. Third, when outside employment takes the form of jobs with some security and legal protection, the corresponding rights that women get can make their economic position much less vulnerable and precarious. Fourth, working outside the home also provides experience of the outside world, and this can be socially important in improving women's position within the family. In this respect outside work may be 'educational' as well. (Sen 1990)

When discussing investment, it is important to differentiate between human potential with its long and multigenerational season of return and the economic investment for a monetary profit. While microloans do not accrue much interest, therefore, a large economic profit, at least the capital is repaid making them sustainable. The human potential return is evident in the following quotations. "Investment in girls' education may well be the highest-return investment available in the developing world" (Summers as cited in Kristof & WuDunn 2009). "Women's empowerment helps raise economic productivity and reduce infant mortality. It contributes to improved health and nutrition. It increases the chances of education for the next generation" (United Nations Development Programme 2006). The loan recipient benefits from loan related education and then in turn, causes the second wave of education that affects the next generation.

When a microfinance loan enables a mother to start a home business, she is able to buy uniforms and release the family's children to attend school. This is the second wave of education linked to microfinance. The primary wave being as the woman herself receives training and community support to launch her business. Now this second wave, allowing her children to go to school is seen as breaking the cycle of poverty. "The report made by the Secretary-General of the United Nations within the context of the Decade for the Eradication of Poverty confirms that universal primary education is central to the fight against poverty" (United Nations Educational, Scientific, and Cultural Organization 2001). "Primary and lower secondary education helps reduce poverty by increasing the productivity of the poor, by reducing fertility and improving health, and by equipping people with the skills they need to participate fully in the economy and in society" (Nduru 1999). "An extra year of primary school boosts girls' eventual wages by 10 to 20 percent. An extra year of secondary school: 15 to 25 percent." (Bicego & Boerma 1993).

The microfinance institution provides compulsory workshops or seminars. The loan recipient attends, finding a group of other recipients already engaged in various stages of their business enterprise. These contacts become an invaluable resource, various business strategies are modeled, and relative successes are examined. Through natural networking the women extrapolate the most value possible from their surroundings. Communities in these developing countries are often well formed and rich with opportunities for the new entrepreneurs to practice. Once women receive the initial capital to enter the game, they are eager to acquire skills that will guarantee success. The alternatives are too heartbreaking to consider.

Advertisements in fashion magazines pull vast revenues with the descriptors "young" and "beautiful." Yet these descriptors spell tragedy in the world of human trafficking. The young and beautiful children of the poor are exploited through sex tourism, prostitution, and pornography.

"Microfinance can break the cycle of poverty and multiply the options available to the poor" (Getu 2006, 152). Lacking the momentum provided by education women and increasingly more, children are targets for human trafficking. "Microfinance can build the ability of the poor and unemployed people to create multiple employment and income opportunities. Those who earn income through the help of microfinance institutions are in turn enabled to support themselves, their children and extended family members. As a result, the number of poor people, mainly women, young girls and children, who are potential targets of human trafficking, is reduced. Employment and income opportunities which traffickers can use as tools for luring vulnerable people cease to be attractive" (Getu 2006, 152). In areas of the world where human trafficking is a constant and increasingly serious problem, microfinance linked with education can be used as a tool to reverse this negative impact. "Microfinance has an inherent ability not only to mitigate human trafficking but also treat its victims. It can offer job and income opportunities to potential targets and survivors of human trafficking as part of the prevention and rehabilitation processes respectively" (Getu 2006, 152).

In September 2000, United Nations member states gathered for the United Nations Millennium Summit and agreed upon a set of eight development targets, which became known as the Millennium Development Goals. The Millennium Development Goals aim to eradicate extreme poverty and hunger, achieve universal primary education, promote gender equality, reduce child mortality, improve maternal health, combat HIV/AIDS, ensure environmental sustainability, and develop a global partnership for development by the year 2015. "Because the MDGs [Millennium Development Goals] are mutually reinforcing, progress towards one goal affects the progress towards the others" (World Bank 2003). Similarly, a total failure towards one goal is likely to have an adverse effect on the total. "Lack of education has caused the limited employment options trafficked persons have been subjected to. Uneducated or poorly educated women, girls and children from poor areas and families are likely to continue to be potential targets of human trafficking" (Getu 2006, 153).

In the face of daunting world poverty, $119.8 billion dollars in humanitarian aid is contributed annually to combat inequities in the world population of 6.7 billion. This money is a justifiable investment in human potential. As with all investments there is hope for a return. Microfinance loans enjoy a favorable return on several levels; first the loan recipient receives capital and coaching to enter the workplace, then the younger members of the family are able to attend school, and finally, even the loan investor is repaid and the money can be reinvested. The microfinance model demonstrates how institutions are currently enjoying a 97-99 per cent repayment rate. This is a legitimate and expansive return on a humanitarian investment. It is imperative that capital be linked to education to result in two waves of benefits: first, success for the loan recipient and second, for her children.

References

Annual Report 2008. Grameen Bank. Accessed February 5, 2010. www.grameen-info.org/index.php?option=com_content &task=view&id=687&Itemid=693.

Bicego, G. T., & Boerma, J. T. 1993. "Maternal Education and Child Survival: A Comparative Study of Survey Data from 17 Countries." Social Science and Medicine 36, 9:1207–1227.

Borges, Phil. 2007. Women Empowered: Inspiring Change in the Emerging World. New York: Rizzoli International Publications.

Development Aid at Its Highest Level Ever in 2008. 2009, March 30. Organisation for Economic Co-Operation and Development. Accessed February 5, 2010. www.oecd.org/document/35/0,3343,en_2649_34 447_42458595_1_1_1_1,00.html.

FAQs. Pro Mujer. Accessed February 5, 2010. https://promujer.org/index.tpl?NG_View=42.

Getu, M. 2006. Human Trafficking and Development: The Role of Microfinance. Transformation 23, 3:142–156.

Kristof, N. D., & WuDunn, S. 2009. Half the Sky: Turning Oppression into Opportunity for Women Worldwide. New York: Alfred P. Knopf.

Nduru, Moyiga. 1999, March. Africa: Urged to Invest in Education of Girls to Reduce Poverty. Inter Press Service. http:/www.twnside.org.sg/title/edu-cn.htm.

Sen, A. 1990. More Than 100 Million Women Are Missing. The New York Review of Books 37, 20:1.

United Nations, United Nations Educational, Scientific, and Cultural Organization. 2001, August. Education and Poverty Eradication. http://www.unesco.org/education/poverty/ news.shtml.

United Nations, United Nations Development Programme. 2006. Annual report
     2006. http://www.undp.org/publications/annualreport2006/.
World Bank. 2003, April. Gender Equality and the Millennium Development
     Goals.
     http://web.worldbank.org/WBSITE/EXTERNAL/TOPICS/EXTEDUCA
     TION/0,,contentMDK:20530049~menuPK:617572~pagePK:148956~pi
     PK:216618~theSitePK:282386,00.html.

Chapter 7: "Sustainable" Microfinance

When Sustainability Fails: A Multi-subject Approach to Assessing Microfinance Programs in Chitwan, Nepal

Yogendra Acharya, Salim Lakha, Anthony Marcus, and Popy Begum

Abstract: This paper is based on empirical research and reports the understandings of small farmers on sustainability, and related issues. The institutional sustainability of microfinance institutions in Nepal has been uneven, despite robust support from national and international development programs. In response to low repayment rates many proposals have been put forward for initiating small farmers' development programs that encourage participation in sustainable microfinance projects. Nevertheless, repayment rates - the crux of sustainability - of farmer-run organizations remain low and are unable to reach required levels. Yet, little research has been conducted to understand small farmers' local understandings of sustainability. It is our argument that without a strong understanding of the divergence between the perspectives and interests of small rural farmers and those of bankers and policymakers microfinance programs are likely to continue to struggle to fulfill their mission of poverty alleviation and sustainability. This study presents the case of rural Nepal from the perspective of small farmers. Our data derives from in-depth individual interviews, and focus group discussions carried out in three farmers' cooperative organizations (the most successful, unsuccessful and the average) from the same geographical area. It demonstrates how the understandings of rural small farmers can contribute to sustainable microfinance and poverty alleviation in rural Nepal.

Keywords: Sustainability, Microfinance, Rural Nepal, Small Farmers, Frame of Reference, Credit Defaults, Repayment Rate, Poverty Alleviation, Local Understandings

Introduction

Various researchers have argued that in democratic societies, small farmers have a right to a participatory role, and full ownership over microfinance organizations – including planning, management, and decision-making (Weitz, 1982: 30-33; Wehnert and Shakya, 2003: 25; Shah, 1999; Sharma and Nepal, 1997:75). The basis of the argument is that farmers have access to local knowledge, which is unknown to official experts. The supporters of this school of thought have argued that microfinance institutions should not be run by public sector organizations, but instead should be self-managed by small farmers who have a built-in incentive to make them succeed (Weitz, 1982: 30-33; Shah, 1999; Sharma and Nepal, 1997:75). In the following article we provide the case study of the Small Farmer Cooperatives Limited (SFCL) in Nepal to suggest the importance and value of this approach to microfinance-based livelihoods development.

The Agricultural Development Bank of Nepal (ADBN) is a public sector development finance institution in Nepal that started the Small Farmer Development Program (SFDP) in 1975 as part of its poverty alleviation responsibilities. Under SFDP, more than 400 sub-project offices (SPOs) were initiated through the 'project approach', which did not succeed because of high transaction costs and low repayment rates. In response, ADBN transferred the SPOs to the small farmers, who created their own organizations at the local level. This initiative received support from the German Agency for Technical Cooperation (GTZ) in 1987 and came to be known as the Small Farmer Cooperatives Limited (SFCL), whichwas legalized under the Institutional Development Program (IDP) in Nepal. The Consultative Group to Assist the Poor (CGAP) cited SFCL as one of the best models for poverty alleviation in 2002, which Wehnert and Shakya, 2003 cite SFCL as a model for successful farmer-run microfinance. Despite these affirmations of success, the repayment rate for SFCLs has remained low and did not meet the level of 70% that the ADBN requires. The overall financial and development indicators remain sub-standard and the sustainability of the institution remains in question (ADBN, 2003). It is, therefore, imperative to understand how the small farmers who manage this program think about sustainability.

Do small farmers think in terms of institutional sustainability? If yes, what is their frame of reference? How do the different socio-economic positionalities that exist among small farmers influence their frame of reference, and the way they understand, prioritize and respond to sustainability discourses and practices? What, in their view, are the major factors that contribute to sustainable microfinance in rural areas? These questions are important to any attempt to discover why credit default rates remain so high among small farmers in these best practice programs. These questions were explored through an in-depth study conducted in 2003 that took a multi-perspectives approach to understanding the consistent underperformance that has marked what have been identified as "best practices" programs.

Some Definitions of Sustainability

From the perspective of most bankers, a microfinance institution is said to have reached sustainability when the operating income from the loan is sufficient to cover all the operating costs (Sharma and Nepal, 1997). This definition adopts the bankers' perspective and sticks to an 'accounting approach' of sustainability. However, Shah (1999) prefers an 'integrated approach' in defining the term sustainability since the 'accounting approach' of sustainability takes only into account the financial aspect of the institution. He defines the term within a broader perspective and uses an 'integrated approach', drawing in other criteria; the ability to obtain funds at market rate and mobilization of local resources – the two key factors that impact an organization's ability to reproduce itself. Therefore, his performance assessment criteria for the financial viability of microfinance related financial institutions are: repayment rate, operating cost ratio, market interest rates, portfolio quality, and the 'demand driven' rural credit system in which farmers themselves demand the loans for their project.

As it appears, from a banker's perspective, the sustainability of microfinance institutions include both financial viability and institutional sustainability (prosperity and self-sufficiency) of the lending institution. Their frame of reference in their definitions is therefore, more financial, administrative and institutionally focused. Small farmers and their communities are expected to embrace these definitions, but they do not always do so.

Aims and Objectives

The aim of this paper is to examine the understandings of sustainability held by small farmers involved in microfinance institutions in rural Nepal. The more specific objectives are to: document the small farmers' frame of reference on sustainability, and record their views of the factors that contribute to creating sustainable microfinance in rural areas from the multiple-perspectives of small farmers.

Method

The study for this paper was conducted in Chitwan district of Nepal. The study took place in three SFCL of successful, unsuccessful and median performance. These SFCLs were taken from Kumroj, Meghauli and Piple Village Development Committee (VDC). The performance assessment criteria and the basis for grading were: repayment rate, profit, number of inactive groups, women's participation, share distribution, internal resource generation and social programs, such as community dairy centers, community irrigation, and local bridge construction. Maximum Variation Sampling Technique (MVST) was used for selecting the most successful and the least successful organizations in the region. The study followed the constructivist research paradigm that examines the understandings and views of small farmers about sustainability of microfinance institutions. The research has used multiple case study method as its research design, and a qualitative approach as a research strategy. Triangulation was accomplished through varied and combined research tools from the social sciences, such as focus group discussions, in-depth individual interviews, and participatory rural appraisal (PRA). A total of 36 small farmers were interviewed. Grounded theory was used both as a research strategy and as a tool for data analysis.

Results

The results of research are presented here under some of the main themes that emerged from the interview data and focus group discussions. The understandings and views expressed by the small farmers of sustainability in microfinance institutions were largely consistent. Do small farmers think in terms of sustainability? Most respondents expressed that they never thought in terms of institutional sustainability when they obtained credit from the SFCL.

Sustainability: Views and Understandings of Small Farmers

A majority of small farmers (excluding landless agricultural workers) did think about sustainability, more in terms of the individual sustainability of their family domestic units than in terms of the success of their organization. Their view was that the prosperity of individuals is the foundation of sustainability for communities and microfinance institutions should depend on a "trickle-up" effect from this individual success. Among this group, those who were serving on an Executive Committee (EC), whose job it was to manage the organization, were able to cite a banker's definition of institutional sustainability. However, these individuals were the primary defaulters, suggesting that their commitment to sharing the banker's definition of sustainability was very limited. For general members, livelihood, personal economic benefit and relief from local indebtedness and sharecropping were the frame of reference to define the term 'sustainability' – an entirely family unit based definition. Executive Committee members gave more emphasis to institutional benefits.

Sustainability is Utility-Based

Several small farmers from the group and intergroup level believed that sustainability described their own personal economic interest. Executive committee member-small farmers (who had spent more than one year on the committee), on the other hand, spoke in favor of institutional sustainability and stated that the major criterion for assessing performance (success / failure) of microfinance institutions (SFCL) was the repayment performance or credit default rate. Therefore, EC members were more focused on repayment rates, despite commonly being in default themselves.

It appears that the main goal of SFCL management was to achieve higher repayment rates by any means, such as taking out new loans of the same amount on the due date to pay the old ones, and restructuring the repayment schedules upon the receipt of a small amount of interest. Small farmers, therefore, had to obtain the loans either from local moneylenders, sell their livestock, land or any other assets, or re-borrow the loans from the SFCL to repay old debts on time.

The farmers believed that such actions could not make the institution better off in the long run. Instead, they thought that such pressure on farmers to repay on time through any possible means would impact negatively on their own situations. Interviews suggested that the financial viability and institutional sustainability of SFCL was of little concern to them. They viewed it as solely a management responsibility.

Small farmers were the least concerned about their institution's long-term financial and economic benefits. For example, one of the respondents asserted, in response to questions about repayment rates for the institution, "I love my land and do not want to lose my land through auction." His view of sustainability was to protect his land from being auctioned, and to satisfy the sustistance needs of his family. He further stated, "...I am bound to sell my land to repay overdue debts, if I don't sell it, it will get auctioned'. Small farmers typically viewed the idea of sustainability and conversion of public sector projects into cooperatives (SPOs) as the "burden of failure" to small farmers rather than the way to self-reliance.

The term 'sustainability' in microfinance refers to "the ability of a microfinance institution to develop a methodology that ensures loans successfully reach the poor, while covering all costs without subsidy" (Unitus, 2005: 4). While a subsidized loan is not issued under a regime of sustainability, the majority of small farmers believed that loans to help them generate income should be either in the form of grants or in a subsidized form, in which institutional sustainability was not important. The attitudes of small farmers towards sustainability of their microfinance institution appeared to be shaped mainly by their perception of immediate benefits they could receive from it.

For instance, local indebtedness and sharecropping were the crucial problems of small farmers in three study areas, and many small farmers were primarily concerned with getting out of debt, rather than taking on more. They tied this to one of their goals, emancipation from sharecropping, fixed contract cultivation, and land leasing. The lending institution's definition of sustainability had little meaning to small farmers since the frame of reference of small farmers was based on livelihood, security, and utility.

Discussion

The small farmers used a utilitarian approach and defined sustainability in terms of direct economic and social benefits to small farmers; whilst the banking and lending institutions and microfinance professionals preferred institutional benefits first. The bankers' perspective is that only a sustainable microfinance institution can deliver long term service to the poor, and such an institution has trickle-down effects in the long run. It appears that small farmers think very little in terms of institutional sustainability when they obtain credit. It seems that both sides use a utilitarian (based on the level of utility and true economic reward) approach. Small farmers believed that if poor people could earn at least a dollar a day, the institutions would automatically grow as a result of prompt repayment of loans and would be sustainable with trickle-up effect. Because money attracts money, this would, in their view, create more demand of credit for income generating projects and more income to fuel them.

Robert Chambers (1983) agrees in certain respects, arguing that the last should be put first and prosperity of the poor is a sine-qua- none for institutional sustainability (Chambers, 1983). Rao (2001) claims that maintaining a socioeconomic benefit for the poor is one of the criteria for sustainable policy (Rao, 2001: 226). Small farmers who never thought in terms of institutional sustainability when they obtained the loans viewed 'sustainability' as simply a policy buzz word designed to impose liability on the poor and the government from responsibility. The most important attribute of the results of this study is the wide range of views and understandings expressed by small farmers involved in the management and use of credit.

As small farmers at the group level did not think in terms of institutional sustainability when they obtained credit, their understandings and frame of reference were different than bankers and the views expressed by EC members. In many cases, the views expressed by the EC members were consistent with bankers, because they were in direct contact with lending institutions (bankers) and microfinance professionals, and were influenced by them. Since EC members perceived institutional credit as an urgent need of small farmers, they believed that a collateral based joint liability approach was the most secure and best alternative, and that sustainability of the institutions would provide prosperity for small farmers. However, the meaning of sustainability to village level small farmers was largely focused on utilitarian needs - what is productive (use of resources) for a lending institution is not productive for small farmers. For example, use of credit for sustainable consumption and daily household expenses was the most efficient, productive and sustainable use for small farmers. For bankers, it is the misuse of loans.

However, there is a deeper problem that may be driving this difference between the perspectives of small farmers and bankers that is the cost of providing microfinance institutions in Nepal. The World Bank (1993) revealed that for the small farmer development program in Nepal to be financially sustainable, they have to increase the lending rate to 42.5% (World Bank, 1993) which is higher than the prevailing moneylenders' rate of 36%. It seems that microfinance service to small farmers at cost plus (cost + profit) interest rate without any subsidy is too expensive. In this situation, small farmers should be provided work rather than unsupervised credit.

Conversion of Public Sector Projects into SFCL: A Burden of Failure

Small farmers viewed the conversion of public sector projects into cooperatives as the "burden of failure" rather than the way to sustainability. Rural development professionals state that improving the quality of life of rural people, and paying special attention to the needs of the poorest is the foundation to build or strengthen local institutions (Dale, 1998 ; Kamarah, 2001). Again, the question of people's participation in the development process is defined and interpreted in different ways, and challenged by some writers. For instance, Buchy (2000) states, ...In the changing political context and economic rationalism (worldwide) it's difficult to know whether governments see public involvement as opportunity to transfer costs and responsibilities from the centre to the periphery or whether government agencies genuinely believe in the long-term value of involving people in running their affairs. The effect of government's withdrawal from rural areas in particular on the capacity of local communities to run their own affairs is not sufficiently studied and understood by the agencies promoting local involvement (Buchy et al., 2000).

Small farmers asserted that the responsibility of running an independent autonomous microfinance institution in a sustainable way is not possible in isolation from their immediate consumption needs. Fisher (2002) argues that the crucial reason why local people often fail to "participate" in local organizations is that they do not feel that these organizations meet their needs (Fisher, 2002). Similarly, IFAD (2000) states, 'policy cannot be mechanically applied. It needs to be adapted to the socio-economic setting of each area' (IFAD, 2000: 1).

It appears that institutional sustainability does not benefit small farmers instantly and sustainability of these cooperatives was not one of their priorities. The national progress report substantiates this fact - the nationwide progress report of the cooperatives shows that there was a remarkably low percentage (16.52%) of internally generated resources (such as savings) and a substantially low percentage of share capital (1.08%) against outstanding loan in 2002/03 (ADBN, 2003). Likewise, the percentage of external sources of overdue loan (SPO source) is higher (19.95%) than the internal (14.99%) in 2003 (ADBN, 2003). Theoretically, the SFCL is supposed to have at least 20% in their capital fund (internally generated) to its total deposits, which is the "entry point level requirement" (RUFIN, 2003: 5).

Conclusions

The small farmers who were involved in the executive committee for more than a year were more concerned about institutional sustainability than others, or at least they were able to effectively draw on and express the key discursive features of institutional sustainability. The majority of non-executive small farmers had some concern for institutional sustainability. However, they defined sustainability in their own way. Their definition and frame of reference for sustainability was entirely different from that of bankers, microfinance professionals, and even the executive committee members who lived and worked in close proximity. The lack of a sense of ownership towards the organization and apathy towards institutional sustainability may provide part of the explanation for high rates of credit default among small farmers. It is confirmed that what is "sustainability" for lending institutions, microfinance professionals, and bankers is not "sustainability" for small farmers. Their frame of reference is more livelihoods focused, and linked to the level of benefit, income, and the economic health of their families – typically defined in terms of basic consumption. The analysis revealed that there is a divergence between the interests of professionals and small farmers, and that this has something to do with the underlying costs of providing sustainable microfinance institutions to those at the economic bottom. The majority of small farmers believed that projects were not viable unless subsidized, and this belief in itself, will likely cause a program to fail.

The most basic demands of small farmers for government action were not however geared primarily towards their own micro-enterprises, but towards the introduction of local industries or factories that could provide them shift work (day and night). This suggests a further problem with the relationship between microfinance projects and the socioeconomic positionality of these small farmers: their vision of how to escape poverty was also not shared with bankers and microfinance professionals. This suggests problems with recruitment and selection of beneficiaries that delivery of basic education and training may be prior to and more significant than simply a lack of convergence between stakeholders over definitions of sustainability. While we would expect a divergence between the interests of professionals and small farmers and differing expectations between lenders and borrowers the huge divide that we found in how these groups defined key program goals suggests the need to reassess project design and delivery, and the sociocultural context within which they are inscribed.

References

Acharya, U., Petheram, R. J. and Reid, R. 2004. 'Concepts and perceptions of biodiversity in community forestry, Nepal,' Small-scale Forest Economics, Management and Policy, vol. 3, no. 3 (special issue), pp. 401-410.

ADBN. 2003. Progress report of Small Farmers Co-operative Limited as of Aswin month 2059/60, Agricultural Development Bank (ADBN), Microfinance Division (MFD), Head office, Kathmandu.

Bajracharya, P. and Bajracharya, S. 1999. 'Strategies for poverty alleviation: An integrated approach,' Agricultural Credit, vol. 31, no. Bi-annual, pp. 15-21.

Buchy, M., Ross, H. and Proctor, W. 2000. Enhancing the Information Base on Participatory Approaches in Australian Natural Resource Management, Land and Water, Australia.

Chambers, R. 1983. Rural Development: Putting the Last First, Longman London.

Chambers, R. 1993. Challenging the Professions: Frontiers for Rural Development, Intermediate Technology Publications Limited London.

Dale, R. 1995. Growth, Development and Poverty, Asian Institute of Technology, Bangkok, Thailand.

Dale, R. 1998. Evaluation Frameworks for Development Programs and Projects, Sage Publications India Pvt. Ltd. New Delhi.

Dhakal, N. H. 2002. 'Marketing in Nepalese Microfinance Institutions,' Agricultural Credit, vol. 34, pp. 9-22.

Fisher, R. J. 2002. 'What Makes Effective Local Organisations and Institutions in Natural Resource Management and Rural Development?,' Seminar on Role of Communities and Institutions in Integrated Rural Development, vol. 15-20 June, Islamic Republic of Iran, p. 8. IFAD. 2000. IFAD

Policy on Rural Finance, International Fund for Agricultural Development (IFAD), pp. 1-19, Rome.

Kamarah, U. I. 2001. Sustainable Rural Development: Semantics or Substance?, University Press of America, .

Rao, P. K. 2001. Sustainable Development: Economics and Policy, Blackwell Publishers Inc. Malden, Massachusetts, USA.

Rood, D. 2005. '$ 20m later, Melbourne Uni shuts its private arm', The Age. Melbourne Wednesday, 8 June 2005.

RUFIN. 2003. Grading System For Excellency in Financial Services Delivery of Small Farmer Cooperatives Ltd., Rural Finance Nepal (RUFIN), pp. 1-8, Kathmandu. Shah, D. P. 1999. 'ADBN and its experience in rural and microfinance attitude,' Quarterly Development Review, vol. XVI, no. 20, November.

Sharma, S. R. and Nepal, V. 1997. Strengthening of Credit Institutions /Programs for rural poverty alleviation in Nepal, In, UN ECOSOC for Asia and Pacific, Bangkok, Thailand. Thieme, J. G. 1963. Handling Storage and Processing of Agricultural Produce, In, Conference on the Application of Science and Technology for the Benefit of the Less Developed Countries : Summary of Proceedings on Agriculture of the United Nations, FAO, Washington D. C., pp. 287-297.

United Nations. 1975. World Economic Survey, Department of Economic and Social Affairs, pp. 102-103, New York.

Unitus. 2005. 'What is microfinance', Unitus: Global Microfinance Accelerator [online], available: http://www.unitus.com/wwd_whatismf.asp [Accessed on 08.04.2005].

Wehnert, U. and Shakya, R. 2003. Microfinance and Armed Conflict in Nepal: The Adverse Effects of the Insurgency on the Small Farmer Cooperatives Ltd. (SFCLs), Rural Finance Nepal (RUFIN), pp. 1 - 46, Working paper 3, Kathmandu, Nepal.

Weitz, R. 1982. Integrated Rural Development: The Rehovot Approach, 3rd edition, Settlement Study Centre Rehovot, Israel. World Bank. 1993. Sustainable Financial Services for the Poor: Building on Local Capacity, Volume I and II: Main Report, Country Operations Industry and Finance Division, South Asia Region.

Chapter 8: Stakeholders' Perspectives on Effectiveness

The Nature of NGO Microfinance in Vietnam and Stakeholders' Perceptions of Effectiveness

Hong Son Nghiem and James Laurenceson

Abstract: The microfinance industry in Vietnam, particularly those sponsored by non-government organisations (NGOs), has experienced rapid expansion in recent years. Yet in spite of this growth, an analysis of their effectiveness has been lacking. In a bid to help address this shortcoming, this paper reports on a subset of data that was obtained during a survey and interview process that incorporated various stakeholders including financial donors, NGO-sponsored microfinance institutions (NMPs), village leaders and NMP members and non-members. Perceptions of NMPs effectiveness are discussed from the standpoint of various stakeholders. NMPs are found to be at a critical juncture. While their activities are widely perceived to contribute to poverty alleviation, their future viability is clouded by donor requirements that they become financially self-sufficient and at the same time certain government policies are making achieving this goal difficult.

Keywords: Microfinance, Vietnam, NGOs, Effectiveness, viability

Introduction

The microfinance industry in Vietnam has been growing rapidly. In particular, the number of non-government organisation (NGO)-sponsored microfinance programs (NMPs) has grown from a mere handful in the early 1990s to currently more than 60 (BWTP, 2005). There is a widely held belief that this expansion has contributed to poverty reduction. For example, comprehensive surveys such as the Vietnam Living Standard Survey (VLSS) show that as the percentage of rural population with access to rural finance programs (i.e., microfinance and others) increased from 23 percent in 1993 to 40 percent in 1998, the poverty rate dropped from 58 percent to 37 percent (GSO, 1994; 2000). However, beyond this largely anecdotal evidence, what has been distinctly lacking is a systematic analysis of the nature and effectiveness of microfinance.

Since 2003, the authors have been involved in a research program that has sought to address these shortcomings. In early 2004, a survey and interview process was conducted in order to collect additional primary data and included various stakeholders such as financial donors, NMPs, village leaders and NMP members and non-members1. The survey and interview process had two main purposes - a. to gain an understanding of the current nature of microfinance in Vietnam such as the objectives of NMPs, their target groups, the financial products they offer, etc, and b. collect both qualitative and quantitative data that would allow conclusions to be drawn on the efficiency of NMPs (i.e., their ability to convert inputs such as labour and capital into outputs such as financial products) and the effectiveness of their operations (i.e., the impact their financial products have on achieving objectives such as alleviating poverty). This chapter reports on and discusses a subset of the data that was obtained. Section 2 provides a brief descriptive overview of rural finance in Vietnam. Section 3 briefly outlines the survey process and elaborates on the findings with respect to the nature of NMP operations. Section 4 draws out two key themes from the survey and interview process that relate to matters of effectiveness from the perspectives of various stakeholders. Section 5 contains concluding comments.

Much of the discussion regarding NMP effectiveness in this chapter is based on data that is qualitative in nature and relates to perceptions of effectiveness rather than what might be termed actual effectiveness. At least in economic research, such data is often looked upon as being the poor cousin of quantitative data and analysis techniques. We respond in several ways. Firstly, there is nothing in the nature of qualitative and quantitative data that make them competing. Ideally, both should be used and research evidence is at its most convincing when both qualitative and quantitative data point in the same direction. Further research drawing on the survey data is planned and will take on a more quantitative orientation. Secondly, notions of inclusiveness and participatory practice in development projects demand that perceptions be given weight in their own right. This is not simply out of deference to some ethical imperative. Integrating perceptions serves a pragmatic end as it is often perceptions that dictate what is and what is not possible and hence actual outcomes. As will later be discussed, this is certainly the case with respect to microfinance in Vietnam. Thirdly, the quantitative analysis of efficiency and effectiveness in microfinance is sometimes problematic. Efficiency analysis is typically based around the specification of a production function that relates inputs to outputs. Yet, in the context of microfinance, it is not even clear what the inputs and outputs should be -savings deposits, for example, could rightly be regarded as both an input and an output. Similarly, deciphering the effectiveness of microfinance programs in tackling poverty (which itself is not amendable to easy measurement) requires the collection of data on an array of control variables since the services provided by NMPs are usually part of a much broader poverty alleviation strategy. Each data series in the array will be costly to obtain and subject to a degree of measurement error. Quite simply, if a researcher wishes to know the effectiveness of microfinance, one of the best means available is simply to ask the various stakeholders for their perceptions.

Overview of Rural Finance in Vietnam

Before the start of the economic reform policy (*doi moi*) in 1986, the formal rural financial sector in Vietnam comprised mainly of traditional credit cooperatives, which were considered representatives of the State Bank of Vietnam (SBV). The first wave of financial sector reform came in 1988 (BWTP, 2005). A key new player to emerge was the Vietnam Bank for Agriculture and Rural Development (VBARD), which was established in 1990 as a policy bank charged with dispensing subsidised credit from the SBV to the rural poor. In 1995, VBARD began transforming itself into a commercial bank. At that time, the Vietnam Bank for the Poor (VBP) was established to take over the reins of delivering subsidised credit for poverty alleviation. The VLSS 2002 revealed that the VBP accounted for 58.26 percent of the total outstanding loans to poor, rural households (Table 1). In 2003, the VBP was reformed as the Vietnam Bank for Social Policies (VBSP) and began to expand further on its branch network as well as target additional groups such as poor students and disabled and migration workers. A distinguishing operational characteristic of the VBSP is that it has a negative spread between the subsidised interest rate it charges on loans and the interest rate it pays to depositors. To cover its policy lending activities, VBSP receives annual transfers from the national government budget and operates as a non-profit entity (BWTP, 2005).

After suffering from a financial collapse in the late 1980s, traditional credit cooperatives were reborn in the form of rural shareholding banks (RSHBs) or People's Cooperative Funds (PCFs). While the number of RSHBs reached 44 by 1995, that number fell to 19 by 2001 and they now play only a marginal role (UNDP, 1996; Llanto, 2000; BWTP, 2005). PCFs were established on the model of the Caisse Populaire system in Quebec, Canada (Hung, 1998). They operate under Vietnam's cooperative law and only provide loans for members, although savings are mobilised from both members and non-members. As of November 2004, there were 901 PCFs in operation. In 2003, this formal financial sector (VBP, VBARD, PCFs) represented over 90 percent of the outreach of rural financial services in Vietnam (BWTP, 2005). Apart from the above institutions, there are government-related institutions such as the TYM fund established in 1993 by the Women's Union of Soc Son district in Hanoi and the CEP fund established in 1992 by the Labour Confederation of Ho Chi Minh City. The main difference between these funds and banks such as VBP is that they do not receive funds directly from the government. Rather, in similar vein to NMPs, their donors include international organisations such as AusAID and the Grameen Trust. Their government connections (such as through the Women's Union and the Labour Confederation) however do provide them with a network that vastly exceeds that of an average NMP. The latest data shows that the CEP fund has reached 50,000clients (BWTP, 2005) and the TYM fund serves nearly 19,000 members (Tran and Yun, 2004).

In addition to the above government-owned and related institutions, NMPs began to merge in the early 1990s. It is these institutions that are the focus of this chapter. Domestic NGO-sponsored programs are few largely because a declaration of separateness from government is still an awkward concept in contemporary Vietnam. NMPs generally function on models derived from overseas experience and can be classified according to three groups, namely Grameen Bank replicas, Village Bank models and Solidarity Group models (Nguyen, 2004). The Grameen Bank model is followed by most NGOs in Vietnam such as Vietnam Plus and Action Aid as well as government-related institutions such as the TYM and CEP funds. In this model, microfinance members establish themselves in groups of five with no family or marriage relations and each person acts asa guarantor for other persons in the group to get loans. Group members meet frequentlyto contribute savings and repay interest and principal by installments. The second model is the Village Bank model, which was originally devised by the International Community Support Organization (FINCA) in the mid-1980s. The main difference between the Grameen replica and the Village Bank model is that the latter involves members actually

holding an ownership share of the institution from its instatement. The NGOs operating this model include Save the Children Japan and World Vision (BWTP, 2005). The third model is the Solidarity Group Model, which was instituted by an American-based NGO, ACCION International. In this model, loans are provided to groups rather than individuals. Members of groups divide the loan equally among themselves. This model has been applied by NGOs such as Save the Children US and Adventist Development and Relief Agency International (ADRA). Apart from the above three models, there is an initiative by the Save the Children US to establish a joint-venture with a private company and a commercial bank to deliver microfinance services on commercial basis. It does not receive any donor subsidy. This venture aims to utilise the hands-on community development experience of NGOs, the fund mobilisation potential of private investors and the labour productivity of commercial banks. Since the venture has only been in operation for about one year, it is too early to gauge its success (Dinh, 2005). Credit extended by institutions such as CEP, TYM and NMPs accounted for around 8 percent of the total to poor, rural households (Table 1).

The rural financial sector in Vietnam also includes an informal sector. Such providers include moneylenders, friends and relatives and rotating savings and credit associations (ROSCAs). Until the mid-1990s, the informal sector was estimated to be the most important source of credit for Vietnamese households, especially in rural areas. According to the results of the VLSS 1992 survey, 73 percent of rural credit was provided by the informal sector (McCarty, 2001a). Although its importance has declined with the expansion of the formal sector described above, according to the VLSS 2002 survey, the informal sector continues to provide 10.71 percent of credit extended to poor, rural households (Table 1). There will always be a niche for informal lenders, particularly as they tend to offer more scope for borrowers to use loans for non-production related purposes.

Table 1. Access of the poor to credit and main providers

Category	Percentage of poor household access to	Providers							
		VPB	VBARD	Other Banks	Job creation programs	PCF	Social organisations	Private lenders	Relatives and friends
Overall	32.46	57.76	23.25	1.11	3.73	2.83	7.98	4.07	6.64
A-Rural/Urban									
Urban	31.36	53.89	19.02	1.09	4.76	2.7	15.63	3.52	5.88
Rural	32.6	58.26	23.79	1.12	3.6	2.85	7	4.14	6.73
B-Household heads									
Male	35.43	58.2	23.81	1.12	3.43	2.63	7.36	4.19	6.77
Female	25.07	56.21	21.29	1.1	4.8	3.52	10.18	3.65	6.15

Source(s): General Statistics Office (2005).

The Nature of NMP Microfinance—Survey and Findings

The Survey

Data for this study comes from two main surveys: an institutional survey and a survey of households. The institutional survey was aimed at NMPs listed in the NGO directory. This directory is maintained by the Vietnam NGO Resource Centre (www.ngocentre.org.vn). NGOs that agreed to participate in the survey and that were based in Hanoi received a questionnaire followed by a face to face interview. Those based outside Hanoi or who had already transferred the program to local partners received a questionnaire by post or email as preferred. Survey responses were received from 44 NMPs operated by 23 NGOs (of which 21 were international NGOs) and were concentrated in the north and the central regions of Vietnam. The focus on these regions was primarily due to time and resource constraints. Nevertheless, given that the majority of NMPs operate in the central and northern regions (McCarty, 2001b), this response affords a reasonable level of confidence that the included sample is representative of the microfinance community in Vietnam.

The household survey was implemented using a stratified sampling design. Initially, 10 NMPs were selected equally from the two regions (five in the north and five in the centre). For each NMP, a list of member villages and non-member villages were defined and a member village was chosen randomly from each list for the 'treatment' group and a non-member village was selected for the 'control' group. To make a proper comparison, the study did not select non-participating villages randomly from the list of all villages that had not received microfinance in the region. Instead, only villages that met eligibility criteria (typically those that were on a government defined list of poor villages) and had not received microfinance services were selected. In each village, households were selected randomly from the list of eligible households. Where a non-member village was not available (i.e., all eligible villages in the area had received the service), an attempt was made to identify eligible households in member villages who had not received the financial services. The household surveys covered 26 villages (of which 17 were member villages) and 471 households (of which 287 were member households). Apart from the survey of households, interviews were conducted with heads of surveyed villages to obtain information on village characteristics and their perceptions relating to microfinance. Village heads are elected by constituents and then approved by the commune people's committee (CPC) to lead the village. Thus, village heads can be categorised as belonging to the local government. Several semi-structured interviews with CPC representatives were also conducted.

In addition to the interviews and surveys described above, group discussions were moderated during two workshops held in Hanoi. The first workshop was held in February 2004 and introduced the research project to stakeholders. It was attended by representatives from the SBV, donors, local and international NGOs and representatives from the Women's Union (WU). The Women's Union is one of five so-called mass organisations in Vietnam (others include the Youth Union, Farmers Union, etc) that act as a bridge between the Community Party of Vietnam (CPV) and society as a whole. It plays an important role in Vietnamese microfinance because the target group of most NMPs is women. Therefore, when a NMP approaches a local government to elicit support for their microfinance program, the WU will usually be assigned as a partnering body. The second workshop was held in May 2004 after the survey and interview process had been undertaken and afforded the opportunity for preliminary findings to be presented and discussed.

Objectives of NMPs

The NMPs that were surveyed were asked to nominate the main objectives of their schemes and to rank the relative importance of these objectives on a three-point scale (very important, important, and less important). Responses were received from 30 NMPs. All indicated that helping the poor access financial services was one of their main objectives and 29 of the 30 ranked it a very important objective. There was also firm evidence to conclude that most NMPs aspire to achieve financial self-sufficiency (ie., no longer be dependent on donor support), with only 2 of the 30 respondents not considering it a main objective of their scheme. Of the 28 NMPs that did consider it a main objective, 25 described it as being important. The third most common objective reported by 14 of the 30 respondents was to generate a profit. This should not be taken to imply that many NMPs have a commercial rather than development orientation. All of the NMPs that nominated generating a profit as being a main objective described it as being less important and also nominated at least one of the other objectives described above as being another main objective of their scheme. Thus, a more nuanced interpretation is that a sizeable proportion of NMPs view generating a profit as a means of better achieving financial self-sufficiency and helping the poor access financial services. Related to this issue is that a regular point to emerge in interviews was that the longer the NMP had been in operation, the higher the priority that tended to be accorded to achieving financial self-sufficiency and generating a profit. This is explained by the fact that while most donor agencies are prepared to provide start-up funds and subsidise the operations of an NMP for a period of time such support is rarely indefinite.

Target Groups and Beneficiaries

Responses were received from 44 NMPs in regards to their target groups and beneficiaries. All identified women as being their target group, especially those who were also members of the WU. The priority given to women by NMPs in Vietnam is consistent with international practices (e.g., the Grameen Bank in Bangladesh). An initially surprising finding was that the institutional survey showed that despite the stated importance accorded to the objective of helping the poor access financial services, on average, only 41.5 percent of microfinance members could be classified as being poor according to the national poverty line. What transpired was that many NMPs preferred to use locally derived measures of poverty to distinguish between the poor and non-poor. One common approach is participatory wealth ranking (PWR) activities, where a selected group of villagers rank all households in the village using a series of indicators such as income, housing condition, household accessories, production equipment, education of children, etc. Sometimes poverty incidence as measured by the national poverty line and the PWR poverty measure differ considerably. For example, an NMP run by the Rural Development Services Centre (RDSC), a Vietnamese NGO to which the first author is affiliated, recorded 60 percent of their members households as being poor using PWR. However, by using the national poverty line only 17 percent would be considered poor. Another possible reason for members being non-poor is that by the time the survey was conducted some had already benefited from program and escaped poverty. Yet another factor that emerged in interviews was that some members, although not considered poor themselves, wished to stay in NMPs to maintain a social network. The poor from ethnic minority groups are on the whole not well represented amongst the ranks of NMP members. In aggregate, members of ethnic minority groups accounted for 29.3 percent of the total members surveyed. This figure may sound impressive given that the percentage of minority groups in the population as a whole is only 13.8 percent (GSO, 2005). However, it is distorted in the sense that it is a mean rather than a median figure. Apart from a couple of larger schemes that focus almost exclusively on ethnic minority groups, the majority have very little dealings with them at all. According to many of the NMPs interviewed, ethnic minority groups, with the exception of the Chinese group, depend mainly on subsistence agriculture and hence the introduction of cash through microfinance services was thought to be of little use to improving their production and livelihood. In an attempt to overcome this problem, some NGOs have introduced in-kind credit or revolving funds of inputs such as seed and animals. Another barrier is that most ethnic minority groups in Vietnam live in remote areas, creating very high transaction costs due to travel difficulties, language barriers, and limited numeracy skills (Che, 2002).

Financial Products

There were only two financial services offered by the NMPs surveyed - credit and savings products. Many NMPs actually described themselves as being Credit and Saving Programs. Other products such as microinsurance and money transfers are rarely available, except in the funds that are connected to the government by virtue of their larger scale and more established networks. For example, the CEP fund provides insurance for health and livestock and the TYM scheme provides death insurance to members and their families. Most of the NMPs interviewed were not enthusiastic about establishing insurance operations. The main reason was because their staff are frugally trained in even basic banking products. Another perceived problem was a lack of insurance product awareness amongst the rural poor in Vietnam that would limit its uptake. The survey also revealed that 79 percent of the credit borrowed by members was for investment purposes. This reflects rules in 69 percent of NMPs that loans are only to be used for production purposes. The most common types of investment from microfinance loans include animal husbandry, crops and off-farm businesses. The proportion of credit extended for on-farm uses was identified by some NMPs as being somewhat incongruent with the microfinance principle of small, regular loan repayments as these types of investment tend to generate seasonal (or longer) fluctuations in income. Of the credit that was extended for consumption purposes, the most common uses were education fees for children, health care and food. All NMPs applied the principle of social collateral rather than physical collateral in their credit service. In the case a borrower defaults, group members are responsible for repaying the loan or face the possibility of being excluded from future loans. Default is also commonly discouraged through the required contribution of compulsory savings, which will be blocked and retained in case of default. Some schemes also invited a representative of local government (e.g., village heads) to the supervision board. Since NMPs are often integrated into other development activities, the local government has an incentive to help NGOs by enforcing intentional defaulters to repay. The design of NMP credit (i.e., small loan sizes and regular installments) is also held to protect against default.

The saving service provided by NMPs consists of a compulsory and voluntary component. In all NMPs surveyed, the compulsory saving account is not for withdrawal unless members want to quit the programs. The purpose of this compulsory account is three-fold. First, it creates a buffer in case of default as described above. Second, it creates a habit of regular saving practice amongst members. Third, the saving fund helps to build an awareness of ownership amongst the members. The amount of compulsory saving required per member household was found to be relatively little ranging from VND 5,000 to VND 15,000 per month. The average rural income in Vietnam is VND 220,000 per person per month (GSO, 2005). Voluntary savings are designed to mobilise additional resources from the community. Opening a voluntary savings account with a NMP can be a convenient and attractive option. For example, the interest rate paid on savings in the NMPs surveyed was around 0.6 percent per month (Table 2). This compared with 0.25-0.4 percent per month on offer at banks such as VBARD at the time. According to current legislation (to be discussed in more detail later), NMPs are only allowed to mobilise voluntary savings from their members.

Table 2. Descriptive data from NMPs surveyed

Indicators	Units	Mean	Median	Minimum	Maximum
Number of members	Persons	2382	800	68	19508
Number of borrowers	Persons	2231	691	48	19608
Average loan size	000 VND	988	787	318	4471
Loan interest rate	Percent/month	1.28	1.2	0.8	1.7
Loan term	Months	14	12	6	36
Number of savers	Persons	2045	631	0	19508
Average saving amount	000 VND	220	149	10	1000
Saving interest rate	Percent/month	0.6	0.6	0.4	0.85

Stakeholders' Perceptions of Effectiveness

In this section we report perceptions surrounding the effectiveness of microfinance from the perspective of various stakeholders including village leaders, donors, NMPs, members and non-members. In order to make the commentary tractable, two basic themes have been drawn from the survey responses and interviews conducted.

Microfinance Programs Were Perceived by Members and Village Leaders as Being Effective in Alleviating Poverty

When members of NMPs were asked what their expectations were when they joined, 95 percent stated that they had expected participation would increase their incomes. When subsequently asked whether their expectation had been fulfilled to date, 99.3 percent reported that it had.

Follow-up questions were asked in a bid to determine what exactly it was about the services provided by NMPs that had led to this positive perception. The most common response was simply that NMPs provided them with access to financial services, particularly credit. Members reported a vital need for credit as the nature of their rural production meant that incomes fluctuated according to season. Members were also asked what they would have done if they had been unable to access a loan from a NMP. A significant proportion (35 percent) said they would have foregone the investment. To the extent that investment is a key determinant of future incomes, the perception that access to credit had improved their incomes is justifiable. It was also interesting to note that 45 percent of members said that had they not been able to borrow from NMPs they would have resorted to borrowing from moneylenders. This is despite the fact that the interest rate charged by moneylenders is usually three to five times that charged by NMPs (McCarthy, 2001a). This willingness to borrow at higher interest rates implies that many would-be borrowers do have access to high return projects. Non-members also reported a positive disposition towards the services provided by NMPs. When asked if they would be interested in joining a microfinance program if one was available in their area and if they were deemed eligible, 99 percent said they would be. The most common reason given for their interest was to gain access to credit services. One caveat that needs to be made clear when reporting the positive perceptions associated with the services offered by NMPs is that the interest rate they charged on loans is in most cases a subsidised rate. The interest rate charged by government-owned banks such as VBP is subsidised even more heavily. This issue will be discussed in more detail later but suffice to say here that the extension of cheap credit will expectedly promote positive perceptions and lead to robust demand.

In regards to the positive features associated with the services provided by NMPs, other common responses were a) 70.1 percent said they liked the simple and quick loan application procedure, and b) 65.1 percent said they liked the flexibility in loan repayments. The average time borrowers reported having to wait for a loan approval was only a couple of days and the paperwork consisted of a one-page loan application form. There were no physical collateral requirements and borrowers typically repaid loans in small monthly installments. In contrast, at least until recently, the standard loan from VBARD required physical collateral, was for a period of three years and required the lump sum repayment of interest and principal. Aside from providing increased access to financial services, one of the chief justifications undergirding the microfinance movement worldwide is that NMPs are better able to serve the poor because they are more flexible and innovative than formal banking institutions. The responses we received lend support this assertion.

Table 3. What are the relative priority areas to alleviate poverty in your community?

Factors	Ranking (percent)		
	Average priority	High priority	Very high priority
Financial services (loans, credit, savings)	3.8	57.7	38.5
Infrastructure (roads, electricity, irrigation)	3.8	50	46.2
Health care	38.5	61.5	0
Education	38.5	57.7	3.8
Production services (agricultural extension, job training, processing)	47.8	47.8	4.3

The perceptions of village leaders were also sought regarding the effectiveness of financial services (including but not limited to microfinance). Village leaders were asked to nominate the relative priority areas for alleviating poverty in their communities. Notable was the fact that financial services, alongside infrastructure, ranked as being the most important priority areas. These two areas ranked ahead of other expectedly worthy areas such as health care and education (see Table 3). The penchant of village leaders for increased access to financial services can also be at least partly explained by the widespread practice of interest rate subsidisation. In this way the practice may be said to distort the priorities of village heads in favour of financial services *vis-a-vis* areas such as education and health care. The fondness of village leaders for financial services and infrastructure might also be explained by the fact that additional resources in these areas result in outputs that are more immediate and visible than spending in education and health care.

Microfinance Institutions Perceived that Government Policies Would Largely Determine Their Ability to Exert a Positive Impact over the Medium and Long Term

When NMPs were asked open-ended questions regarding what they considered to be the main factors promoting and hindering their operations in Vietnam, the role played by the government came up prominently in both instances. On a positive note, it was said that it was not uncommon for the local government to provide operational support. This support often came in the form of an in-kind staffing subsidy through the WU. In addition, the local government also sometimes provided free (or heavily subsidised) office space. One NMP also reported that best practice in microfinance had been promoted through the official media.

On a more negative note, two issues stood out. Firstly, 93 percent of NMPs raised the official policy of government-owned banks extending subsidised credit. This point turned out to be closely related to the fact that when NMP members were asked what they disliked about the services NMPs offered, 51 percent responded that the interest rate they levied on loans was too high. Interviews with

NMPs revealed the problem was primarily that members made judgements regarding the suitability of the interest rate by comparing it with the rate charged by government-owned banks. At the time of the interviews, for example, the VBP was charging 0.7-0.8 percent per month whilst the typical NMP charged around 1.2 percent per month (Table 2). The rate charged by NMPs was on a par with that charged by VBARD. What is important to note is that NMPs reported to being effectively duty bound not to charge in excess of this rate since to do so would be to invite claims of exploiting the poor. NMPs contended that their members were largely unaware that the interest rate charged by banks such as VBP was a subsidised one. Lenhart (2000) has claimed that the interest rate offered by the VBP at the time was around half that which would be consistent with cost recovery. Along similar lines, some NMPs stated that their members felt they were obligated to provide lower rates of interest since they were billed as development programs.

The implication here is that as long as government-owned banks offer subsidised interest rates, it can be expected that NMP members will express dissatisfaction regarding the interest rate charged by NMPs. This perception presents a serious conundrum for NMPs in Vietnam. While members report to benefiting from the programs in place, if the official policy of interest rate subsidisation is maintained NMPs will be limited in their ability to charge an interest rate that would be consistent with financial self-sufficiency. And as was noted earlier, while donor organisations typically accept responsibility for subsidising operations during the initial set-up period, over time they expect the programs will become self-sufficient.

The second major hindrance - raised by 82 percent of respondent NMPs - was related to the regulatory framework surrounding NMPs. At the time the surveys and interviews were conducted, NMPs were operating without any supporting legislation that defined and protected their operations. Some also complained that government policies relating to matters such as labour recruitment and taxation requirements were unclear. In this respect, one might expect that the decree released in March 2005 on the organisation and operation of microfinance institutions in Vietnam would be welcome. And in many ways it was. For the first time, NMPs had a formal document that defined the types of financial services they were permitted to engage in and were given legal protection covering their operations. However, while it is still too early to confidently predict the long run impact of this legislation, there are some worrying issues. The decree by the SBV sets out minimum legal capital requirements for NMPs. For those that do not accept voluntary deposits, the minimum legal capital requirement is VND 500 million (~$US 32,000). For those that do, the requirement jumps to VND 5 billion (~$US 320,000) report (ADB, 2003) for the Asian Development Bank (ADB) and the SBV on the regulatory framework surrounding microfinance institutions in Vietnam, Price Waterhouse Coopers wrote that the typical range for microfinance institutions internationally was between $US 60,000 -$US 100,000. Data from our survey showed that only 32 percent of NMPs had start-up capital of more than VND 500 million and no NMP had VND 5 billion. According to the decree, NMPs that do not satisfy these minimum requirements within two years, will be required to stop their microfinance activities.

Aside from the interest rate being considered too high, the next most common criticism of NMPs, which was raised by 42 percent of member respondents, was that the loan size on offer was too small. From the perspective of the NMP, smaller loans served several beneficial ends. Firstly, they helped to screen the rich out from accessing to microfinance. Having physical collateral, the rich would often prefer to access credit through one of the banks such as VBARD rather than incur the opportunity costs that relate to borrowing money from an NMP (regular meetings, etc). Secondly, it was considered a training process for the poor to manage their loans. Thirdly, the small loan size allowed the NMP to reach more clients. The latter is a practical consideration forced upon NMPs already heavily reliant on donors for loanable funds. The ratio between local funds (ie. from member savings) and total loanable funds amongst the NMPs surveyed was on average just 19.3 percent. There were only three programs in the sample that had a ratio of more than 50 percent. From a poverty reduction standpoint, this constraint is worrying since the small average loan size and ensuing complaints imply that some potentially productive projects are going unfunded due to the lumpy, indivisible nature of investment (McKinnon, 1973). While there may well be an economic justification for concluding that NMPs should offer larger loans, there is clearly an interplay between this issue and the government policies raised above. It is hard to see how NMPs will be able to attract the additional funds they need to be able to offer larger loans when they are hamstrung with respect to the interest rates they charge (because of the subsidised interest rate in government-owned banks) and in accepting voluntary deposits from members and non-members (by legislation restricting their services to members and imposing high minimum legal capital requirements).

Conclusions

NMPs in Vietnam are now at a critical juncture. Somewhat ironically, the question marks over their future are in spite of their own continued professed dedication to helping the poor and the perception of members, non-members and village leaders that their operations do contribute to poverty alleviation. Now that many institutions are at least several years old, sponsoring donors are increasingly expecting them to become financially self-sufficient. At the same time government policies such as subsidising official interest rates and instituting high minimum legal capital requirements make it very difficult for these institutions to attract a volume of savings that would be consistent with financial self-sufficiency. A constricted savings volume also contributes to the situation whereby NMPs are forced to choose between offering smaller loans to a greater number of members or larger loans to fewer members.

If these issues remain unaddressed, two scenarios are likely to eventuate - neither of which is appealing from the perspective of helping the poor. The first is that donors will pull the plug on programs that fail to reach financial self-sufficiency or they will be forced to close by the government for failing to reach minimum capital requirements. The second is that current NMPs will switch from their current development orientation to more commercial objectives in order to survive - they will, in effect, cease to be microfinance institutions that focus on poverty alleviation. If financial markets in developing countries were complete and not subject to market failure, a distinction need not be drawn between development and commercial objectives. In reality however, many market failures do exist and there are often large divergences between the financial and social returns to lending (Kane, 1983). Both of the above scenarios would be extremely unfortunate given that nearly 70 percent of poor rural households in Vietnam still do not have access to vital credit services (Table 1).

References

Asian Development Bank (ADB). 2003. "Annex 1: Microfinance framework", Assessment report of TA 3741-VIE: Preparing the Framework for Microfinance Development, Hanoi, Vietnam.

Banking With The Poor (BWTP). 2005. Profile of Vietnam, http://www.bwtp.org/ (26.04.2005)

Che, P. L. 2002. "The Challenges of Microfinance in Highland Areas", Vietnam Microfinance Bulletin, Vol. 1, September 2002.

Dinh, A.T. 2005. (pers. comm.), Discussion on the establishment and operations of Binh Minh Co. Ltd.

General Statistics Office (GSO) 1994. *Vietnam Living Standard Survey 1992-1993*, Statistics Publishing House, Hanoi, Vietnam

General Statistics Office (GSO). 2000. *Vietnam Living Standard Survey 1997-1998*, Statistics Publishing House, Hanoi, Vietnam

General Statistics Office (GSO). 2005. Data of the Vietnam Living Standard Survey and other surveys, http://www.gso.gov.vn/default.aspx?tabid=217 (18.04.2005)

Hung, D.V. 1998. "Study Case: People's Credit Funds in Vietnam", Report Presented to Development International Desjardins, Quebec, Canada.

Kane, J. 1983. *Development banking: an economic appraisal*, Lexington, MA: Lexington Books.

Lenhart, K. 2000. "The Influence of Donors on Microcredit Sustainability: A Case Study from three Microcredit in Vietnam, The Vietnamese Bank for the Poor, Save the Children UK, and NIKE", Evans School of Public Affair, University of Washington.

Llanto, G.M. 2000. "Vietnam", The Role of Central Banks in Microfinance in Asia and the Pacific: Countries Studies, Asian Development Bank, pp.334-55

McCarty, A. 2001a. "Microfinance in Vietnam: A Survey of Schemes and Issues", Report presented to the DFID and the State Bank of Vietnam, Hanoi.

McCarty, A. 2001b. "The Institutional and Legal Structure of Microfinance in Vietnam", Working Paper No.2, DFID and the State Bank of Vietnam, Hanoi.

McKinnon, R. 1973. *Money and capital in economic development*, Washington, DC: Brookings Institution.

Nguyen, T.A. 2004. "Notes from Preliminary Review on Microfinance for Poverty Reduction in Vietnam", Ford Foundation, Hanoi, Vietnam.

Tran, N.A. and Yun T.S. 2004. "TYM's Mutual Assistance Fund, Vietnam", Case Study No. 3, CGAP Working Group on Microinsurance

United Nations Development Programme (UNDP). 1996. *Catching Up - Capacity Development for Poverty Elimination*, Hanoi

Chapter 9: Microfinance as a Means of Alleviating Poverty

Trickle-Up Economic Development: A Critical Examination of Microfinance Programs

Jonathan H. Westover

Abstract: With Muhammad Yunus being recently awarded the Nobel Peace Prize for his pioneering approach and sustained effort in addressing the problem of poverty, microfinance programs have continued to grow in usage and popularity. There are numerous studies that demonstrate the tremendous successes of such programs throughout much of the underdeveloped world. However, the universal effectiveness of microfinance institutions in alleviating poverty is still in question, and not free from debate. Much of the evidence cited for the successes of microfinance and microcredit are merely anecdotal or involve in-depth case-study approaches, which provide vivid examples and rich details of the impact and effectiveness of specific programs in specific locations at a specific time, but generally fail to achieve a more rigorous standard that would allow for research findings to be more widely generalized to other contexts. Some more rigorous studies have been conducted and more are surely to follow, but in the meantime, NGO leaders and government policy makers must exercise caution and restraint in applying the microfinance approach universally as a means of alleviating poverty. This chapter reviews some of the recent research into the effectiveness of microfinance programs and proposes areas for future directions in the continued research of microfinance programs.

Keywords: Microfinance, Microcredit, Economic Development, Poverty

Introduction

Poverty has different meanings to different people and is the source of much debate in the public arena. This is largely due to the fact that there are many potential causes of poverty, ranging from those that could be categorized as causes stemming from one's personal choices and actions, causes stemming from structural constraints and inequalities in society, and causes that arise from government welfare entitlement programs. As a result of such a wide and diverse array of potential poverty causes, there are an equally large number of proposed policy interventions and solutions designed to eradicate the problem of poverty, some addressing each of the different areas mentioned above. One potential solution that has been increasing in popularity, and controversy, in recent years is the area of microfinance. Despite the increased popularity, what is the record of such programs? Furthermore, what is the effectiveness/ ineffectiveness of such programs on reducing poverty? Finally, what are the predominant methodological approaches in the microfinance literature? As with any intervention strategy, as the number of microfinance programs instituted throughout the world continues to increase, formal investigation into the effectiveness of such programs is important.

In this chapter I will provide evidence from the existing literature on microfinance to show the current performance record of such programs and the effectiveness/ineffectiveness of such programs on reducing poverty. Furthermore, I will discuss some criticisms of the microfinance approach to eradicating poverty and provide a critique of the methodological foundation of microfinance as a whole, as well as the increased number of impact studies that have been conducted in recent years. Finally, I will draw several conclusions on the appropriateness and effectiveness of microfinance programs in addressing the problem of world poverty, while providing several suggestions for future research directions in this developing field.

Review of Literature

Article Selection Method

For this literature review, I conducted an EBSCO Host database search of peer-reviewed academic journal articles between the years of 1996-2006, using the search terms, "microfinance and poverty," and "microcredit and poverty." This search produced over 100 article abstracts, which I read to determine which articles I would include in the review for this paper. While reading through the abstracts and skimming through the methods and findings sections of these articles, I quickly found that there is a large body of less "rigorous" research in this area, including microfinance institutions program impact studies and a large number of studies that used qualitative or more of a case studies approach. I therefore decided to focus my review on those articles that utilized some form of quantitative data and analysis, and where possible, a broader study scope (rather than focusing on just one program or one town). This reduced the number of articles dramatically, yielding the final six studies to be reviewed in this chapter.

In addition to the peer-reviewed journal articles, I also used some references to popular media sources and visited a few microfinance practitioner-based websites to provide what may be viewed as the popular mainstream perspective.

Background to Microfinance

Poverty is a world-wide poverty epidemic. Figure 1 below illustrates that though extreme poverty rates have been declining across many regions of the world in recent decades, high rates still persist. Furthermore, it is estimated that about one-sixth (500 million of an estimated 3 billion) of poor people throughout the world have access to formal financial services (World Bank, 2005). This represents a large gap in access to such services.

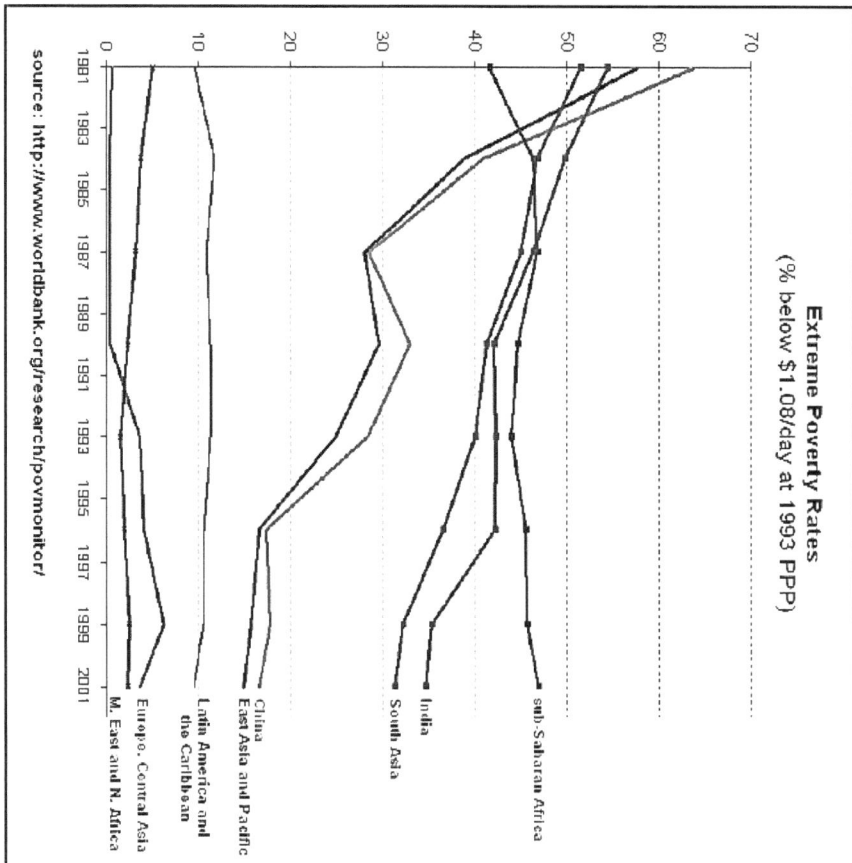

Figure 1. Extreme Poverty Rates in World Regions

One approach to reducing this gap that has increased in popularity in recent years has been the formation of microfinance institutions (an estimated 7,000 microfinance institutions serving approximately 16 million poor individuals in developing countries) (World Bank, 2005). However, Figure 2 illustrates the large gap that still persists between need and the access of microfinance services available to the world's poorest families.

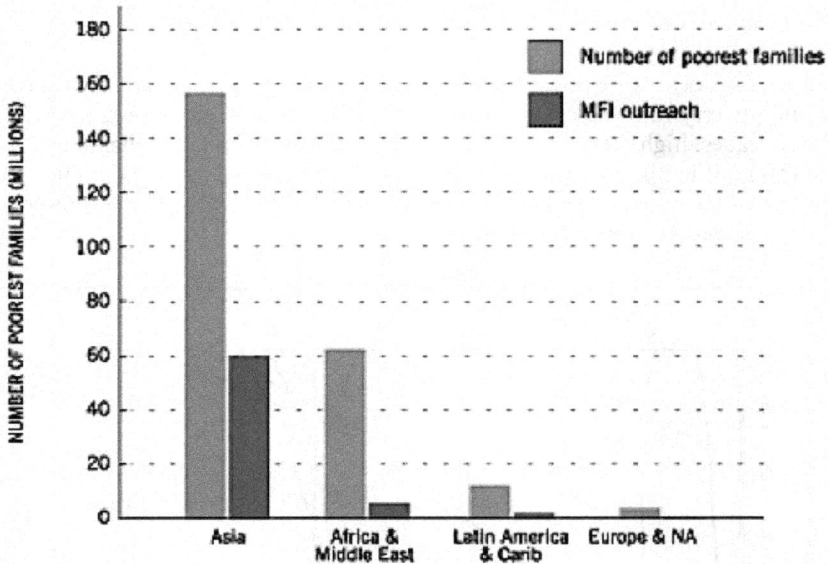

Figure 2. Access to Microfinance Services
Source: www.unitus.com/wwd_whatismf.asp

The idea of microfinance started in Bangladesh around 1976 with Muhammad Yunus and Grameen Bank (recently awarded the Nobel Peace Prize for his work). Microfinance refers to financial services offered to low SES individuals that are excluded from the traditional financial system (considered "unbankable"— lacking collateral, steady employment, and a verifiable credit history). Aspects of microfinance, such as microcredit, are designed to help lift individuals, families, and communities out of poverty by providing small amounts of start-up capital for entrepreneurial projects, which will then presumably help individuals to generate income, build wealth, and exit poverty.

One aspect of microfinance that distinguishes it from the traditional financial system is the "joint liability concept," where groups of individuals, usually women, group together to apply for loans, and hold joint accountability for repayment of the loan. The premise is that providing low SES individuals access to financial services will better enable poor households to move away from subsistence living, to a future oriented outlook on life and an increased investment in nutrition, education, and living expenses. Furthermore, microfinance is unique as a development tool because of its potential to be self-sustaining (both reducing poverty and maintaining a profitable business) (Business Week, 2005).

Reported Strengths/Positive Impacts of Microfinance Programs

A variety of studies have found a few key strengths and positive impacts produced by the implementation of microfinance programs in poor and impoverished areas of the world. First, microfinance programs can be an effective way to provide low-cost financial services to poor individuals and families (Miller and Martinez, 2006; Stephens and Tazi 2006). Second, such programs have been shown to help in the development and growth of the local economy as individuals and families are able to move past subsistence living and increase disposable income levels (Khandker, 2005).

In addition, many studies (primarily microfinance institution impact studies and academic researcher qualitative or case studies) have shown that microfinance programs were able to reduce poverty through increasing individual and household income levels, as well as improving healthcare, nutrition, education, and helping to empower women. For example, standard of living increases, which help to eradicate extreme poverty and hunger, have occurred at both the individual and household levels as a result of microfinance programs (Khandker, 2005). Furthermore, it has been demonstrated by some research that microfinance programs increase access to healthcare, making preventative healthcare measures more affordable to the poor. In addition, more children are being sent to school and staying enrolled longer (Morduch, 1998). Finally, it has been shown that such programs can help borrowers to develop dignity and self-confidence in conjunction with loan repayment, and self-sufficiency as a means for sustainable income becomes available. Since microfinance services are primarily focused on women, it is argued that this leads to the empowerment of women and the breaking down of gender inequalities, through providing opportunities for women to take on leadership roles and responsibilities (Goetz and Gupta, 1995).

Reported Problems/Negative Impacts of Microfinance Programs

In contrast to the various positive impacts and strengths of microfinance programs listed above, other studies (more quantitative, with appropriate treatment/control frameworks and comparisons made across larger samples) have found several key problems and negative impacts produced by the implementation of microfinance programs in poor and impoverished areas of the world. First, some studies have shown that microfinance programs benefit the moderately poor more than the destitute, and thus impact can vary by income group (better-off benefit more from micro-credit) (Copestake et al., 2001; Morduch, 1998; Dugger, 2004). Second, most microfinance programs target women (due to higher repayment rates), which may result in men requiring wife to get loans for them (Goetz and Gupta, 1995). Third, examples exist of a vicious cycle of debt, microcredit dependency, increased workloads, and domestic violence associated with participation in microfinance programs (Copestake et al., 2001; Morduch, 1998). Fourth, studies have shown that there are low repayment rates in comparison with traditional financial institutions (Miller and Martinez, 2006; Stephens and Tazi, 2006), thus possibly contradicting one of the key strengths listed above, that such programs can lead to empowerment and increased self-confidence through responsible loan repayment. Fifth, there have been reports of the use of harsh and coercive methods to push for repayment and excessive interest rates (Business Week, 2005; The Financial Express, 2005). Finally, concerns have been raised that the reliance on microfinance programs to aid the poor may result in a reduction of government and charitable assistance ("privatization of public safety-net programs") (Neff, 1996).

Microfinance as a Means to Alleviate Poverty?

Based on the findings reported above, there are mixed conclusions as to the overall impact of microfinance institutions. This leads us to the key question of this paper: What is the effectiveness/ ineffectiveness of microfinance programs on reducing poverty? Some studies have found marked decreases in overall poverty levels, including declining levels of extreme poverty (Khandker, 2005), while other studies do not find the same direct effect (Morris and Barnes, 2005; Kan, Olds, and Kah, 2005; Goetz and Gupta, 1996). Still, other studies provide mixed results (Copestake, Bhalotra, and Johnson, 2001; Morduch, 1998). Thus, the academic literature is mixed in regards to the specific impact that microfinance has on alleviating poverty. In what follows, I will review these studies, briefly discussing the study designs and key findings.

Microfinance Helps to Alleviate Poverty

The only study, among those selected for review in this paper, that was both more rigorous in design and reported very clear and direct effects of microfinance programs on poverty was Khandker's 2005 article, "Microfinance and Poverty: Evidence Using Panel Data from Bangladesh." This research examined 1,638 households that participated in two waves of the BIDS—World Bank 1991/92 and 1998/99 survey in Bangladesh. Khandker found that moderate poverty in the sample villages declined 17% between the two waves of the survey, and extreme poverty declined 13%. Among those households that participated in the microfinance programs, the poverty rate declined 20% in the same period, with more than half of the nearly 3% annual moderate poverty decline among participants attributed to the microfinance programs alone. He further found that access to microfinance programs contributed to the reduction of both moderate and extreme poverty of individuals (particularly women) as well as for the village as a whole—where inflow of microfinance funds to rural areas impacted the local economy— and raised per capita household consumption for both participants and nonparticipants.

Microfinance Does Not Help to Alleviate Poverty

Despite the very positive results reported by Khandker, other studies reported more findings that were much muddier. Kan, Olds, and Kah (2005) studied the evolution, sustainability, and management of ten microcredit institutions in Gossas, Senegal, using a mixed-methods approach to study design, utilizing socioeconomic surveys, semi-structured interviews, and ethnographic research over a period of three years. They found that microcredit institutions have helped to create some positive change, but that there was no clear and marked evidence of poverty reduction that was attributable to the microfinance programs studied and stated that the expectations of what microcredit can do to help lift communities out of poverty is "a bit too optimistic" (p. 146).

Morris and Barnes (2005) attempted to provide an overall assessment of the impact of microfinance, and examined the impacts of three microfinance programs in Uganda (FINCA, FOCCAS, and PRIDE). Utilizing survey data collected via random sample from each of the three program areas (for both program clients and non-clients), baseline data was first collected in the winter of 1997, and then the survey was repeated in the winter of 1999 to assess impact. The researchers did not find that microfinance programs help to alleviate poverty in program areas, though results from these impact studies indicated positive impacts of these microfinance programs on both program participants' entrepreneurial business endeavors and within their own households. The authors further found that microfinance programs help to reduce financial vulnerability of poor individuals through the diversification of available income sources and the accumulation of assets.

Mixed Results

Though most of the studies already previously cited found some mixed results of the role that microfinance programs play in alleviating poverty, a few other studies clearly did not come down on one side or the other. Copestake, Bhalotra, and Johnson (2001) also attempted to provide an overall assessment of microfinance programs and used a mixed-methods approach, utilizing a questionnaire-based sample survey of PULSE participants, a secondary survey on drawn on a larger population of businesses and households, and qualitative focus-group discussion and key informant interviews. The researchers noted that "expectations are high, but evidence of the impact of microcredit remains in short supply" (abstract) and that the number of rigorous studies still remains small (p. 82). However, 57% of program participants reported feeling better off overall, though some borrowers are made worse off financially through involvement with the microcredit programs. Further, the researchers found that the microfinance programs benefited the moderately poor more than the destitute.

Morduch (1998) attempted to look specifically at the role microfinance plays in helping the poor, and reported mixed results, including some positive and some negative impacts of microfinance in alleviating poverty and helping the poor. Morduch used survey data collected in 1991/92 by the Bangladesh Institute for Development Studies, in collaboration with the World Bank, covering 87 villages and nearly 1800 households. Survey data was collected at three points during the collection period to capture seasonal variations in household circumstances. Morduch found that the microfinance programs benefited the moderately poor more than the destitute. Further, he found that households that are eligible to borrow and have access to the programs do not have notably higher consumption levels that control households. Additionally, he found that households eligible for programs have substantially lower variation in consumption and labor supply across seasons, thus the most important potential impacts of microfinance programs are with reducing one's financial vulnerability, and not necessarily poverty.

Critique of Existing Literature

As demonstrated in the review section of this paper, the findings in the literature on the effectiveness and impact of microfinance programs vary. Many impact studies and other similar assessments find great strengths and positive impacts of such programs on reducing poverty, while other studies report that such positive impacts may be over-reported and even inaccurate, while pointing out some fundamental flaws with such study designs. The question is, which group of studies is correct, and to what extent? In what follows I will briefly provide some methodological critiques of the current body of research in trying to address this question.

At this point in the literature, there are few stringent evaluations of microcredit programs generally viewed as credible by experts. Much of the literature reporting positive results of the impact of microfinance programs in reducing poverty fails to meet a rigorous level of study design and statistical analysis, using qualitative methods, looking at single cases or specific areas or regions, using cross-sectional data, analyzing self-reported measures, and using non-random sampling procedures, resulting in findings that cannot be easily replicated nor generalized to all programs. In contrast to the common qualitative and case-study approaches in the less rigorous body of research, only a handful of studies use sizeable samples and appropriate treatment/ control frameworks to answer the questions of real impact and effectiveness. As Morduch said in his critique of the existing literature methodology, "While strong claims are made for the ability of microfinance to reduce poverty, only a handful of studies use sizable samples and appropriate treatment/control frameworks to answer the question" (1998, p. 1). Until more such studies are conducted and findings reported, we must take the findings of less rigorous impact studies with a grain of salt and not be too quick to generalize findings of the impact and effectiveness of a specific program, in specific location, at a specific time, to other cases.

Future Directions

I am encouraged by the increasing popularity of the growing microfinance movement and recognize it as a pioneering approach to addressing the problem of poverty. There are numerous studies that demonstrate the tremendous successes of such programs throughout much of the underdeveloped world. However, despite the increase in the popularity of microfinance programs and the vast amount of research conducted to date, there are two key areas for future research into the effectiveness of microfinance programs.

First and foremost, more stringent evaluations of microcredit programs are needed. Various feasibility and impact studies have shown the financial viability of such programs in being self-sustainable institutions, but the question of the effectiveness and impact on the poor of such programs is still highly in question. Many studies use a case-study approach to looking at the effectiveness of a given program in a given region at a given time, but few effectively measure the impact of multiple programs. To be able to say once and for all that these programs are or are not effective at reduce poverty will require a large sample of programs with data that can be rigorously analyzed, with replicable methods and generalizable findings.

Second, there are considerable practical debates surrounding the implementation of microfinance programs that have yet to be answered. These debates include a fundamental theoretical debate between large-scale, top-down funding of major development projects versus small-scale, bottom-up funding to individuals and households as a means of alleviating poverty. Additionally, there are questions surrounding the potential of microfinance programs to cannibalize other programs, including government assistance and aid. Furthermore, there are still questions as to the potential of microcredit hurting the poor and creating a kind of microcredit dependency. Finally, as microfinance programs are geared almost exclusively to woman, there is a debate about the appropriateness of such a policy and the possible exploitation of women. Therefore further research needs to be conducted to examine these facets of microfinance programs.

Conclusion

Despite the popularization of microfinance in the mass media and the many positive findings that are reported in some feasibility and impact studies, there are also many studies that report some negative impacts of such programs and fail to find a direct link between microfinance program involvement and poverty reduction. Thus, at this point, NGO leaders and government policy makers must exercise caution and restraint in applying the microfinance approach universally as a means of alleviating poverty and continue to conduct rigorous research that will better answer the questions addressed in this paper.

References

Copestake, James, Bhalotra, Sonia, and Johnson, Susan. 2001. "Assessing the Impact of Microcredit: A Zambian Case Study." *The Journal of Development Studies*, Vol. 37 (4), p. 81-100.

Dugger, Celia W. 2004. "Debate Stirs over Tiny Loans for World's Poorest." *New York Times*.

Goetz, Anne Marrie andGupta, Rina Sen. 1996. "Who Takes the Credit? Gender, Power and Control over Loan Use in Rural Credit Programmes in Bangladesh." *World Development* Vol. 24 (1), p. 45-63.

Kah, Jainaba M.L., Olds, Dana L., and Kah, Muhammadou M. O. 2005. "Microcredit, Social Capital, and Politics." *Journal of Microfinance*, Vol. 7 (1), p. 121-151.

Khandker, Shahidur R. 2005. "Microfinance and Poverty: Data from Bangladesh." *The World Bank Economic Review*, Vol. 19 (2), p. 263-286.

"Large NGOs Becoming Rockefellers." *The Financial Express*, November 22, 2005.

"Micro Loans, Solid Returns: Microfinance Funds Lift Poor Entrepreneurs and Benefit Investors." *Business Week,* May 9, 2005.

Miller, Jared, and Martinez, Renso. "Championship League: An Overview of 80 Leading Latin American Providers of Microfinance." *Microbanking Bulletin*, April 2006.

Morduch, Jonathan. 1998. "Does Microfinance Really Help the Poor? New Evidence from Flagship Programs in Bangladesh." *MacArthur Network, Princeton University*.

Morris, Gayle, and Barnes, Carolyn. 2005. "An Assessment of the Impact of Microfinance." *Journal of Microfinance*, Vol. 7 (1), p. 40-54.

Neff, Gina. 1996. "Microcredit, Microresults." *The Left Business Observer* Vol. 74.

Stephens, Blaine and Tazi, Hind. "Performance and Transparency: A Survey of Microfinance in South Asia." *Microbanking Bulletin*, April 2006.

Part 3: Social Entrepreneurship and Microfinance Education

Chapters 10-12 make up Part 3 of the book, which focuses on social entrepreneurship and microfinance education. Chapter 10 looks at the universtity's role in promoting "new" entrepreneurship. Chapter 11 looks at educating the socially conscious entrepreneur. Chapter 12 looks at educators as social entrepreneurs.

Chapter 10: Universities Promoting "New" Entrepreneurship

Universities and the Next Generation of Entrepreneurship

Jianhong Xue

Abstract: Arguing that three interwoven factors, including globalization, the advancement of technologies, and the theme of sustainable development, have been shaping the new world development, this paper explains the opportunities and challenges that modern universities are facing. While describing how universities' roles and functions are extended and expanded in the context of globalization and new communication technologies, this paper also points out the requirement that the theme of sustainable development has posed on universities. Considering that economic entrepreneurship in modern universities is necessary in exploring their potential in knowledge-based economic production, this paper argues that universities have great responsibility in promoting the next generation of entrepreneurship by which economic activities should conform with strong social and moral values. Implications for both university initiatives and government policy towards universities are discussed.
Keywords: Universities, Globalization, New Knowledge and Technology, Sustainable Development, Entrepreneurship

Introduction

After the end of the Cold War, institutional changes in many countries have made communications and interactions among people all over the world much easier. Frequent and massive exchanges between individuals, organizations, and countries are also supported by the advancement of information and communication technologies. Consequentially, large scale economic development has occurred in many parts of the world, especially in major developing countries like China, India, and Brazil, where about 40 percent of the world's population reside. Such rapid and massive economic development and growth in the developing world along with the affluent-driven and unrestricted consumption pattern in major developed countries have brought alarming environmental concerns. Therefore, the idea of sustainable development has been gradually accepted as a new theme of our new world development. These all suggest that three major interwoven factors have been shaping world development: the process of globalization, the advancement of new technologies, and the new theme of sustainable development. While globalization and technologies make factors of production, especially human capital, much more moveable and productive, the distributional effect of human capital and the way that international trade is conducted would have a huge impact on the future order of human societies in the world. Meanwhile, the theme of sustainable development requires changes in our systems of beliefs, by which more responsible human behaviors in business practices and daily activities can be sufficiently induced, and thus, social, economic, and environmental sustainability could be achieved.

In such a new phase of the world development, universities play increasingly important roles because that they are directly involved with these three factors that are shaping new world development. In the process of globalization, universities have been extending their reach to many regions and areas and gaining powers in the distribution of human capital, knowledge and technologies. In new knowledge production and technological development, universities even have much more direct involvement, resulting in the rise of university entrepreneurship in knowledge-based economic activities. Moreover, since universities are places where human ideas are frequently originated and exchanged, they are critical institutions in propelling the formation of new human systems of beliefs by which the theme of sustainable development can be realized. That is, while universities are being shaped by these factors, they are also shaping new world development through their unique institutional roles or functions. However, less attention has been paid to the roles or functions that universities should exert in meeting the opportunities and challenges in the context of globalization, new technologies, and sustainable development. Therefore, the objective of this short paper is to provide a helpful discussion on the roles, problems, and potentials of modern universities in the new phase of world development. Important policy implications for universities and governments can be drawn.

While reviewing the traditional roles and functions that universities have in human society, Section II of this paper explains the new or extended roles and functions for modern universities in the context of globalization and knowledge-based economic production. Section III of the paper discuses the problems and challenges that universities are facing today, particularly those that are posed by the theme of sustainable development. In Section IV, while describing the trend that modern universities become more entrepreneurial through growing participation in the knowledge-based economic development, the paper further argues that the new generation of entrepreneurship that universities need to promote should not be merely an economic one, but a combination of economic and social entrepreneurship. Section V of the paper summarizes important issues regarding university policy making in the new world development. Social and moral responsibilities in university entrepreneurial development are emphasized.

The Role of Universities in the New Era

As social institutions, universities have played important roles and functions in human society. Although such roles or functions are complex and vary over time, scholars have tried to explain them from different perspectives. While describing the relationship between economic return and investment in human capital, Becker (1962 and 1964) has used expenditure in education, training, and healthcare as a proxy measure of human capital. In explaining the economic and social value of education, Schultz (1963) has considered education as not only an important input in the production function of individual, firm, and the aggregate economy, but also as a critical input for individual utility and social welfare function. Since universities provide a critical part of education and training, they have a significant role to play in human capital formation, economic production, and social welfare creation. To analyze the academic and social functions of universities in the United States, Boyer (1990) has identified four categories of scholarship that universities offer to society: the scholarship of teaching, the scholarship of discovering, the scholarship of application, and the scholarship of integration. We may often refer to them as teaching, research, professional practice, and incorporation of diversified knowledge and thoughts. While acknowledging such fundamental roles of universities in providing education and research for economic production, this section of the paper further explores the institutional functions that universities have in the production of new knowledge and innovation as well as in the distribution of human capital and technologies.

First, I argue that universities serve as institutional platforms that enhance knowledge and innovative production. Unlike ordinary economic production, knowledge and innovative production originally takes place inside individual human minds. Information, including existing knowledge and any other random or recorded signals, serves as inputs for such productions. However, information and knowledge, as inputs for innovative production, have distributional attributes that require frequent exchanges between individuals. As Hayek (1945) has put it, "the knowledge of the circumstances of which we must make use never exists in concentrated or integrated form, but solely as the dispersed bits of incomplete and frequently contradictory knowledge which all the separate individuals possesses" (p. 519). This suggests that, in order to make new knowledge or innovative production, reallocation or exchange of information and knowledge among individuals is necessary. Xue (2007a) has argued that the firm is "a physical place and a social device that provides geographic, social, and technical proximities to individuals, and thus, increases the frequency and relevancy of the exchange of information and knowledge" (p. 19). Therefore, universities as a special type of firm can be seen as institutional platforms that facilitate exchanges of information and knowledge, and thus, innovative production. How such a role of universities can be enhanced is an important topic of university policy.

Second, in the new era, major advancement of information and communication technologies and an increasing scale of globalization have enhanced the traditional roles of universities and expanded their new institutional functions in the development of human society and regions. Feldman (2003) has used the word "regional anchor" (p. 312) to explain the role of existing biotechnology firms in the formation of biotechnology industry clusters in certain regions. She suggests that certain existing technology firms in a particular region serve as anchors that not only attract skilled labor pools and related intermediate industries to the region, but also lead scientific innovation and industry practice in the region in a specific direction by providing expertise and knowledge about scientific application, technical development trajectories, and product markets. Based on Feldman's characterization of certain existing firms as regional anchors, Xue (2007b) has suggested that universities play similar roles in the region and has named two types of regional anchors, "anchor universities" and "anchor firms" (p. 60). This paper further argues that, in the age of globalization and advanced technologies, such regional anchors play an increasingly important role in the distribution of critical resources, such as human capital, knowledge, and technological innovations, and thus, the competitiveness of regions. Universities play such a role for the region by attracting talents and internalizing extremely important economic exchanges and transactions for new knowledge and technological productions. Many universities in the United States have most excellently demonstrated such roles in both national and regional economic development and growth. For example, universities in the United States have had large portions of foreign graduate student enrollment in the fields of science and engineering (Oliver, 2007). In the two famous high technology industry clusters, "Silicon Valley" in California and "Route 128" in Massachusetts, many new firms have been started by foreign-born U.S. university graduates (Saxenian, 1994 and 2002). These all inform us that the role of anchoring played by the presence of many outstanding universities in these regions cannot be overlooked. In the process of globalization, individuals become increasingly mobile. Hence, the superiority of universities is the key in exerting such a role of anchoring. Universities as both institutional platforms and anchors have great importance to regional economic development.

Problems and Challenges of Modern Universities

From the above discussion, one may realize that, given an increasingly large scale of globalization equipped with advanced communication technologies, universities have far more reaching power beyond geographic, national, and cultural boundaries. This definitely creates great opportunities for modern universities. While recognizing these opportunities for universities in the new era, we should not ignore the problems and challenges universities encounter. There are many such problems and challenges that universities are facing today, this section of the paper only focuses on the problems and challenges that the theme of sustainable development has posed on universities.

In the past two decades, since the publication of the Brundtland Report, *Our Common Future* (World Commission on Environment and Development, 1987), much attention has been paid to the idea of sustainable development. As the scientific communities have made progress in revealing evidence showing unwanted impacts of human activities on the environment, the idea of sustainable development has become more acceptable. However, how to make the theme of sustainable development operational is a major challenge to human society. Given their scholarly and institutional functions described above, universities should have strong responsibilities in working towards a practical phase of sustainable development because of the following reasons.

First, the key requirement of sustainable development is to reduce the negative impact of human activities on the natural environment and on the health of human society as a whole, thus, avoiding unwanted and disastrous consequences. Evidently, human beings have often behaved destructively on the basis of their lives both consciously and unconsciously. Therefore, it is necessary to evaluate the existing human systems and beliefs that govern human behaviors. Universities, as the most important institutions in which human beliefs and ideas are formed, should have a major role to play in moving the idea of sustainable development to a practical phase. Nevertheless, some of the human systems or beliefs based on academic thoughts or theories have limitations in achieving the goal of sustainable development. For instance, in mainstream economics, the market price mechanism has been long believed to be the dominant force in coordinating allocation of resources. In such a theoretical framework, market price, based on the quantity of supply and demand, is considered the invisible hand to governing the exchanges of economic goods and production; and it is argued that optimal allocation of resources can be realized under such a price system. Logically, and to a certain extent, price has an impact on demand. However, the problem is that human wants seem to be unlimited. To maximize their utility, individuals do not restrain their consumption. For example, the price of oil is about tripled in the last decade or so, but the quantity demanded for oil has similarly increased. Another problem under the price system is that profit maximization has been considered the paramount objective of the firm. To maximize profit, firms do not care much about the consequences of certain unhealthy business operations. As a result, there are large unhealthy components of our economy under the governance of the so-called price mechanism. This can be further demonstrated by the following examples. It is well-known that overwhelming scientific evidence has shown that the health risk of smoking is very high, yet the tobacco industry in many countries in the world has accounted for a large portion of their economies. While food shortages have frequently occurred in many parts of the world, the profit motive drives certain countries or regions to use their agricultural land for growing opium. Even in the pharmaceutical industry, under profit-seeking behavior, cold-medicine is often found to be no better than drinking water. Apparently, the price-mechanism has its limitation in achieving sustainability because it would not automatically prevent irresponsible activities and behaviors that are harmful to the natural environment, human health, and social stability. Since the idea of sustainable development involves consideration of the needs for future generations, high ethical standards are essential. Universities should put more effort into devising and enforcing a better human system of beliefs in which the moral component should be emphasized.

Second, human beings live in an increasingly human-made technological world, and much of the new technological innovations and products are created by university researchers or graduates. However, many technological innovations have dual uses. For example, there are both civic uses and destructive uses of technologies, such as nuclear technology, laser technology, biotechnology, aviation technology and so on. While many technologies, like "green" technologies, can be used to save resources and improve the quality of life, many human-made technologies have also been employed to destroy millions of human lives during many wars and conflicts. Today, there are still tons of technological weapons in stock, and more powerful new technologies in the form of weaponry continue to be produced by humans with the capacity of destroying the entire human population and the planet. Similarly, academic knowledge can be used for different purposes. As technologies are made more portable with new means of delivering them, the control of inhumane deployment of many technologies becomes more difficult. Universities, as producers of these technologies or knowledge, should have responsibilities in controlling the trajectories of technology development and the rights in technology transfer and commercialization.

Third, in the new era, there is exponential growth and increasing complexities of new knowledge and technologies, which are largely created in universities. While these new knowledge and technologies create great economic value and improve the quality of life, the distribution of them may also raise questions on the university's role in society. One widely recognized problem is the so-called "digital divide". As a very large portion of the world's population does not have sufficient education and access to technological means, universities may create inequality in society. Another problem is that some life-supporting technological means have hardly been distributed to a hefty portion of population. For instance, as increasing amounts of resources have been used in medical education, research, and facilities, many populations in the world still do not have adequate and timely healthcare, even in the developed world. Similarly, many agricultural technologies are capable of increasing food production, but food shortages and hunger can still be seen in many parts of the world where these technologies are simply unavailable. To a certain extent, these examples have signaled the problems of delivering university-produced technologies and services to society, in which economic cost is only one. Universities should stretch their full potential to meet moral obligations in applying these university-produced, life-supporting technologies.

Universities and the Next Generation of Entrepreneurship

Given the fact that the new economy in the world has a growing portion of knowledge-based components, universities are increasingly involved in economic production. As previously discussed, new communication technology and globalization have granted universities much greater institutional power in the creation and distribution of knowledge and human capital. As a result, while continuously providing their traditional socio-economic functions in human society, universities have much more and direct participation in economic activities and value creation, especially in areas of new knowledge and technological production. Literature has suggested that there is rising economic entrepreneurship in modern universities. For instance, Dill (1995) indicates that American research universities have entered an "entrepreneurial" stage with a substantial scale of technology transfer activities. These activities include patenting and licensing, supporting small business development, stimulating research and technology transfer in a particular area of technology under university-industry joint ventures, providing business incubation services, and investing university resources in start-up companies and spin-off enterprises based on university technology. Etzkowitz (2003) has also described the changing phase of universities in the transition from the "research university" to the "entrepreneurial university." While Subotzky (1999) argues that university-business partnership may lead to growing market-like behaviors in university faculty and personnel, Eun, Lee, and Wu (2006) has found that "university-run enterprises" are popular in China. Certainly, university entrepreneurial activities would increase the rate of innovation, and thus, the competitiveness of nations and regions. Therefore, it is important for national and regional policy makers to recognize the significance of supporting university entrepreneurship.

Acknowledging the critical importance of university entrepreneurship in knowledge-based economic development, one should be aware that universities have great responsibilities in making sure that such entrepreneurial development works towards the goal of sustainable development. Under the theme of sustainable development, society needs a new type of entrepreneurship by which economic, social, and environmental sustainability can be secured by responsible human activities and business practices. That is, the new generation of entrepreneurship should include two inseparable components, economic entrepreneurship and social entrepreneurship. I maintain that universities should bear great responsibilities and play a leading role in such entrepreneurial endeavor because of the following. First, as producer of new knowledge and technologies, universities should control the trajectories of both the development and utilization of them since the dual uses apply to many technologies in which the negative impact of these technologies can be catastrophic. This could become a much more serious issue as technologies are made more powerful and portable. Second, as important institutions where ideas are exchanged and the systems of human beliefs are studied, universities need academic entrepreneurship in discovering a more effective and integrated human system of beliefs and in providing education to students with great social responsibility and values. Third, as institutional anchors, universities have to pay attention to the distributional effects of education and research given that the "digital divide," poverty, and other social problems still widely exist in society.

Conclusion

In conclusion, rapid globalization, advancement of technologies, and the theme of sustainable development have represented a new phase of the world development in which universities play more important roles and functions in human society. To reach their potential, universities should realize both opportunities and challenges they are facing in the critical stage of the world development. First, since the new economy has been increasingly comprised of knowledge and technologies, universities have become major economic players given their role as institutional platforms for knowledge production. Also, as institutional anchors in the globalizing world, universities have far more power in the creation and distribution of human capital, knowledge, and technologies. Therefore, it is resourceful for universities to become entrepreneurial in the era of technologies. How to foster entrepreneurship in the area of technological innovation and commercialization should be one of the top priorities for the policy making of universities. Meanwhile, the theme of sustainable development requires universities to be aware of their social and moral responsibilities in their entrepreneurial development. There are three important issues that universities need to address: (1) the impact and limitation of the theoretical human system of beliefs in governing individual and organizational behaviors; (2) the unwanted consequences of the utilization of university-produced new knowledge and technologies; and (3) the increasingly uneven distribution of new knowledge and technologies and the need of more effective distribution of them among society. Therefore, as important institutions where not only new knowledge and technologies are produced, but also human systems of belief are formed, universities should support the next generation of entrepreneurship, by which economic activities must conform with social and moral responsibilities. University management, faculty, and students should take leadership roles and initiatives in the development of both economic entrepreneurship and social entrepreneurship. In order to do so, they must not compromise important principles and values while participating in economic activities. In addition, local, regional, and national governments should fully recognize the institutional roles and functions of universities in knowledge production and the development of the new economy. While providing adequate support for university research, governments need to put more emphasis on how to best commercialize and distribute university-produced knowledge and technologies to society.

References

Becker, G. S. (1962). "Investment in Human Capital: A Theoretical Analysis," *Journal of Political Economy*, 70(5), 9-49.

Becker, G. S. (1964). *Human Capital*. New York: Columbia University Press (for NBER).

Boyer, E. L. (1990). *Scholarship Reconsidered: Priorities of the Professoriate*. San Francisco: Jossey-Boss Publishers.

Dill, D. D. (1995). "University-Industry Entrepreneurship: the Organization and Management of American University Technology Transfer Units," *Higher Education*, Vol. 29, No. 4, pp. 369-384.

Etzkowitz, H. (2003). "Research Groups as 'quasi-firms': the Invention of the Entrepreneurial University," *Research Policy*, Vol. 32, No. 1, pp. 109-121.

Eun, J.H.; Lee, K.; and Wu, G. (2006). "Explaining the 'University-run Enterprises' in China: A Theoretical Framework for University-Industry

Relationship in Developing Countries and Its Application to China,"
Research Policy, Vol. 35, No. 9, pp. 1329-1346.

Feldman, M. P. (2003). "The Locational Dynamics of the US Biotech Industry:
Knowledge Externalities and the Anchor Hypothesis," *Industry and
Innovation*, Vol. 10, No. 3, 311-328.

Hayek, F. A. (1945). "The Use of Knowledge in Society," *The American
Economic Review*, Vol. 35, No. 4, pp. 519-530.

Oliver, J. (2007). "First-Time, Full-Time Graduate Student Enrollment in Science
and Engineering Increases in 2006, Especially among Foreign Students,"
National Science Foundation, retrieved on March 2, 2008 at
http://www.nsf.gov/statistics/infbrief/nsf08302/

Saxenian, A. L. (1994). *Regional Advantage: Culture and Competition in Silicon
Valley and Route 128*. Cambridge, Mass.: Harvard University Press.

Saxenian, A. L. (2002). "Silicon Valley's New Immigrant High Growth
Entrepreneurs," *Economic Development Quarterly*, Vol. 16, No. 1, pp.
20-31.

Schultz, T. W. (1963). *The Economic Value of Education*. New York: Columbia
University Press.

Subotzky, G. (1999). "Alternatives to the entrepreneurial university: new modes
of knowledge production in community service programs," *Higher
Education*, Vol. 38. No. 4, pp. 401-440.

World Commission on Environment and Development (Brundtland Commission),
1987, *Our Common Future*. Oxford: Oxford University Press.

Xue, J. (2007a). "Essay One: Hidden Transactions, Entrepreneurship, and
Economic Development," in *Three Essays on Entrepreneurship: Theory,
Measurement, and Environment*, Dissertation, University of Missouri-
Columbia, May 2007.

Xue, J. (2007b). "Essay Three: The Region as an Entrepreneur's Opportunity Set:
an Empirical Analysis in the Case of Technology Entrepreneurship in
the United States," in *Three Essays on Entrepreneurship: Theory,
Measurement, and Environment*, Dissertation, University of Missouri-
Columbia, May 2007.

Chapter 11: Educating for Socially Conscious Entrepreneurship

Reshaping Gandhi's Humanistic Model of Education: Towards a 'Socially Conscious' Entrepreneurship Education

Vijaya Sherry Chand

Abstract: In recent times higher education in developing countries has been seen as primarily 'application-oriented' and geared to the demands of rapidly expanding markets. At the same time, concern about the role of education in developing values for sustainable human development, has grown. The philosophy of "Basic Education", developed by Mahatma Gandhi (1869-1948), seems to combine these two elements—technical and humanizing. The educational theory that he drew from it, no doubt in the historical and social context of colonialism in India, emphasized the integration of fact and value, cognition and affect, the subject and the object, the learner/ human being and her environment and nature. In contrast to the absolute claims to truth and knowledge of modern science, Gandhi stressed the contextuality and relativity of all human knowledge. Education and 'training', according to Gandhi, are organically linked, and based on the fundamental as¬sumption of the goodness of human beings and an awareness of the impact of all actions on oneself, society and nature. His vision, radical at that time, is in consonance with what various post-modern approaches advocate as humane and sustainable, and provides a framework for examining the role of humanities education in the development of humanistic values. This paper is based on the experiences of ten rural institutions which have applied Gandhi's theory to a three-year rural studies humanities degree programme for at least 20 years. While the pressure to focus on job-oriented education has been severe, the model is trying to evolve into a humanities-technical education mix that aims at developing 'socially conscious' entrepreneurship and a greater focus on learning from people's knowledge.

Keywords: Humanistic Education, Values in Education

Mahatma Gandhi (1869-1948) is well known as the "father" of India's struggle for freedom from Great Britain. His philosophy of education—*Nai talim* (New Education), more popularly called 'Basic Education'—and the theory he derived from it have not, however, found much space in educational discourse ever since the schools based on his theories were wound up a few years after independence in 1947. But a small and unique network of rural colleges (*vidyapiths*), which continues to base itself on Gandhi's philosophy of education, offers us an opportunity to revisit this philosophy, examine the stresses it has been subject to, and identify the future directions that a curriculum based on it needs to take, if the original educational intent is to be preserved.[1] This network of colleges is based in the western Indian state of Gujarat and aims at creating self-reliant, rural service-oriented graduates, who will undertake rural transformation (Pancholi 1974: 144-157). The colleges offer a three-year Bachelor in Rural Studies (BRS) program to students who have completed 12 years of schooling. The program is designed around one of the following curriculum streams: agriculture and animal husbandry, people's education, home science, dairy science and forestry. The total number of students who graduate every year from the network is about 1000. This paper first describes Gandhi's educational philosophy and its application, and then discusses the directions that this humanistic philosophy needs to take if the network's colleges are to retain the original curricular intent of the philosophy.

The Basic Education Philosophy and *Vidyapith* Practice

The theory—an extremely self-conscious one—and the social philosophy underpinning the curricular practice of the *vidyapiths*, may be positioned in a specific historical and social context, namely the experience of colonial rule in India and the dynamics of the freedom struggle. During colonial rule, there was an emphasis on the role of the "enlightened outsider" in selecting and shaping what was 'valid' knowledge (Kumar 1991). This emphasis led to a devaluation of the skills and knowledge of the people or "the masses", as a result of interpreting material poverty as proof of cultural weakness and decadence.[2] A 'weak' or 'deficient' culture, in the eyes of the 'enlightened outsider', could not be the epistemological basis for an instrument of social change like education. The result,

---

[1] This paper is based on a study of ten such colleges, carried out at two different points of time. The first stage of understanding how teachers, students and administrators interpret the philosophy was carried out during 1994-95. The progress of these institutions was re-assessed through a series of discussions during late 2004 and early 2005. Methods of data collection included a mix of surveys and interviews of students, alumni and teachers, and analysis of a variety of institutional documents. The second round of the study relied entirely on individual interviews and group discussions. However, the author has been involved with the colleges since 1998. As of 2004, there were 18 such colleges, most of them established in the mid-1980s.

[2] This aspect of the colonial legacy harks back to Calvinist theology which saw material poverty as a manifestation of original sin and predestination to eternal damnation. Ashis Nandy's *The Intimate Enemy* (New Delhi: Oxford University Press, 1983) highlights the way in which Calvinist Protestantism enabled the colonizers to create ideological homologies between the 'incorrigible native' and the 'reprobate child', both needing 'correction' and 'education'.

therefore, was a growing dissociation of the curriculum from the students' everyday life. The identification between the educated property-holding Indian and the British was cemented by a common perception of the masses as ignorant and illiterate because of their moral and cultural 'decadence'. Therefore, "none of the skills, crafts, arts and knowledge that the illiterate masses possessed could impress the educated Indians, including teachers, as being worth learning. These forms of culture became symbols of ignorance and decadence...." (Kumar 1991: 15). At the same time, the independence movement also witnessed a struggle over the field of education. As Kumar (1991) notes, the value-orientations that underpinned educational debates at this time comprised a set of three quests—for justice, for identity and for 'progress'. The justice orientation demanded educational opportunities for the downtrodden, without focussing on colonial injustices or questioning the colonial educational model. The quest for self-identity took the form of a confrontation with the colonial model through an emphasis on classical/ high culture and a religio-cultural revival. This cultural revivalism, unfortunately, only achieved the entrenchment of a sanskritised Hindi[3] in large parts of India as the symbol of a liberated identity, and a slowing down of the spread of mass literacy. The quest for progress was often equated by many leaders of the nationalist movement with the European model of industrialization.

All three orientations left hierarchical social structures intact and were, therefore, rejected by Gandhi. His critique of colonial education and its devaluation of the knowledge of the masses, and his misgivings about the value-orientations underpinning the responses to this education, have also to be placed in the context of his criticism of Western civilization and its development model. The latter has been discussed elsewhere. In the context of this critique, Gandhi wanted to see colonial as well as revivalist education give way to a system which would help India create an alternative concept of progress which basically demanded the development of the political[4] and institutional capacities of the people; in other words, social restructuring, before launching out on material growth. Gandhi's experience of famine relief work convinced him that work and not charity was needed to enhance self-respect. This insight was translated into one of the fundamental principles of Basic Education. The valorisation of work may have also been influenced by an early reading of Ruskin's *Unto This Last*. Gandhi also drew upon the experiences of the various *ashram* (residential) schools set up by his followers in Gujarat.[5] All these influences led him to move

---

[3] The national language, spoken by a large number of Indians.

[4] Gandhi's critique of modern industrialization was spelt out in his newspaper columns from South Africa (Gandhi [1939] 1990).

[5] The ashrams were aimed at educating tribal children. The "tribal question" had engaged many social reformers, including those of Gandhian inspiration. The Gandhian workers who went into remote tribal areas are credited with taking the first concrete steps for the formal education of tribal youth in Gujarat (see Joshi 1989). These social workers had a broader agenda of social reform and believed they were turning out workers who would act as "leaven to raise the lump" (Mahadev Desai, quoted in Hardiman ([1987] 1995: 8), the lump, rather derogatorily, referring to the tribals. This negative aspect of the relationship between the Gandhian social reformers and the people they set out to reform, is reflected in historical accounts written by the reformers which deny the tribals any agency (ibid.: 6-8).

from an exclusive focus on teaching a productive craft (work for its own sake) to "work" as a medium of learning.

The centrality of learning through a craft over a fairly long period of time is a crucial element of the "teachers' dimension" of Gandhi's curricular plan.[6] Such learning was to combine three elements: the craft, the social environment of the children and their natural environment. That is, the teachers themselves would have to look at the educational possibilities of the craft and of daily incidents, to "correlate" common actions with the educational value of those actions. Thus, though the theory did not depart from the traditional view of the teacher as a morally superior being, and did not seek a change in the traditional pedagogical relationship, the teacher was given a great deal of autonomy in curricular matters. The curriculum plan combined those subjects which "naturally belong together", into fields of studies like social studies and general science. Each subject had "units", which bore a close relationship to life. For example, in general science, some of the units were food, water and fire. The teacher was supposed to weave these into the life experiences of the children and to come up with a set of "learning experiences", which had to be graded according to the children's maturity levels. Gandhi, however, went to the extent of placing the economic value of the craft at the base of experiential learning (Ramanathan 1962: 21-22). Thus, apart from the pedagogical value of the central craft, Gandhi justified the craft's introduction into the curriculum in terms of self-sufficiency, so as to maintain a school's autonomy.

Though schools which followed Gandhi's educational approach were set up in many parts of India, by the 1960s it had became obvious that the experiment was in decline. From its very inception the model had been subject to criticism, and doubts had been expressed regarding (a) the merits of self-supporting schools versus the orthodox belief that school education should be funded by the State; (b) the ethical implications of making children work, and (c) the feasibility of the idea.[7],[8]

In summary, the crucial features which distinguish the curricular intent of Basic Education from that of the formal mainstream system of education derive from the radical, alternative model of development which Gandhi visualized for India and his rejection of the mainstream colonial model. Nandy (1992) has highlighted some dimensions of this rejection, especially the problematic of the 'secular' scientific worldview "[which] promises 'true' knowledge and the control and predictability which goes with such knowledge, only when a person (1) isolates or splits off his cognition from his feelings and ethics and (2) when he partitions himself off from the subjects of his enquiry emotionally". Many

---

[6] This emphasis in Gandhi's educational philosophy, also closely linked to his stress on the dignity of labour, stands in sharp contrast to the Western and Indian classical traditions in education with their insistent valorisation of the mental/ intellectual life over the manual/ menial.

[7] Gandhi (1951), Section V contains Gandhi's replies to the initial criticisms of his plan.

[8] See Naik (1975c: 27, 1975a, 1975b) for a discussion of the opposition to the model from the classes in power as well as the masses. Kurrien (1983) and Weiner (1993: 11-12) focus on the model's 'conceptual inappropriateness' in the context of universal elementary education and its non-feasibility. Kumar (1991) focuses on the more radical features of the model as the reasons for its marginalization. Basic Education tried to replace the literacy, literature and mathematical sciences combine with crafts which, in the traditional order of things, were the domain of the 'lower' castes and 'untouchables'.

features of modern life like the "emphasis on a negotiable, market-oriented concept of equality and the totally instrumental, non-sacramental concept of nature" may be seen as the "indirect expression of this aspect of modern science and its attempt to become universal by being . . . amoral and dispassionate" (Nandy 1992: 130-131). Alongside the philosophy underpinning this kind of science, Gandhi rejected the ideology of modern technocracy which produces a "mechanomorphic concept of society" and derives social priorities from it. "To such a society the humanness of man is an embarrassment" (ibid.: 135). In contrast, Gandhi used "plural concepts of science and technology" judging technology not only by what it did but by what it symbolized, treating proper technology as part of his social and political programmes. Hence, so-called "oddities" like his emphasis on the *charkha* (the spinning wheel, to produce hand-made cloth). Hence too his emphasis on learning through a craft and understanding its scientific principles.

In contrast to the splits (mentioned above) required by modern science, Gandhi emphasized the integration of fact and value, cognition and feeling, 'subject' and object, learner and environment, the human being and nature—an emphasis which was the foundation of his notion of *ahimsa* (non-violence), (Parekh 1989: 155). In contrast to the absolute and objective truth and knowledge claims of modern scientism, Gandhi emphasized the contextuality and relativity of all human knowledge (ibid.: 156). These aims and assumptions underlay the formulation of Basic Education. It is such a radically alternative vision that various postmodern, environmentalist and politically-conscious groups advocate today as humane and sustainable. This is especially the case with Gandhi's critique of modern technocracy, his emphasis on the valorisation of local knowledges and crafts, and his emphasis on the connection between human beings and their natural environment. His focus on learning through a craft, however, consciously draws on John Dewey's pragmatic model of 'progressive' education.[9] In some sense he also anticipates postmodern attitudes in this eclectic mixture. However, the fact remains that while his philosophy of knowledge, the knower and the act of knowing anticipated the radical postmodern questioning of the Western scientific paradigm, there was never any attempt to extend this questioning to traditional authoritarian pedagogical structures.[10]

To return to the Basic Education vision, it also happened that the theory was unable to establish its relevance for school education, given the tensions that existed with regard to its position on "work". In response to this failure, the applicability of the educational theories of Basic Education to higher education was seriously explored in Gandhi's home state, Gujarat. Older students would possibly see the need to "correlate" technology with social, human and

[9] Aronowitz and Giroux (1997: 13) highlight a contradiction between progressivism and the postmodern: "the progressives want to make room for the excluded within the established culture; in contrast, postmodernism asserts no privileged place, aside from power considerations, for the art works, scientific achievements, and philosophical traditions by which Western culture legitimates itself."

[10] The ambiguity of Gandhi's approach, compared with postmodern critical pedagogy becomes evident in the light of Giroux's account of the latter in Giroux (1997).

environmental development, and would perhaps be more amenable to being educated through the medium of work.

The Basic Education Model in Rural higher Education

A policy initiative in the early years of independent India supported the establishment of rural colleges which followed the Basic Education philosophy. Nanalal Bhatt (1883-1961) founded the first such institution, Lok Bharati, in 1953. The innovation he introduced was to develop agriculture and animal husbandry as Basic Education crafts, in contrast to artisanal work. Lok Bharati adopted the motto, *Avidyaya mrityum teertva/ Vidyaya amritam ashnute*. This motto (which is in Sanskrit) is derived from the *Kathopanishad*, one of the sacred texts of the Hindus. "He who knows *vidya* (humanities) and *avidya* (technical knowledge) uses *avidya* to overcome *mrityu*, the sadness of death, and can achieve *amrit*, peace of mind" (Pancholi 1974: 178, translated from Gujarati). Buch (1992: 18-19) recalls Bhatt's explanation in the following words: "*Avidya* is the labour and skill needed to earn ... bread ... and *vidya* is the conscious feeling of indebtedness to society translated into action whenever needed." By the mid-1980s, the number of such rural colleges had reached 18, and so a formal network was established. The colleges follow a philosophy that is built around the principles described above. Integrating theoretical learning with practical work is seen as a key curricular goal: observations, field work and assignments, which link learning from practice with the concepts taught in the classroom, are key aspects of classroom approaches. There are well-laid down norms for the number of hours of on-campus and off-campus work to be put in, and for the manner in which this time is to be distributed. At the same time, the valorisation of manual labour and of the skills of those caste groups which have occupied the 'lower' rungs in the traditional social hierarchy, is integrated into a study of the humanities—including history, social studies and vernacular literature. Apart from the humanities and technical subjects, an ancillary component deals with people's education and topics of interest to the students.

Emerging Pressures on the Educational Model

The model, as it was put into practice, was designed as a response to the "social failure" of mainstream higher education. This failure was evident in the systematic bias against the access of underprivileged sections of society to higher education, and in the contribution of higher education to the phenomenon of graduate unemployment. Hence the Gandhian model's emphasis on rural youth and educating them to become 'self-starters' who would undertake 'rural trans-formation'. Over the years, this educational model has been subjected to criticism and pressures from within—from the alumni, students and many faculty members. Though the criticisms relate to three themes, we focus here on the criticisms of the values that underpin the model's social and technical entrepreneurship goal.[11]

---

[11] This section draws on the surveys and discussions conducted by the author as part of the network's attempt to reform its curriculum. The first set of criticisms refers to the bias of the colleges towards

While the value base which governs the norms of *vidyapith* functioning is quite obvious to the graduates, the most important expectations from the curriculum veer towards a desire to improve "self-reliance/ vocational/ self-employment skill levels". These two dimensions—the value base and skill expectations—reflect a familiar tension between the conceptions of the terms 'education' and 'training': education as a preparation for life and individuality, training as specific education which is vocationally relevant. Depending on which conception one adopts, the goals of pedagogy can range between changing society for the better on the one hand, and reproducing society, on the other. While such an antithesis between education and training has been questioned for a long time (see for instance, Bridges 1993), it is possible to see the pressure for change on the *vidyapith* curriculum as an expression of concern about the need for students to be able not just "to make choices intellectually but be able additionally to pursue them practically by acting in and upon a competitive social world" (ibid.: 43).

Gandhi saw this point and formulated a model in which "education" and "training" were organically linked, through the inclusion of a 'Humanities' component which served as an anchor for infusing the principle of learning through the medium of a craft into the technical component of the curriculum. The only difference is that he did not aim it at survival in a "competitive social world". His model was based on the fundamental assumptions of the goodness of human beings, cooperation and "correlated action"—awareness of the effects of action on the self, society and nature. These assumptions relate to contemporary concern about what is referred to as "sustainability"—of resource use, development and human society in general. However, as noted in Chand (2001), over time, the Humanities segment came to be identified as a component which operated in parallel with the Technical and Ancillary components of the curriculum, and "went along an independent path". Rather than acting as a base for the values implied by key themes like rural transformation, sustainability, the centrality of learning from a craft, and a humanitarian and development-oriented outlook, the Humanities component came to be seen as a set of 'subjects' which dealt with culture, social development, political science, world history and Gujarati language and literature. Thus, a key proposition that was formulated midway through the study on which this paper is based, was that the Humanities segment of the curriculum had lost its original curricular intent to serve as an anchor for the values underpinning the alternative vision of society and social development formulated in the early years of the model's establishment. This proposition was explored further. The main direction such exploration took was towards "recovering" the role of the Humanities, and two themes emerged as crucial if the relationship between the value base and the skill expectations of the model had to be realigned to the current socio-economic contexts that the graduates enter.

---

the marginalized sections of society; occupying as it does a 'de-valued' and marginal niche in higher education, the model is likely to continue as "education for others". The second refers to the tendency among some of the newer colleges to focus more on the certification function and downplay the importance of creating 'self-starters'.

Re-contextualizing the Entrepreneurship and 'Craft' Linkage

If various crafts became ends in themselves, the result might be excessive specialization and an overlooking of the final aim of all crafts (according to the Basic model)—to "educate" the whole human being. This would, however, happen only if the model lapsed into the dichotomous view of "education" and "training" mentioned above, instead of maintaining Gandhi's organic view. To prevent this, enterprise/ skill training needs to remain firmly anchored within the values of cooperation and sustainability. In other words, the Humanities have to be redefined to incorporate the technical and institutional ideas emerging from contemporary social action in the areas of sustainable agriculture, environmentally-sound developmental interventions and people-driven innovations at the grassroots. This is best brought out by a significant strand of thought within the network, which sees the need to adopt 'alternative development' as a theoretical underpinning for *vidyapith* education, and to link it with the issue of entrepreneurship. Reaffirming the fundamental values of the *vidyapith* model of education through such a re-orientation of the 'craft' or enterprise dimension of the education is seen by this group of educators as one of the most important challenges facing the *vidyapiths* today. Such a shift has serious implications for the constitution of the subjects that comprise the humanities—teaching sociological thought, natural resource management, development economics, gender and development, and new trends in the thinking on sustainable development, would require a new set of competencies.

If a reoriented humanities program is to build on the *vidyapiths'* original conception of "work" (through which learning has to take place), serious reflection on how its constituents relate to the conception of work as 'socially-useful' is called for. Work, in *vidyapith* education, insofar as it is related to learning, takes three forms (Bhatt [1946] 1983: 347-349). The *adibhowtik* concept of manual work (sheer physical labour undertaken out of necessity) has to be transcended quickly into the *adidhaivik* form of work (work interlinked with education or reflection on work). A student has to transcend even this form of work to reach the *adhyatmik* form of work, which goes beyond individual learning into socially-useful action. While reaching the third form takes effort, this stage should be reinforced as a "non-negotiable" pedagogical principle since it conveys the core of Gandhian education. While the colleges did innovate by moving from artisan work to agriculture, dairying and outreach education, they have perhaps failed to innovate further in evolving new vehicles for the third form of work. New opportunities being thrown up by rural enterprises, value addition to people's knowledge, and social work that seeks economic rewards for innovative artisans, are now being examined for their potential as *adhyatmik* form of work.

Re-conceptualizing the Convergence of the Vocational and Liberal Imperatives in Education

Recovering the curricular intent of the Humanities component also calls for a pedagogical reorientation, especially given the model's reluctance to question traditional authoritarian pedagogical structures. Feinberg's two paradigms of education's social function—a primarily economic and vocational function and a primarily political and cultural function (Feinberg 1983), reflect the familiar dichotomy between the vocational role and the liberal role of education. However, the distinction between a vocational and a liberal education is not an absolute one. Models of education like Gandhian Basic Education have attempted an integration of the two roles. An integration or convergence of general and vocational education is also necessary in the context of the "need for increased democratization of education and training systems..." (UNESCO 1986: 307). Bridges (1991) relates this convergence to the shift in emphasis from teaching to learning. This focus on learning (student-centred/ independent/ experiential learning, negotiated curricula etc.) results from a perception that the world is not only changing rapidly, but that such change is "discontinuous", and demands new behaviour or "re-tooling" for change. There is a danger that preparing for such change may be based on a pragmatic theory of knowledge which may be criticized for leaving "too much unchallenged". Thus, preparing students for change should not be limited to equipping students with the skills needed for "re-tooling". Rather, it is essential not to neglect the "breadth of perspective" which provides the substantive contexts—socio-economic, political, moral—and meaning to the narrow "re-tooling" skills. Equipping students with such an ability to discriminate is akin to the liberal project of "rational autonomy". Independence and autonomy are often undermined by the lack of certain ordinary capacities like the ability to speak one's mind in a group or to access information, and by the power-ridden social structures which form the context of educational institutions. New trends in student-centred pedagogy, like Giroux's analysis of critical pedagogy mentioned above, have the potential to develop the students' personal autonomy and critical awareness, while developing their technical skills.

In the context of *vidyapith* education, convergence among the humanities and technical subjects, and ancillary activities like outreach and extension programs, was designed to provide students with the necessary "breadth of perspective". However, as noted by many *vidyapith* teachers, the subjects under the humanities label have tended to become disengaged from the overall curricular aims. A periodic re-interpretation of the Humanities as an integrating theoretical underpinning for the *vidyapith* model has been missing. Such re-interpretations would have helped clearer discussion of emerging dilemmas, in a 'public' and democratic arena. Two examples noted by the graduates and teachers are recounted here. The liberal imperative of the *vidyapith* model has failed to deal with the conflicting interpretations of "a key private enterprise value like the profit motive as not an absolute priority." The value is seen as a priority only within an overall concept of value addition and growth of "social wealth" which derives sustenance from certain orientations like cooperation, sustainability, organizational efficiency and viability. This is the dominant vision which underpins the views of many teachers on the matter. But there is another viewpoint which considers that socio-technical entrepreneurship education does imply that private enterprise within a liberalizing economy and the profit motive should provide the basis for the formation of graduates through a "practical" curriculum like the *vidyapiths'*. This position is closer to the dominance of "operationalism" (Barnett 1993) and a privileging of the technical-knowledge-constitutive interest of Habermas (1971). It may also perhaps indicate recognition of the limited role of a localized and radical curriculum in countering powerful emerging economic arrangements. Jansen (1990: 33), while discussing the failure of the 'Education with Production' project in Zimbabwe, cites the "glaring contradictions in the broader economy" as one of the main reasons for the failure: "any notions that a localised pilot project can produce a curriculum that will negate the powerful social and economic arrangements under existing capitalism is pure fantasy". This is an example of the dilemma that a convergence of the vocational and liberal imperatives needs to deal with.

A second example is teaching sustainable development, in which the principles of "building upon what people know" and valorising the innovations of agriculturists, pastoralists, artisans and other grassroots people, are important. Generating returns for the people from their knowledge and adding value to their innovations, are key opportunities thrown up by recent market-oriented economic developments. These call for developing decentralized entrepreneurial networks, identifying and registering innovations and opportunities (including the legal formalities that may have to be instituted to protect intellectual property rights), and a greater focus on market research and developing products which are more in tune with sustainability values (herbal pesticides and vegetable dyes, for instance). They also demand the development of a whole range of new skills in the graduates, in addition to the creation of attitudes and behaviours consistent with an entrepreneurial personality. The Humanities component has failed to develop a theoretical platform for incorporating these themes into the technical component of the curriculum.

Concluding Note

Given the philosophy of *vidyapith* education, the move from the vocational and self-employment perspectives towards responding to the entrepreneurship imperative—which demands a convergence of the vocational and liberal aspects of education—may be easier to accommodate. The emphasis on entrepreneurship in *vidyapith* circles is often presented as a return to, or a reinforcement of, the original aim of *vidyapith* education. But it is necessary to recognize that the original socio-economic context of 'rural transformation' may no longer be valid, though the goal itself may still be appropriate. Also, the shift demands a reconciliation of emerging private enterprise values with the values of social development implied by Basic Education. One way of doing this, as indicated by this study, is to develop in the graduates a broader understanding of adding value to existing entrepreneurial trends in rural contexts and to the knowledge and innovations of grassroots people like agriculturists, pastoralists and herbalists. However, given the poor socio-economic backgrounds from which the colleges draw their students, the model of education also needs to develop appropriate risk assurance mechanisms. In other words, if students are venturing into something new, some form of a risk fund and risk-sharing mechanisms need to be developed. Group entrepreneurship is one possible means for sharing risks. Other models of "fostering" students who undertake entrepreneurial initiatives may also be possible. This is an important co-curricular task for the colleges, on which very little work has been done. Without this preparation, it will not be possible for the network to respond to the future curricular direction indicated by many teachers and alumni: reinforcing the 'socio-technical entrepreneurship' aim of *vidyapith* education.

References

Aronowitz, S., and H. A. Giroux. 1997. *Postmodern education*. Minneapolis: Minnesota University Press.

Barnett, R. 1993. Knowledge, higher education and society: A postmodern problem. *Oxford Review of Education* 19 (1): 33-46.

Bhatt, N. [1946] 1983. *The pathway of education* (in Gujarati). Reprint, Sanosara: Lok Bharati Prakashan.

Bridges, D. 1991. From teaching to learning. *The Curriculum Journal* 2 (2): 137-51.

———. 1993. Transferable skills: A philosophical perspective. *Studies in Higher Education* 18 (1): 43-51.

Buch, N. P. 1992. *Lok Dakshinamoorti: 1938-1992*. Sanosara: Sarvoday Sahakari Prakashan Sangh.

Chand, Vijaya Sherry. 2001. Curriculum reform in the *Gram Vidyapiths*: Background paper for workshop of *vidyapith* principals and directors. Ahmedabad: Ravi J. Matthai Centre for Educational Innovation, Indian Institute of Management. Mimeo.

Feinberg, W. 1983. *Understanding education: Towards a reconstruction of educational inquiry*. Cambridge: Cambridge University Press.

Gandhi, M. K. [1939] 1990. *Hind swaraj or Indian home rule*. Ahmedabad: The Navajivan Trust.

———. 1951. *Basic education*. Ahmedabad: Navajivan Publishing House.

Giroux, H. A. 1997. Crossing the boundaries of educational discourse: Modernism, postmodernism, and feminism. In *Education: Culture, economy, society*, eds. A.H. Halsey, H. Lauder, P. Brown, and A. S. Wells. Oxford: OUP, pp. 113-130.

Habermas, J. 1971. *Knowledge and human interests*. Translated by Jeremy J. Shapiro. Boston: Beacon.

Hardiman, D. [1987] 1995. *The coming of the devi: Adivasi assertion in Western India*. Delhi: Oxford University Press.

Jansen, J. D. 1990. Curriculum policy as compensatory legitimation? A view from the periphery. *Oxford Review of Education* 16 (1): 29-38.

Joshi, V. 1989. A century of tribal education in Gujarat. In *Studies in educational reform in India. Vol. 3, Reform towards equality and relevance*, ed. P. R. Panchamukhi. New Delhi: Himalaya Publishing House.

Kumar, Krishna. 1991. *The political agenda of education*. New Delhi, Newbury Park, London: Sage.

Kurrien, J. 1983. *Elementary education in India: Myth, reality, alternative*. New Delhi: Vikas Publishing House.

Naik, J. P. 1975a. *Elementary education in India: A promise to keep*. Bombay: Allied Publishers.

———. 1975b. *Equality, quality and quantity*. New Delhi: Allied.

———. 1975c. *Policy and performance in Indian education, 1947-74*. New Delhi: Dr. K. G. Saiyidain Memorial Trust.

Nandy, A. 1992. *Traditions, tyranny, and utopia: Essays in the politics of awareness*. Delhi: Oxford University Press.

Pancholi, M. 1974. *Sarvodaya and education* (in Gujarati). Part II. Sanosara: Lok Bharati.

Parekh, B. 1989. *Colonialism, tradition and reform: An analysis of Gandhi's political discourse*. New Delhi: Sage.

Ramanathan, G. 1962. *Education from Dewey to Gandhi: The theory of Basic Education*. Bombay: Asia Publishing House.

UNESCO. 1986. *The integration of general and technical and vocational education*. Paris: United Nations Educational, Scientific and Cultural Organization.

Weiner, M. 1993. If not now, when? Politics of primary education. *Future* 29-30:11-14.

Chapter 12: Teaching Social Entrepreneurship

Educators as Social Entrepreneurs: A Different Approach to Teacher Training

Yehuda Bar Shalom, Eyal Bloch, and Yonatan Glaser

Abstract: Future teachers will face challenges that are unknown in the educational field of the present. It seems that more than ever, the future teacher will have to display the ability to adapt to changes, understand societal and cultural issues deeply, and to create and maintain a sense of community. (Bar Shalom, Bloch and Peretz, 2007). The four walls of the classroom, which used to define a clear boundary between the class and "the world out there", seem to become more fluid, fragile, and open to outside influences. Therefore, the future teacher is expected to be proactive and have the skills needed in creating partnerships with the surrounding community (Bar Shalom, Bloch and Peretz, 2007, Bar Shalom, 2006, Epstein & Sheldon, 2006, Sanders, 2005, Sanders et al, 2002). As a strategy to help future teachers adapt to the demands and challenges of the future, The David Yellin College of Education in Jerusalem created, in conjunction with the Jerusalem municipality, a program in Social Entrepreneurship, which aims to help future teachers become educational leaders who have a capacity to generate social change in the context of the classroom and the surrounding community.

Keywords: Social Entrepreneurship, Teacher Training

Introduction

Future teachers will face challenges that are unknown in the educational field of the present. More than ever, the future teacher will need the ability to adapt to changes, to understand societal and cultural issues deeply, and to create and maintain a sense of community. (Bar Shalom, Bloch and Peretz, 2007). The walls of the classroom, which used to define a clear boundary between the classroom and "the world out there," will become more fluid, fragile, and open to outside influences.

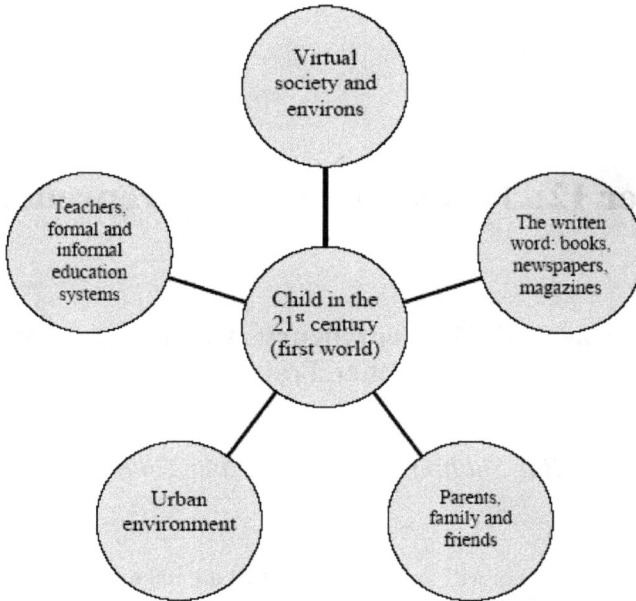

Diagram 1: The Forces that Shape and Educate 21st-Century Children

Therefore, the future teacher is expected to be proactive and have the skills needed in creating partnerships with the surrounding community (Bar Shalom, Bloch and Peretz, 2007, Bar Shalom, 2006, Epstein & Sheldon, 2006, Sanders, 2005, Sanders et al, 2002).

Diagram 1 emphasizes a powerful new player influencing the child's education. Virtual reality has already entered class life in ways that traditional teaching is not equipped to deal with. For example: a teenager girl bursts out crying in the middle of a lesson and runs out of the class; later the teacher finds out that her boyfriend had sent her an SMS that he was breaking up with her.[1] This mundane example indicates the complexity and challenge lying ahead of the teachers in particular and society in general.

In addition to changing roles, boundaries and influences in the complex business of meaning-making, there is an increasingly powerful voice in the educational community advocating for greater community involvement on the basis of normative rather than pragmatic grounds. This stream of educational thought argues that the very purposes of education are not only grounded in the desire for the development of the learner's intellectual and emotional life, cultural

---

[1] True example reported to us by an Israeli teacher.

competence and vocational skills, but for her connection to society and desire and ability to contribute meaningfully to its positive evolution. Even if the surrounding milieu was not changing as it is, this broad school of thought – carried forward by educational practitioners and academics, community groups and educational organizations – argues for increased attention to what they variously call citizenship education, democracy education, leadership development, justice education, and futures thinking.

As a strategy to help future teachers adapt to the demands and challenges of the future and become the co-shapers of the societies in which they live – local, national and international - the David Yellin College of Education in Jerusalem created, in conjunction with the Jerusalem Municipality (The Department of Social Services), a program in Social Entrepreneurship. The program aims to help future teachers become educational leaders capable of generating different organizational and social relations that will frame the educational experiences they offer their students. They become capable of enacting social change in the context of the classroom and the surrounding community. Even though it is implicit in the program directors' approach, whether or not the student teachers should be trained to, themselves, create leadership development opportunities for their school students, remains an open question.

At the end of the three-year program, the students receive a joint diploma from David Yellin College and the Jerusalem Municipality. Both institutions felt that they had something to gain from the synergy generated by the college and municipality working as a team. The college brings the formal educational know-how, while the municipality brings extensive practical knowledge from the fields of community work and informal education. The idea was to create a synergy that is greater than the sum of its parts. The individuals behind the program's inception are the former dean, Dr. Itai Zimran, the current dean, Dr. Anna Rousseau, and the head of the Social Services Department at the Jerusalem Municipality, Mr. Yossi Sharabi. The program staff consists of Dr. Yehuda Bar Shalom and Mr. Eyal Bloch, and Ms. Rachel Peretz, senior social worker from the Jerusalem Municipality (The Department of Social Services).

The Ideal Teacher as Social Entrepreneur

Social entrepreneurs are individuals who show an ability not merely to criticize a given social or communal problem, but to identify a solution, find partners to help in its implementation, and ultimately generate the desired social change. In some cases they have the ability to turn a crisis into an opportunity. They are not "just dreamers" they are dreamers, visionaries, and do-ers. They seem to be "married" to their cause and difficulties do not deter their enthusiasm. (Bar Shalom, 2006, Drayton, 2006, Bornstein, 2004). Social entrepreneurs are not interested in profit. Therefore, mission-related impact is their main criterion for gauging success. Of course, social entrepreneurs need resources and even wealth, but these are seen as means to an end. (Dees, 1998)

We envision a new generation of teachers who will seek to become social entrepreneurs. They will have the ability not only to be effective teachers in subject matter but will also use their subject matter as a springboard for addressing current communal, national and global issues. They will be able to inspire and educate their students in new ways, empower communities, and generate social change. They will create effective partnerships with the surrounding communities while locating additional resources to make their initiatives succeed. One of the writers of this paper, Eyal Bloch, is a model for social entrepreneurship. After many years of teaching experience from kindergarten to university level, Eyal Bloch now acts as a social and educational entrepreneur. He has created and developed educational models for coexistence and cooperation that have been duplicated throughout the world. He founded and coordinated the "AllinPeace" movement, which organizes "Peace Olympics" for children from areas of conflict throughout the world. Eyal Bloch has also worked with visually impaired youth from the Zulu nation in South Africa, who became the "heroes" of the AllinPeace children due to their ability to run 240 km in four days! Since 2000, Eyal has been involved in developing programs for bridging visually-impaired and seeing students in cooperation with the Centre for Studies of the Blind at the Hebrew University in Jerusalem.

David Yellin College and Jerusalem Municipality Educational Social Entrepreneurship Program Design

The First Year

The first year provides students with the theoretical foundations of social entrepreneurship, presenting many examples from successful educational initiatives in Israel and abroad that have achieved change in specific communities. A key focus is programs that have succeeded in empowering students and communities who belong to marginalized and excluded groups, such as Meier's Central Park East School in New York, (Meier, 2002, Wood, 1992); Bialik School in Tel Aviv, which serves mostly children from migrant workers families (Bar Shalom, 2006); Neve Shalom school, which integrates Arabs and Jewish students; Keshet School, which integrates religious and secular Jewish students (Bar Shalom, 2006, Weil, 2000); and Kedma School, which empowers students from marginalized Mizrachi communities (Aram, 2007, Bar Shalom, 2006, Bairey Ben Ishai, 1998). The common denominator of all of these schools is that their leaders have proven themselves to be social entrepreneurs able to create frameworks suitable to the social and cultural needs of the students and the surrounding communities. School was not the only model utilized. Students were also exposed to social entrepreneurs who generated changes in the fields of social services and informal education. One of the most important examples was the analysis of Uri Amedi's work in the "Heart of the City" Project of Jerusalem. Amedi is a veteran social entrepreneur who has managed to bring together people from diverse backgrounds to create an ambience of tolerance and coexistence despite the problems central Jerusalem has known. His work is an excellent example of building a democratic civil society by the people and for the people.

One of Amedi's biggest achievements was the transformation of the city's open market workers, usually seen as a subversive and "criminal" population, into a democratic self-run community. Another famous program is Amedi's intervention in favor of the Palestinian children working in the Mahane Yehuda market. He created a program, together with Palestinian social workers, that enabled these children to regain some of their childhood in their harsh life conditions. Uri's work has been a very important teaching model for the students. They were impressed by the depth of Uri's three-dimensional model whereby he strives to use the center of Jerusalem as a laboratory to work on what he perceives are the three biggest problems that Israeli society faces, namely the tension between the religious and secular Jews; between Mizrachim (often underprivileged Jews of North African and Asian origin), Ashkenazim (Jews of European origin), and the national tensions between Jews and Arabs.

Other progressive and experimental models are examined critically. For example, democratic and progressive schools in Israel and abroad certainly offer a new way of looking at the educational experience. The program helps students carefully examine the possible societal price of the way these institutions seem to mostly attract students from middle class backgrounds (Bar Shalom, 2006, Hecht, 2005, Zimran, 1991). Other important theoretical foundations are critical pedagogy (Giroux, 1996, Mclaren, 1989, Freire, 1993), alternative ways of thinking, (such as DeBono's *Six Thinking Hats*, 1999), and an examination of the pros and cons of the increase in third sector activity in the west in general and in Israel in particular (Gidron, et al, 2000).

Second Year

The second year is devoted to advanced learning in social entrepreneurship. In the second semester, each student, in conjunction with the Jerusalem Municipality, is assigned to do field work in social projects such as working with disadvantaged youth in community projects or working in a radio show for visually impaired people designed and operated jointly by students and blind people and broadcast over the college's radio station. The two teachers from the college, together with the facilitator from the Jerusalem Municipality, supervise the students' activities in the field. Each student reports during the semester and gives a final report at the end of the year. The practical work in the field has proved itself to be a worthy endeavor for the students. It enables them to identify a range of tools and strategies that they expect will prove useful in the regular school setting. This experience offers them opportunities to grow as educators capable of integrating formal and informal education in their future work.

The Third Year

In the third year, the students prepare a seminary paper requiring them to conduct research on an educational initiative. We particularly encourage students to research an initiative that they themselves have created i.e. an action research project on their social entrepreneurship. Other students' research proposed initiatives that may or may be not implemented in the field.

The third year is open to other students who have not participated in the first two years but who have a leaning to educational entrepreneurship. These students can write the research paper, but will not be eligible for the dual diploma with the Jerusalem Municipality. This option has been effective for veteran teachers who decide to return to school and take some courses. This course has been relevant for those who wish to explore their field from the point of view of social entrepreneurship.

Examples of Student Initiatives

From questionnaires and ongoing evaluation of the program, we can see that a majority of students feel that the skills learned in the program, especially the meeting with social entrepreneurs, created positive change in the way they view their unfolding educational career in general and the possibility of generating change in particular. Along the way, we have seen students engaging in new and exciting initiatives. Here are a few examples.

Ela's field placement in the second year was in a low-income neighborhood in Jerusalem. Together, with the local community worker, she engaged in dialogue with neighborhood children and educators. As a group, they came to the conclusion that they would like to do something to improve the aesthetic appeal of the neighborhood. An joint committee decided that painting the huge trash containers with children's art would make a lively addition to the neighborhood. Ela turned to the David Yellin Arts Department which was happy to provide students to undertake this project as part of their own learning requirements. We see here a simple win-win situation in which the resources exist and just the social entrepreneur was needed to tie them together. The project was very successful and received local media attention.

Ravit is a veteran teacher who decided to join the research seminar in her third year because she wanted to generate changes in her field. She is the vice principal of Keshet School. The school itself is an example of a social entrepreneurship initiative by Ruti Lehavi. She created the first Israel school in which orthodox and secular Jewish children, who are normally segregated, study in a bi-cultural school that seeks to strengthen pluralistic values and acceptance of the "other" (See Bar Shalom, 2006, Weil, 2000).

During this research year, Ravit came to the conclusion that what is missing in the Keshet School is the informal component. She came up with the idea of creating a youth movement that would operate according to the school values. She checked this idea, sending questionnaires to parents and students, leading focus groups, and engaging in dialogue with staff members. She concluded that the idea seemed feasible to all those involved and the initiative has now been implemented in the school.

Karnit and Noa worked with the "Aleh" association for the blind. They met with visually impaired students and asked them about their needs and aspirations. It emerged that there is no radio broadcast addressing the needs and concerns of blind people. With the guidance of the Aleh staff, they joined forces the David Yellin College and recruited resources available there. The college radio station had a broadcasting slot, but did not always know exactly how to use it. The new radio program, created jointly by the social entrepreneurship students and blind students from the "Aleh" organization, serves the blind community in the city and the surrounding communities.

All these three examples reflect a process of needs assessment, planning, and implementation. Furthermore, we see that the social entrepreneurs/educators use and integrate available resources to create projects whose outcomes were previously unattainable. They developed what we call "social entrepreneurial thinking"' - a way to address a need or void in the community with a win-win action. We are sure that they will use this ability as future teachers in the field. In support of this view, Ravit, who already is a veteran in the field, testifies in a letter that the program changed her mind set about possible solutions to social and cultural problems in her school.

The Significance of the Program

In questionnaires and discussions that we have conducted with the students during the last three years, we have discovered that the students felt that the exposure to the actions, philosophies and fields of social entrepreneurs has given them skills that were not accessible in other college courses. Furthermore, the exposure to the philosophy of social entrepreneurship and to social entrepreneurs gave them fresh ideas about new possibilities in school community relations and in community development in general. The students particularly liked the combination of visits to the field, hands-on placements, and theoretical classroom discussions.

We believe that the days are gone in which teachers can or should hope that the school walls will protect them from the world "out there" (Elkind, 1997). This program attempts to develop some responses to the burning question of how to train teachers in the changing world we live in (Hargreaves, 1998).

Additional Theoretical Considerations

At a deep, primary level the program seeks to offer a meaningful response to the dystopian tendencies so influential in Israel and the western world today. Despite the apparent wealth, knowledge and power available to citizens and their governments, there is deep ambivalence about whether we are in fact proceeding down a path of progress and positive social transition or one of increasing dysfunction and non-sustainability. Futures Thinking is a discipline and a pedagogy that has taken on the challenge of helping students envisage a positive future using eclectic methods of social analysis and investigation (Slaughter and Bussey, 2005). This approach shares with some approaches to citizenship and democracy education the need to develop the interpersonal and emotional qualities necessary to embody effective and worthy agency. Hannah Arendt, Martha Nussbaum and Maxine Greene are particularly strong sources to draw on in this regard with their respective notions of deliberative argumentation, compassion and imaginative action (Waghid, 2005).

An additional source of theory we draw on is that of service-learning. A field developed in the USA for over two decades, it has attracted extensive empirical and analytical research. While used in many different settings and for different purposes, including as an adjunct to studies in diverse disciplines, personal growth and citizenship development (Eyler and Giles, 1999), its use in the context of citizenship education is of particular interest to us. A strong theoretical basis that distinguishes between the different 'types' of citizens that programs seek to develop, is most compelling (Westheimer, Kahne, 2004).

In proposing this typology, the authors do not suggest a hierarchy per se, as each kind of citizenship understanding, commitment and behavior is necessary for a dynamic and healthy democratic society. They do claim that the last is rarely sought. Even when it is what a program declaratively seeks, there is often a huge dissonance between the declared goal – which embraces the Justice Oriented Citizen - and the actual impact of implementation – which does not. (Westheimer, Kahne & Rogers, 1999). In the examples given in this article:

- **Ela's** bin-painting project is a case of encouraging **Participatory Citizenship**
- **Ravit's** school-based youth movement is unclear, without us knowing more about what values and kinds of citizenship the youth movement itself engenders.
- **Karnit** and **Noah's** radio with and for the blind project goes much closer to reflecting the development of a **Justice Oriented Citizen** in that it addresses root causes of the problem, namely lack of access creating inequality of service and information availability.

This model enriches our thinking and is an important ancillary to the concept of social entrepreneurship. It ensures that we continue to put in front of students the full range of possible actions as social entrepreneurs – not only the more widespread model of the personally responsible citizen and the participatory citizen, but also the Justice oriented citizen. It also helps us and the students be discerning in relation to the ways society benefits from the outcomes of specific student actions and

	Personally Responsible Citizen	**Participatory Citizen**	**Justice Oriented Citizen**
DESCRIPTION	❖ Acts responsibly in his/her community ❖ Works and pays taxes ❖ Obeys laws ❖ Recycles, gives blood ❖ Volunteers to lend a hand in times of crisis	❖ Active member of community organizations and/or improvement efforts ❖ Organizes community efforts to care for those in need, promote economic development, or clean up environment ❖ Knows how government agencies work ❖ Knows strategies for accomplishing collective tasks	❖ Critically assesses social, political, and economic structures to see beyond surface causes ❖ Knows about social movements and how to effect systemic change ❖ Seeks out and addresses areas of injustice
SAMPLE ACTION	❖ Contributes food to a food drive	❖ Helps to organize a food drive	❖ Explores why people are hungry and acts to solve root causes
CORE ASSUMPTIONS	❖ To solve social problems and improve society, citizens must have good character; they must be honest, responsible, and law-abiding members of the community	❖ To solve social problems and improve society, citizens must actively participate and take leadership positions within established systems and community structures	❖ To solve social problems and improve society, citizens must question and change established systems and structures when they reproduce patterns of injustice over time

From "What Kind of Citizen? The Politics of Educating for Democracy" American Educational Research Journal. Volume 41 No. 2, Summer 2004, 237-269. Joel Westheimer, University of Ottawa. Joseph Kahne, Mills College

The Future

Whereas programs to develop entrepreneurship in the context of MBA studies at business schools is widespread and has attracted comparative research (Twaalfhoven, 2001), programs such as the one under review are still in their relative nascence. As the program evolves, we will increasingly draw on new thinking and practice designed to build new self-conceptions and tools for the teachers of the future. In addition to giving additional attention to how the wisdom and insight of citizenship education, democracy education, leadership development, justice education and "Futures Thinking" can find their place in the course, additional tools we will draw on are: ecological thinking, process thinking, chaotic thinking and possibilities thinking. These will all strengthen future teachers' capacities to imagine a new reality (Greene, 2002) and to have a sense of ownership over their new social initiatives (Bygrave, 1994).

References

Aram, A. (2007). 'A Model for Teacher Mentoring of Poor and Minority Children: A Case Study of an Urban Israeli School Mentoring Program,' *Mentoring & Tutoring: Partnership in Learning*, Volume 15, No. 1.

Bairey Ben Ishai, A. (1998). Teacher Burnout and Consciousness-Complexity: An Analysis of the Mentors at Kedma. Harvard School of Education. (unpublished doctoral thesis.)

Bar Shalom, Y. (2006). *Educating Israel: Educational Entrepreneurship in Israel's Multicultural Society.* New York: Palgrave McMillan.

Bar Shalom, Y. Bloch, E. & Peretz, R. (2007). 'The Social Entrepreneurship Program at the David Yellin College of Education,' *Bimchlala* (19) (Hebrew).

Bornstein, D. (2004). *How to Change the World: Social Entrepreneurs and the Power of New Ideas*, Oxford: Oxford University Press.

Bygrave, W.D. (1994). *The Portable MBA in Entrepreneurship,* New York: John Wiley & Sons.

DeBono, E. (1999). *Six Thinking Hats,* Boston: Back Bay Books.

Dees, J. G. (1998). The Meaning of 'Social Entrepreneurship', http://www.fuqua.duke.edu/centers/case/documents/dees_sedef.pdf

Drayton, B. (2006). "Everyone a Changemaker: Social Entrepreneurship's Ultimate Goal," *Innovations,* Winter 2006.

Elkind, D. (1997). "Schooling and Family in the Postmodern World. Rethinking Educational Change with Heart and Mind," in A. Hargreaves (Ed.), *ASCD Year Book* Alexandria, VA: Association for Supervision and Curriculum Development.

Epstein, J. L. & Sheldon, S. B. (2006). 'Moving Forward: Ideas for Research on School, Family, and Community Partnerships', in C. F. Conrad & R. Serlin (Eds.), *SAGE Handbook for Research in Education: Engaging Ideas and Enriching Inquiry,* Thousand Oaks, CA: Sage Publications, pp. 117-37.

Eyler, J. & Giles, D. E. (1999). *Where's the Learning in Service-Learning?,* San Francisco: Jossey-Bass.

Freire, P. (1993). *Pedagogy of the City.* New York: Continuum.

Gidron, B., Katz H., & Bar, M. (2000). *The Israeli Third Sector 2000: The Roles of the Sector,* Beersheva: Israeli Center for Third Sector Research and the Israeli Third Sector Database, Ben-Gurion University of the Negev. (Hebrew)

Giroux, H. A. (1996). *Fugitive Cultures: Race, Violence, and Youth*, New York: Routledge.

Greene, M. (2002). *Variations on a Blue Guitar: The Lincoln Center Institute Lectures on Aesthetic Education,* New York: Teachers College Press.

Hargreaves, A. & Fullan, M. (1998). *What's Worth Fighting for in Education?* , Buckingham: Open University Press.

Hecht, Y. (2005). *Democratic Education: A Story with a Beginning.* Tel Aviv: Keter. (Hebrew)

McLaren, P. (1989). *Life in Schools: An Introduction to Critical Pedagogy in the Foundations of Education*, New York: Longman.

Meier, D. (2002). *The Power of Their Ideas: Lessons for America from a Small School in Harlem,* New York: Beacon Press.

Sanders, M. G., Jones, G. A. & Abel, Y. (2002). 'Involving Families and Communities in the Education of Children and Youth Placed at Risk', in S. Stringfield & D. Land (Eds.), *Educating at Risk Students,* Chicago: National Society for the Study of Education Yearbook, pp. 171-88

Sanders, M. G. (2005). *Building School-community Partnerships: Collaboration for Student Success*, Thousand Oaks, CA: Corwin Press.

Slaughter, R. & Bussey, M. (2005). *Futures Thinking for Social Foresight*, Australia, Tamkang University Press (with Foresight International)

Twaalfhoven, Dr. B. (2001). *Developing Entrepreneurship Programs in MBA Schools: A Contrast in Approaches by a survey of 7 business schools*, at http://www.efer.eu/pdf/RP-WilmaJuliaAContrastinApproachesFeb2001.pdf

Waghid, Y. (2005). 'Action as an Educational Virtue: Toward a Different Understanding of Democratic Citizenship Education', *Educational Theory*, Volume 55, No. 3, pp. 323-342.

Weil, S. J. (2000). *The Unique and the Unifying: Religious and Secular Schoolchildren and their Parents at Keshet School.* Jerusalem: The NCJW Research Institute for Innovation in Education, The Hebrew University (Hebrew).

Westheimer, J., Kahne, J. & Rogers, B. (1999). 'Learning to Lead: Building on Young People's Desire to "Do Something"', *New Designs For Youth Development,* Volume 15, No. 3

Westheimer, J. & Kahne, J. (2004). 'What Kind of Citizen? The Politics of Educating for Democracy', *American Educational Research Journal*, Volume 41 No. 2, Summer, pp.237-269.

Wood, G. (1992). *Schools that Work: America's Most Innovative Public Education Program,.* New York: Plume.

Zimran, I. (1991). *What? Are You a Kid?,* Jerusalem: Carmel. (Hebrew).

Part 4: Cases in Social Entrepreneurship

Part 4 of the book is made up of four cases, each looking at issues surrounding social entrepreneurship and microfinance. Chapter 13 explores the role of social entrepreneurship in South Africa. Chapter 14 looks entrepreneurial intentions in Kenya. Chapter 15 looks at microfinance in Vietnam. Chapter 16 looks at educational centers and microfinance in India.

Chapter 13: The Role of Social Entrepreneurship in South Africa

Ten Years Down the Road of a Transition Economy the Role of Social Entrepreneurship

Ethel Brundin, Eslyn Isaacs, Kobus Visser, and Caroline Wigren

Abstract: Over the past 10 years South Africa has shown its capacity to engage in solving its own political, economic and social problems. Statistics clearly show that its small, medium and micro enterprise sector has made valuable contributions to economic growth, employment creation and the Gross Domestic Product. During the period of a new democracy, the number of new businesses created has increased by 34%, which indicates that entrepreneurship and opportunities do exist. Social entrepreneurs are part of this increase and these activities. The purpose of this paper is to explain the role of social entrepreneurship and its implications for a sustainable development in the region of the Western Cape in South Africa. In doing so, we offer a framework for understanding and explaining social entrepreneurship. In general, social entrepreneurship is a process of finding creative and innovative ways of solving social problems, which may result in economic and social empowerment, development and upliftment of disadvantaged communities. From four cases and a set of interviews, we can conclude that social entrepreneurship must be viewed as an iterative process where individual characteristics, skills, environmental conditions and relationships interact and where personal profit-making and social development co-exist. Furthermore, and within this setting, we conclude that social entrepreneurship is a new epithet on an old phenomenon

Keywords: Entrepreneurship, Social Entrepreneur, Empowerment, Upliftment

Introduction

Small business development and promotion are crucial for job creation and poverty alleviation in South Africa. According to a *World Bank Report* (2001:2), "the number of people living in absolute poverty (living below the dollar-a-day poverty line) fell from approximately 40% in 1981 to 21% in 2001".

The 2001 Census showed that South Africa's population was about 44.8 million (*Statistics South Africa*, 2003), of whom 79.0% were classified as Blacks, 9.6% White, 8.9% Coloured and 2.5% Asian. It is estimated that the population growth rate is approximately 2% (*Liberty Learning Centre*, 2003). The current growth rate of 1.9% is totally inadequate to stimulate the economic activities to such an extent that big business will create jobs and contribute to poverty alleviation. It is argued that the small, medium and micro enterprise (SMME) sector can make a positive contribution to job creation. This is already evident from the fact that in 1995 SMME contribution to the Gross Domestic Product was 32.7%, while in 2001 it was already 36.1% and employed 44% of the workforce in 1995, which increased to 53.9% in 2001. The total number of employees in 1995 was 3.5 million and increased to 7.0 million in 2001 (*State of Small Business Development in South Africa,* 2002). It is clear that this sector is important for job creation. This prompted the government to develop a policy for SMME and entrepreneurship development (*National Strategy for the Development and Promotion of Small Business In South Africa, 1996*). According to this document there were about 800,000 small, medium and micro enterprises in 1995. In 2001 this figure had grown to 1,079,000, an increase of 34.5% (*State of Small Business Development in South Africa*, 2002).

From the figures above it becomes evident that the situation needs focussed attention and that small, medium and micro enterprises do play an important role in job creation that can make a contribution to poverty alleviation. It is, however, obvious that this sector alone will not eradicate poverty. It is a social problem and requires social involvement, such as non-governmental organisations (NGOs) or people with visions, creativity, innovativeness and passion for community development. NGOs are by definition "organized and operated for some benevolent purpose completely unrelated to the economic advancement of its founders and those who support it financially" (Lasprogata and Cotton, 2003:74) and are under governmental law.

In this article the authors take an interest in social entrepreneurship and social entrepreneurs. Social entrepreneurship involves creative and innovative ways of approaching and solving social issues at the same time as it might create economic output. We draw on social entrepreneurship in South Africa in the context of the geographic area of the Western Cape. More specifically, the focus is on the poorest parts of the Western Cape, namely the townships and previously disadvantaged groups. The term "previously disadvantaged groups" is generally being used when referring to Blacks, Coloured and Asian South Africans who until 1990 were not allowed to take part as entrepreneurs in mainstream economic activities.

Drawing on four stories depicted through the eyes of the social entrepreneurs and a set of conversations with representatives of NGOs, we illustrate how dependent a developing country is in terms of social entrepreneurship and how social entrepreneurs help motivating and stimulating entrepreneurial activities that together and in a long-term perspective will enhance growth aspirations and be part of the embryo of a new infrastructure in the Western Cape area.

The purpose of this article is to explain the role of social entrepreneurship and its implications for a sustainable development in the region of the Western Cape in South Africa. In doing so, we offer a framework for understanding and explaining social entrepreneurship.

We conclude that in order to understand social entrepreneurs, we need to view social entrepreneurship as an iterative process. An interaction takes place between individual characteristics, skills and outcome. The social entrepreneurs move between the urge to earn money and to look out for their own success and the urge to create jobs and wealth for others. Moreover, in this process of profit-making and social development where also legitimacy and rules of the games are created, the key to social development seems to be within the locus of control of the entrepreneur him/herself. The assertiveness is of decisive importance in establishing, maintaining and developing sustainable relationships with the community inhabitants, as well as with community leaders. Furthermore, we are inclined to conclude that social entrepreneurship is a new word for an old phenomenon.

The article consists of four parts: First, we define social entrepreneurship and set out some questions for this study. Then, we give an account of the four cases of social entrepreneurs. This leads to a discussion where we argue that social entrepreneurship must be viewed as an iterative process where individual characteristics, skills, environmental conditions and relationships interact. We conclude with some implications derived from our study.

Social Entrepreneurship

Research endeavours have failed to provide a universal definition of entrepreneurship (Shane and Venkataraman, 2000; Davidsson, 2003). In addition, new concepts have been added to the research agenda. Traditional entrepreneurship focuses on maximizing the rewards for the entrepreneur, often ignoring the social dimensions (Lasprogata and Cotton, 2003; Mair and Marti, 2004). This approach is parallel to the capitalism concept and has been deserted over the years, and it is today not acceptable to look for either purely egoistic motives or organizational profitability only. The importance of the social environment and the upholding and/or creation of social value have increased in importance over the years. As a consequence, social entrepreneurship has turned up on the agenda as a complement on the outer end of a continuum ranging from traditional to social entrepreneurial activities (Hibbert, Hogg and Quinn, 2002 in Mair and Noboa, 2003a; 2003b).

Social entrepreneurship is used in different contexts and various definitions exist. Mair and Noboa (2003a; 2003b) have selected the following three as a guide to formulate an alternative definition:

- "The initiatives of non-profit organizations in search of additional revenues after facing cuts in government support, cuts in individual and corporate giving, increased competition, more social needs and pressure from fund providers to merge or downsize;

- The initiatives of independent social entrepreneurs aiming to alleviate a particular social problem;
- The socially responsible practices of commercial businesses engaged in cross-sector partnerships".

Social entrepreneurship can thus be found within the voluntary sector in social enterprises pursuing a social purpose (Thompson, 2002), among individuals where the entrepreneur is committed to 'do good' for society and within profit-seeking businesses for various reasons, such as seeking legitimacy and enhancing profits. Furthermore, the social mission is considered the prime force and is the driving force for pursuing an entrepreneurial opportunity (Mort, Weerawardena and Carnegie, 2003). Social entrepreneurship is therefore an entrepreneurial approach to solve a social issue.

Mair and Noboa's (2003a; 2003b) view on social entrepreneurship is in line with Mort et al. (2003) when they concluded that the concept stands for the "innovative use of resource combinations to pursue opportunities aiming at the creation of organizations and/or practices that yield and sustain social benefits". Seelos and Mair (2004) contend that the combination of the two wordings 'social' and 'entrepreneurship' is as diverse as the concept entrepreneurship in itself. They argue that the phenomenon needs to be related to the outcome which, according to them, is sustainable development. They suggest that social entrepreneurship derives from a continuum between two outer poles with the profit motive of the social entrepreneur at one end and the social motive of the social entrepreneur at the other end, resulting in a 'win-win' situation for society, as well as for the social entrepreneur somewhere in the middle.

Social entrepreneurship is also associated with a range of characteristics (Dees et al., 2001, 2002; Lasprogata and Cotton, 2003; Hibbert et al., 2001; Pomerantz, 2003). These are a drive for social mission; recognition and relentless pursuit of a mission; ability to find new ways of providing a service, innovation, adaptation and engagement in continuous learning; negligence of limited resources as a hindrance; and accountability to other people.

As a consequence, it is evident that social entrepreneurship is also breeding a new group of entrepreneurs, namely social entrepreneurs. These often operate in social organizations and/or a specific social setting, for example in a third-world setting, or an area of poverty.

Social Entrepreneurs

A common feature for social entrepreneurs is that they care about their local communities and "listen to the 'voice of the community' and respond in meaningful ways" (Thompson, 2002:416). Furthermore, social entrepreneurs are associated with leadership qualities (Mort et al., 2003; Thompson et al., 2000) and other individual characteristics such as the willingness to take risks (Brinckerhoff, 2000; Mort et al., 2003), being prone to change (Waddock and Post, 1991; Bornstein, 1998, 2004; Prabhu, 1999; LaBarre et. al., 2001; Mort et al., 2003), and possessing innovative and entrepreneurial characteristics (Reis and Clohesy, 2001; Pomerantz, 2003; Waddock and Post, 1991).

Even if traditional and social entrepreneurs have been associated with similar qualities, some researchers argue for differences between them as depicted in exhibit 1 below (Steenkamp, 2004: 2; Rwigema and Venter, 2004:512):

For-profit (profit-driven) entrepreneurs	Social entrepreneurs
Strength from own personal skills and knowledge.	Strength from collective wisdom and experience.
Focus on short-term financial gain.	Focus on long-term capacity.
No limit on scope of ideas.	Ideas limited by mission.
Profit is an end, reinvested for further profit or pocketed for self-enrichment.	Profit is a means, put into serving people.
Being in charge of their own destiny – rather than being beholden by an employer	Enable the organization to become sustainable and through this process be in charge of their destiny.

Exhibit 1. Differences Between For-Profit Entrepreneurs and Social Entrepreneurs.

For the purpose of this article, we lend ourselves to the approach that social entrepreneurship is, on the one hand, a societal gain in social value creation and, on the other hand, an individual gain by the entrepreneur in satisfying his/her needs also beyond pure monetary profit by sharing his/her innovations and insights (Seelos and, Mair, 2004; Mair and Noboa, 2003a; 2003b). This definition thus points to a) the outcome on a societal level as well as b) the personal gain in both social value and monetary terms for the individual social entrepreneur him-/herself.

Within the field of social entrepreneurship, we can sense a theoretical as well as an empirical dilemma insofar that there is no agreement on the frames within which we can place social entrepreneurship. The concept can be either very narrow in its focus, including pure non-profit endeavours with a clear social mission to more broad approaches, including "businesses organized as for-profit entities and hybrid organizations mixing non-profit and for-profit elements" (Lasprogata and Cotton 2003:69). Lasprogata and Cotton[1] claim that this situation has led to some challenges being under way. For instance, the competition between different kinds of social enterprises has increased, governmental funding has decreased, a range of scandals (such as the Red Cross in New York City) has damaged the reputation of these institutions and measurements for outcome are required. The situation in South Africa is slightly different. Being a 'new' democracy, NGOs are not questioned *per se* at this stage; they are rather seen as

---

[1] Drawing on the non-profit scholar Lester M. Salamon: "Holding the Center: America's Non-profit Sector at a Crossroads" (1997; on file with Lasprogata and Cotton).

necessary means for the government to ease and speed up the process of creating sustainability. Furthermore, funding to the NGOs has been generous and without requirements for detailed statements of accounts. The main interest has been devoted to encouraging entrepreneurship and to start up businesses with the help of NGOs without really questioning their relevance.

Taking the situation in South Africa one step further, we claim that NGOs probably play a major role in facilitating community development; however, it is more important and more interesting to focus on the prime target for creating possible sustainability, namely the entrepreneurs themselves. How are these entrepreneurs related to social entrepreneurship? What relationship is there between the NGOs and the entrepreneurs? Is it possible to suggest a framework that mirrors the diversity of opinions within the field and that rhymes with our approach to social entrepreneurship?

The Empirical Material

Our empirical material is from the Western Cape of South Africa and is illustrated by conversations with four entrepreneurs who showed a strong social responsibility. The choice of cases was made with accessibility as well as security in mind. We had to rely on the earlier established network between the academia and the 'field' in order to get in touch with these social entrepreneurs. None of the conversations have been taped since we believed that the tape recorder could restrain the conversation. The Swedish authors carried out two of the four conversations and were both present to secure the quality of the conversations and to avoid as much as possible misunderstandings based on cultural differences. In the other two cases the conversations have been carried out by South Africans; in those cases only one researcher was present. Women tell three of the four stories. The businesses are owned and managed by females (two Africans and one coloured) and one male (Muslim). The inclusion of women is highly relevant since they traditionally do not own businesses and since there are few female role-models. There is also reason to believe that the businesses in this article (bed and breakfast, restaurant, day-care centre) are traditional female businesses. Each conversation lasted for about 2-3 hours. In all four cases the enterprises were visited on site.

Conversations have also been carried out with representatives of NGOs. This was to understand their roles and how they contribute to increasing entrepreneurial activities. Through interviews with NGOs it was possible to get a better understanding of the environment in which the social entrepreneurs live and run their firms. The conversations with NGOs lasted for about one hour each. In all cases, except for Open for Business, the conversations were carried out in their offices. Exhibit 2 below presents a summary of the NGOs that were interviewed. The material from the interviews with the NGOs is used in our analysis to strengthen our case.

Name of the NGO interviewee	Purpose of the NGO
BON (Business Opportunity Network) Wendy Summers, CEO	Founded in 1995. Supports local economic development by working for previously disadvantaged industries (e.g. cleaning, security and construction industries). BON is the intermediary between the SMMEs and the actors they face when founding and starting a business (e.g. banks). 2000 members. 98% of the people getting in contact with BON are blacks.
KHULA Finance Xola Sithole, CEO	Founded in 1995. Owned by the Ministry of Trade and Industry and facilitates SMME development by pushing access to finance by giving credit guarantees. The smallest loan is 50,000 Rand. About 70% of the ideas are brought to the bank, and about 10% of these receive a loan.
MAPPPSeta (Media, Advertisement, Printing, Publishing, and Packaging) Dave Thomas, CEO and Belinda Petersen.	An educational authority, with a facilitating function. The Department of Labour and the Department of Finance has structured the different sectors and sub-sectors of the industries in RSA up into 25 SETAS (initially 27) based on education and training. The role of the setas is to identify the needs of the sectors, identify gaps regarding skills and to influence the educational system.
Open for Business (OFB) Denise Dookoo, Project Manager	Open for Business is developed from the Canadian model where all service providers for small businesses is located under one roof. OFB is a co-operation between the local government and the bank and mainly for unemployed people between the ages of 18 – 35.
WECBOF (Western Cape Business Opportunities Forum) Lesley Africa, CEO	Founded in 1995 on the initiative by local business people, academics and 'prominent' members of the economic community. The prime goal is to assist previously disadvantaged small and medium enterprises with finance and training in order to identify, create and encourage business opportunities within the Western Cape region. WECBOF has over 500 members and appoints and rewards The Business Person of the Year.
Clotex (Western Cape	Clotex was founded in 1999 and is directed towards the

Clothing & Textile Service Center) Averill Appollis, Manager	clothing and textile industry in the Western Cape with the vision to increase employment and international competitiveness. Clothing is the largest industry in the Western Cape. The main target is black and coloured women and the main tasks are to identify potential opportunities for networking between SMMEs and client companies, to give advice, help with trade contracts and to provide training and counselling. The two major stakeholders of Clotex are The Department of Trade and Industry and The Department of Economic Affairs, Agriculture and Tourism. .

Exhibit 2: NGOs, Persons Approached and the Purpose of the NGO.

Methodologically, we rely on an interpretive approach (Burrell and Morgan, 1979; Alvesson and Sköldberg, 1994). The aim of the interpretative approach is to create a further understanding of social entrepreneurs. However, we extend this understanding to explanations, as well as consequences, as a basis for theory generation. To deepen our understanding about social entrepreneurs there is a need to learn about the stories these entrepreneurs tell, how they tell them and the cultures they are embedded in. Moreover, interactions need to be understood in the socio-cultural context they belong to (Steyaert, 1997), which will be best done through a qualitative approach (Hjort et al., 2003).

Next, we will give account of the four stories, told by Thope Lekau, Jean Williams, Nomalungelo (Lungi) Kobus-Khaye and Sedick Jappie, respectively.

Thope Lekau: Founder of Kopanong Khayelitsha

In 1999 Thope Lekau turned her house into a bed and breakfast. It was the first bed and breakfast (B&B) in Khayelitsha, a township with about 800,000 inhabitants in the Western Cape area. Before starting the B&B she worked for NGOs with community development projects in rural areas. In 1999 she started to work part-time with the B&B. It was when she was working as a guide for township tours that she realized that there was a market for a B&B in Khayelitsha.

A team of three to sixteen persons work for Thope. She offers accommodation, guided township tours and food for those who book in advance. Regarding business she says: "You should dream big, but start small." Thope has an academic background. From 1997 to 1999 she studied at the University of Pittsburgh in Pennsylvania. She considers education to be very important. However, it is not only 'schoolbook' knowledge that is important: tacit knowledge is as important as explicit knowledge. If a person wants to learn, s/he can learn from everything, by participating and watching how and what other people do. But s/he has to take learning seriously, she says. Entrepreneurs need to be coached. They have to learn to run a business, to learn to keep record of incomes and expenses, according to her.

Thope identifies a certain need among the female community members. They turn to her for advice regarding founding and running a business. She considers herself as a consultant but says that the women would not go to other places and ask for help, such as support organizations. Few people are familiar with consultants and they do not even know what they can do for them. It is easier for them to turn to her for help since she is one of them. Her ambition is that some of them might start a business, which would lead to job creation, which, further on, would contribute to the development of the township. She says that small-scale entrepreneurship is probably the way for communities like Khayelitsha to develop further. She considers herself to be a role-model for others and her driving force is not money: "What's fulfilling is to know what I have achieved and that I am happy and content because of it." She wants to pass on the entrepreneurial spirit to others and share her "little knowledge with others".

Another important quality of an entrepreneur, stressed by Thope, is that s/he learns to delegate to others. She is considering having someone else in the township to bake her breads, a special type boiled in water, which her mother baked and which was frequently served in her parental home. By serving this bread, she has, in a way, turned poverty into a business idea. Another example is ginger-beer. Foods and drinks that always have been frequently served among the poor people have suddenly become a specialty. Local people are involved as suppliers.

A great many dedicated people in South Africa work at the grassroots level, according to Thope. They are important coaches and they start a snow-ball effect by inspiring others to start their own businesses, too. To Thope, an entrepreneur takes a risk and he/she leaves his/her bed every morning with a plan for the coming day. Thope contends that entrepreneurship is about planning and sticking to the plan. Being a successful entrepreneur is about managing the time well. What is most important is to "seize the moment". Thope is engaged in training other B&B start-ups until 2010, when the World Cup in soccer takes place in South Africa.

Jean Williams: Founder of a Day-Care Centre

Jean Williams was born in 1949 in Raithby, a small missionary community situated about 70 kilometres from Cape Town. She went to primary school and continued to secondary school. During her childhood and adolescence she learned the hands-on skills such as baking, sewing, cooking, farming and she even assisted the local shopkeeper as a sales assistant.

Having finished secondary school, she joined Schneider Clothing as a sales assistant in Bellville, where she worked for approximately 16 years. She commuted to work by train. Talking with people on the train she realized that many newly-wed young couples were moving into the area. Due to the high interest rates on bonds, the wives were forced to continue working, even after the birth of their first child. As there were no pre-primary school facilities, they had to leave the child with the neighbour, who often exploited these struggling families. She realized that there was a business opportunity, but at the same time presented an opportunity to help a community that was facing a major problem.

Jean gave up her secure job and started a day-care centre. She advertised on a Friday and two days later she had 20 confirmed customers. She started to operate from a room in the house. She collected the children at their homes and in the evening she dropped them off again. There was no time to employ any assistants and she was forced to rely on her family to lend a hand. The number of customers grew, which forced her to employ people and buy a bigger vehicle for transportation of the children. She later moved to bigger premises with more employees and even more vehicles. She currently employs 6 people and has about 150 children, two drivers, three vehicles and a car. Her husband, who retired in March 2004, assists her with the transport of the children. The children who graduate are enrolled in the nearby primary schools. Because of the good relationship that was built over the years, the parents still depend on Jean to collect the children in the morning and take them to school and collect them at the school in the afternoon and keep them until the parents return in the evening. This has led to another opportunity of operating an after-school centre. Currently, there are about 10 such day-care centres following Jean's example.

Jean is also the co-ordinator for a group of approximately 120 senior citizens, who meet thrice a week for a meal and doing handicraft work. The church initially provided the funds for the meals, but she has explored fundraising opportunities and government departments for financial assistance. Now, the Department of Social Welfare and Pensions is providing financial assistance. About 22 voluntary people, 20 women and 2 retired males carry out the activity, preparation of the food and care of the senior citizens. In addition to the financial assistance from the Department of Social Welfare and Pensions, they have regular fundraising events, such as barbecuing, baking and handicraft sales or concerts. The funds generated enabled the team to take the senior citizens on weekend, or even weeklong, outings. Most of these women come from disadvantaged backgrounds and many would never have seen the places that they have visited during the past five years.

Jean has discovered that many of the senior citizens are often maltreated by their children and are forced to give their monthly pension allowance to them. Many of these senior citizens have to move from family member to family member, often left homeless. Her next project is to raise funds to either buy a house, or convert it into a shelter for senior citizens in the Eerste River- Blue Downs area. She has appointed a principal for the day-care and after school centre, which enables her to concentrate on the other projects.

Nomalungelo (Lungi) Kobus-Khaye: Partner in Masande Restaurant and Founder and Owner of Ayanamkela Xhosa Restaurant

Lungi hails from Kensington, Cape Town. She started her career as a nurse. In 1995 she and five other nurses decided to open and run a restaurant on a part-time basis to supplement their low monthly income. They started their restaurant from a rented house in the well-known Gugulethu, about 20 kilometres from Cape Town. After a while they were forced to close the business as the home-owner decided to use the premises for other purposes. Due to this setback, four of the friends decided to quit. Lungi and a friend of hers restarted the business at

Crossroads, in partnership with the Zenzele Trust. They were approached by Karel le Roux, a manager of one the many projects of Mfesane (an NGO that promotes self-help and business start-up schemes for women) to manage the restaurant as they were two experienced restaurateurs. This Christian organization, which had been in existence for almost 25 years, aimed to improve the living conditions of various township communities. André was the manager of the Zenzele project which is aimed at helping people who are interested in starting businesses. This was the help that they were looking for. Since then, they have never looked back.

Lungi appointed a marketing manager and a chef. Mfesane provided the land and buildings. The Masande Restaurant, as it was known, was owned and strategically managed by five directors. Zenzele Trust appointed three of them. This agreement ensured that Zenzele shared in the profits of the restaurant, which would be ploughed back into community projects.

The two owners had one goal in mind and that was to showcase the Xhosa tradition to the tourists. This would contribute greatly to the profit-making opportunities of their restaurant. According to the owners, this restaurant would, for the first time, give the people from Cape Town a taste of the following: home-made "sonka samanzi" (steamed bread), and "papa nolusu" (porridge with tripe) with sour milk while the tourists are learning Xhosa and Xhosa traditions. It was a hit from the very start, and the tourists streamed to the restaurant. According to the owner, many foreign tourists have walked in with a copy of the brochure, which had been given to them by their friends.

Lungi suffered a major setback in 2001 when her partner passed away. However, the activities at the restaurant went ahead full steam. The restaurant changed into an academic meeting place. Academicians brought groups of overseas colleagues. With the acceptance of catering for groups, it was also easier to provide live concerts, as bookings were made in advance. In addition to the live concerts, visitors can also view and buy the handmade beadwork, clay pots, carved and painted items. These are products made by people within the community. Lungi is well-supported by local businesspeople to whom she provides catering and finger lunches. She is still involved in nursing on a full-time basis. In addition, she also trains members from the community in needlework and baking.

Due to her community involvement and business acumen, she was invited by the Department of Trade and Industry to accompany a group of businesspeople to attend the 2001 Global Summit. In 2001 she was voted businessperson of the month by WECBOF, SANTAM (one the large short-term insurance companies) and KFM 94.5 (one of the large radio stations in the Western Cape).

In 2002 she left the Masande Restaurant to start her own restaurant from her newly- acquired home in Montana. She named it Ayanamkela Xhosa Restaurant, meaning "my clan/people welcome you". Upon moving into her new premises she was only able to seat 20 customers and with her own capital she has renovated her place comfortably to seat 120 customers. The restaurant has accommodation facilities for 4 people. She currently has 3 people in full-time employment, 3 part-time and 6 –10 casuals.

Her hard work and quality of service have resulted in many awards. In May 2002 she received the "Good food and wine" award. In September 2003 she was runner-up in the ETEYA (Emerging Tourism Entrepreneur of the Year award) award and in November 2003 she was a finalist in the Cape Tourism awards. Lungi is still involved in other community projects and her organization is currently involved in an AIDS campaign; sewing; arts and music; parents' guidance; vegetable; and flower garden. She is currently the co-ordinator of the Flower garden. This pilot project is operated from Vukukhanye Public Primary School in Gugulethu. She has also been approached by the Tour Operators Association to join their network. Her philosophy is to help building the nation, through hard work and involvement in business and community projects.

The Story of Sedick Jappie of Superior Cabinet Doors

The story of Sedick Jappie dates back to 1985 when he was a second-year law student at the University of the Western Cape (UWC). The times were politically turbulent and eventually the university was closed down. Sedick wanted to be an entrepreneur and he wanted to run and manage his own company, since he is a person who wants to be in command. This was forbidden at the time and he therefore started to work for an American company. However, it was hard to advance, being surrounded by whites, and therefore he had difficulty in settling into a stable work environment. Eventually, he managed to get around the laws by becoming associated with a Chinese person, who was considered White. Together they built a company that made canvas, carports and garage doors. Two years later the company went insolvent. Sedick believed it was a good learning experience; he learned all about starting and managing a business - what mistakes to avoid and that it is dangerous to grow from an artisan to an entrepreneur without training. During this time he completed two years' of legal studies. The firm went bankrupt, but was restarted in 1987. It was registered as "Sedick Jappie (Pty) Ltd" but trading as Gordon's Joinery. His former business partner Gordon became a silent partner. The business grew but Sedick needed to borrow money. As a result of the lessons learned, the loan was maximised to the value of his house and the outstanding mortgage. In 1994 he bought his friend's shares and operated as a sole proprietor manufacturing kitchen cupboards. Sedick wanted to grow and was keen on trying out a new concept – MDF material – for his kitchen door cupboards. In order to get funding he sold his company to two former employees and trained them together with his wife and son to start off, and the employees also acquired foreign financial assistance. Sedick Jappie then started *Sedick Jappie Superior Cabinet Doors* with three other workers in the company. At this time he was not scared of borrowing money and the company today has 60 employees with an annual turnover of R12 – 15 million. He operates from an industrial area at the border of Kuils River. The customers are mainly situated in the Western Cape area and the local market is number one to Sedick – even if the company has started export to Tanzania, United Arab Emirates (Dubai) and Saudi Arabia (Jeddah).

Sedick is aware of his needs and to him life is about working less and earning more. He thrives on challenges, always sees a need to restructure and to think ahead. However, he also gains pleasure in providing and creating jobs. Sedick supports charity and "upliftment programmes". He works though a range of support agencies in order to develop the community, such as WEBCOF, WESGRO, The Cape Town Regional Board for SMME Opportunities for Rural Areas, Debasa (funded through the World Bank to assist start-ups) and the governing body of the school. Sedick says that it is necessary to focus on the future, but one must not forget one's past. So far, blacks and coloured have gained political freedom but not economic freedom. One of his tasks in life is to "smooth out" the differences between the past and the future. The greatest challenge to the Western Cape area is job creation. Sedick says that "you have to work together to get a momentum. If we can create jobs, social problems are solved and dignity restored. If you teach a man to fish he will get sustainability for life". The main problem for black people is that they are not assertive enough. Self-confidence comes through knowledge, which makes education and training the prime priorities in previously disadvantaged areas.

Sedick argues that support agencies are needed but there is too much politics and not enough deliveries. Furthermore, they are not entrepreneurial enough and do not work systematically on all levels. Politicians are most often academics and do not see the problem and do not work systematically at all levels. According to Sedick, they also seem to get occupied more with issues related to personal gain, especially in times of elections. The infra-structure is lagging behind and housing and services, among other things, are badly needed. However, also existentialistic and philosophical matters, says Sedick, need urgent attention.

Discussion

This discussion is based on the stories about the four entrepreneurs but also on understandings gained from the interviews with the NGOs.

From our stories about Thope, Jean, Lungi, and Seddick we identify that they all are involved in activities that are related to a caring for the community as well as for traditions. The activities are either their main activities or side activities:

	Main activity	**Side activity**
Caring for the community	*Jean:* day-care centre, after school activities Lungi: Nursing *Seddick:* Manufacturing kitchen door cupboards	*Thope:* training women Jean: Caring for the elderly *Lungi:* Aids campaigns *Seddick:* Charity and upliftment programs through NGOs
Caring for traditions	*Thope:* Bed & Breakfast with traditional food focus *Lungi:* Restaurant with Xhosa traditions	*Jean:* Handicraft work *Lungi:* Traditional hand craft and food

Exhibit 3: Main and Side Activities Carried Out by the Social Entrepreneurs

Caring for the community involves the possibility to indirectly or directly create job opportunities. Caring for traditions involves the interest of keeping kinship or clan/tribe traditions alive. Main activities are those from which the four earn their livings. From the quadrant we can draw the conclusion that all entrepreneurs in focus have many and varied pursuits and that there are social elements in all their doings.

A common underlying issue is the monetary aspects: To the manager of Clotex the driving force is to see the women when they leave in the end of the week with their earnings and the satisfaction of being appreciated for their work. This is also mirrored by the following statement by the CEO of BON: "One of the challenges of the future is the micro sector, where it will go and how they get out of the grey economy is hard to say."

Besides activities and monetary aspects, a set of features can be recognized that seem to be present in all the stories. These are displayed in Exhibit 4 below and are further commented below.

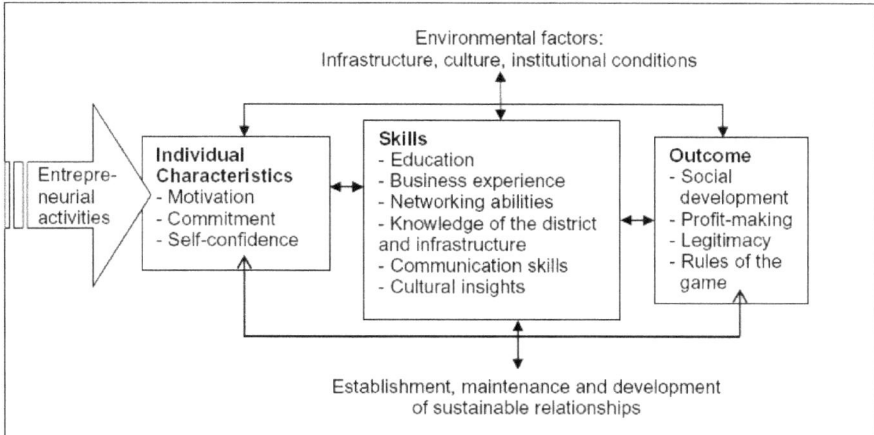

Exhibit 4: Social Entrepreneurship as an Iterative Process

Environmental Factors

Environmental factors refer to factors more or less beyond the control of the social entrepreneur. These are infrastructure, institutional conditions and the culture. The social entrepreneurs illustrated here are active in a special environment of former disadvantaged areas. The Apartheid regime created certain institutional conditions that are still present, and the people in these areas still live in a historically anti-entrepreneurial culture, in poverty and segregated residential areas within the townships themselves. The traditional 'black identity' (Adam and Moodley, 1993) is still present with its traditional elements and rural customs where 'street wisdom' is part of a natural living. The most evident proofs today of environmental factors are the infrastructure, but also in the minds of the inhabitants who suffer from a lack of solid educational backgrounds and lack of confidence.

From our stories we can conclude that all of the four social entrepreneurs are familiar with the environment and its conditions. Even if the settings differ from the most miserable to less miserable, they have been brought up in this specific background. Within the framework of the institutional environment we also find a range of NGOs, such as the ones mentioned elsewhere in this paper: BON, Clotex, Khula, MAPPP Seta, Open for Business and WECBOF. The social entrepreneurs in our study have a solid knowledge about their operations and, above all, how to approach them and take advantage of their offerings. However, recent research in South Africa has shown that business owner-managers in general lack knowledge and information about NGOs. Since our contact with the entrepreneurs has been established through the University of the Western Cape, it could very well be so that we have met with those who have more public positions and who are part of the networks of the NGOs.

Individual Characteristics

Individual characteristics are characteristics that are hard to learn, but can either be inborn or developed through life experiences, such as motivation, commitment and self-confidence. From the CEO of BON we hear that "we are the speaking partner. They [Blacks and Coloured] are taught and trained in the school of thought that they are not allowed to speak. They do not dare. They need someone who helps them. Those who have not been through the process do not know. Not even how to go to the bank." Fundamental reasons for this perceived lack of motivation, commitment and self-confidence in this context have been presented by Visser (1997) when he concludes that the majority of South Africans have grown up with no school or home tradition of business, innovation or entrepreneurship; the majority of the population has no notion of themselves as 'resource creators'; they come from a background where their predecessors have been marginalized from the economic mainstream, thereby precluding them from owning property, businesses and the ability to create wealth; and disadvantaged communities and economic minorities have had few role models to motivate and guide them in their career development.

The social entrepreneurs here seem to 'be made of the right stuff'. Their personal characteristics differed but they had in common a specific motivation including a willingness to start a business, to take the risk and the responsibility that follows from that decision. They are, therefore, particularly committed to their task and a lot of self-confidence that has been acquired in different ways including education, and support from family and friends. When the social entrepreneurs here started their businesses they were either driven by a necessity to do so, or identified a specific opportunity. For instance, Sedick Jappie entered into business from a necessity to get an income, whereas Jean Williams saw an opportunity to solve a problem. In either case they initially started their businesses with monetary profit as a goal.

Skills

Skills can be learned and accumulate in explicit as well as tacit knowledge. In our cases all four entrepreneurs have over the years acquired skills that have played a major role in their business life. All of them are well-educated in general but have also learned considerably about starting and running a business (entrepreneurship in a wide sense) over the years. Sedick Jappie started out as a law student and had the opportunity to test his business skills within the frame of a friend's failure. Thope Lekau was educated overseas and is fostered in the American entrepreneurial 'go spirit'. Nomalungelo Khaye has started at least two businesses over the years. Prime skills that have proven to be of crucial importance in our cases are knowledge about the infrastructure, the existing networks and abilities to 'network' in different layers, ability to communicate on several levels and being one of the same in the cultural environment. Above all, the social entrepreneurs have the ability to move back and forward between different settings, make use of the right institution at the right time and put it into a wider 'whole'.

The NGOs work with training, which is important. Wendy Summers stresses that one of the most important roles for BON is to de-mystify the "big documents", which are needed when one starts and runs a business. However, the training does not necessarily have to be schoolbook training only. To the entrepreneurs it is more important to, among other things learn how to keep record of company income and expenses. Skills and knowledge about how to access finance, training and opportunity are underdeveloped according to WECBOF's spokesperson. Entrepreneurs need someone to open the doors for them and help them get in contact with the right person. The CEO of BON agrees: "Whites have friends and families who can give them access to technology for example, while Blacks and Coloureds do not."

Outcome

Social development can be defined as activities making a difference for the social environment (or local community) in which the social entrepreneurs operate. Seelos and Mair (2004) combine social needs on three different levels (individual, societal and those of future generations) when they define sustainable development. In this paper we have chosen the wording 'social development' since we argue that in the areas we find our social entrepreneurs, social development is a pre-requisite for sustainable development. It is too early to use the label sustainability.

The social development the four entrepreneurs create is not revolutionary – it comes in small steps, such as giving employment to people, sharing their experience and knowledge with others who want to start their own businesses, being role models to neighbours and close friends.

The contribution to social development mainly comes as a value addition. Along the way, the social entrepreneurs have become aware of their abilities to extend their knowledge into a wider social context. Examples of this are Thope's extension of the business within the local township area and Nomalungelo Khaye's organization, which is currently involved in a community project fighting AIDS, mainly as a result of being successful in her ordinary business operations. Sedick Jappie is heavily engaged in NGOs and other social activites. We draw the conclusion that the outcome of the entrepreneurial endeavours is both profit making and social development. Sedick had to find a way to support himself when the university was closed down and he also claims that he wanted "to earn a lot and work less." Nomalungelo (Lungi) started a business in order to increase her monthly income. When Thope and Jean identified opportunities, it was with the idea that it could support them, and maybe also be profitable business.

Legitimacy is understood as a generalised perception or assumption that the actions of an entity are desirable, proper or appropriate within some socially constructed system of norms, values, beliefs and definitions (cf. Suchman, 1995). To gain legitimacy in this context is equal to successfully starting a business and thereby creating an audience, to survive with the business and possibly become profitable and last, but not least, be 'taken for granted'. The process of legitimacy is eased by the fact that the social entrepreneurs know the actors on different community levels and are perceived as 'one of the locals'. The individual characteristics combined with the skills enhance the legitimacy of the entrepreneur, and the entrepreneurs in focus have all gained legitimacy accordingly. On the other hand, the social activities may be a way for the social entrepreneurs to quicker gain legitimacy.

Considering that South Africa is a nation of only ten years of age, tremendous changes have taken place and still are taking place in the areas where 'our' social entrepreneurs operate. In operating their businesses they do not have many business codes to rely on, rather they have to create them along the way. Therefore, one important outcome of the entrepreneurship activities are that they learn and develop 'rules of the game' (North, 1990), knowledge that is spread to future entrepreneurs. By socializing others into the system, and the way of thinking and acting, more people learn what to do and how to do it. The best trainer is probably one who has done it him- or herself, a person who comes from the same community as the entrepreneur. To Thope Lekau, the entrepreneurs have an important role to fulfill since few women would go to support agencies; they prefer to go to the entrepreneur whom they know from their own community. This implies that the social entrepreneur becomes the extended arm of the NGO, who instead devotes time to 'package' and 'commercialize' their services. The CEO of BON says: "I can package the organization, I can do it, but I am hating it. Then I am running a firm again, it should be funded. If BON adds value, it should not be done as a business." Social entrepreneurs have the skilfulness and abilities to develop, to bring about change and to influence entrepreneurial processes in their respective communities. Furthermore, these skills have been successfully applied to engage the resources of government and private sector organisations to understand the needs of disadvantaged communities and to 'buy into' the concept of caring for a community. In all probability, the skills of 'positive manipulation', creating networks, accessing resources and a heightened sense of awareness creation of potential service providers all contribute (even in small ways) to the social and economic upliftment and advancement of these communities.

Sustainable Relationships

This whole framework of social entrepreneurship as an iterative process relies on the ability of the entrepreneur to establish, maintain and develop sustainable relationships. For example, the individual characteristics of social entrepreneurs (i.e. motivation, commitment, self-confidence) influence the outcome of their interventions (i.e. social development, profit-making, legitimacy and understanding the rules of the game) by applying a distinct set of community skills (i.e. experience of the local environment, networking abilities, unique knowledge of the district and cultural insights). Through network skills, the entrepreneurs gain access to strategically important resources.

In sum, we argue that social entrepreneurship is an iterative process, where the social entrepreneurs are aware of and knowledgeable within his/her institutional and cultural environment, and have the motivation and self-confidence to start a business. Within this framework, activities are taken that are fostered by education, business experience, networking abilities, communication skills and cultural insights. Even though all factors interact and the borders between them are blurred, an overall issue that stands out is the importance of relationships – relationships that cannot become sustainable unless the social entrepreneurs possess certain individual characteristics and skills and know how to make use of them in their environment.

Implications

In this paper we have illustrated that social entrepreneurship matters to the new democracy of South Africa. Initially, we provided some rather depressing figures regarding poverty but there are people out there fighting against them. We have also illustrated that social entrepreneurs have important features in common that make a difference to the regional development of the Western Cape in South Africa. Cook, Dodds and Mitchell (2003:66) argue that social entrepreneurship is relieving "the government of the responsibility for social problems because it puts the onus for reform onto the community". This postulation does not hold in a society such as South Africa, in which a system of ethnic socialism left disadvantaged communities destitute and devoid of support structures. It is exactly these social entrepreneurs who invest their "sweat equity" for the common good of the community. In the absence of the social entrepreneur, these communities will still be backward and 'stuck in the mud'. As Emerson and Twersky (1996) argue, "Social entrepreneurs have their roots in the history of community service and development. This history of commitment to social justice and economic empowerment is what feeds their passion for the creation of social purpose business ventures". Furthermore, evidence by Harding (2004) suggests that social entrepreneurs tend to come from mainly, but not predominantly, economically disadvantaged groups and areas and they leverage social entrepreneurial activities as mechanisms for engaging the labour market for the disadvantaged areas.

Turning back to our initial question "What relationship is there between the NGOs and the entrepreneurs?", we are inclined to claim that there is a risk for NGOs to fall in the trap of alienating themselves from grassroot entrepreneurial processes The relationship between the social entrepreneurs and the NGOs is not self-evident. There are examples where we clearly see that the representatives of the NGOs focus on building their own organisations instead of focusing on building up relationships with future entrepreneurs. The reason might be that they want to be strong in order to survive and/or that they sense a future competition between NGOs. However, in order to enhance social development the closeness to the local community is of decisive importance. The individual social entrepreneur can be the bridge between the NGOs and the local future entrepreneur but this is not enough – the representatives need to find new ways of increasing this important bonding. Otherwise, the future might hold a similar development as that pictured by Lasprogata and Cotton (2003) in the American context.

One of our main concerns in this paper was to ascertain whether a frame of social entrepreneurship can bring some order into the diversity regarding the concept of social entrepreneurship. Furthermore, we wanted to investigate how 'our' entrepreneurs are related to social entrepreneurship. In our framework, social entrepreneurs are not entirely different from entrepreneurs; they contribute to social development and, thereby, improve the infrastructure of the communities they serve. They promote and influence economic development and create employment opportunities in areas which are not that well-served and supported by both public and private sector initiatives. Furthermore, these social entrepreneurs vividly illustrate a need to extend the approach social entrepreneurship and conclude that social entrepreneurs are driven by an urge to earn their own money and look out for their own success, and in doing so, realize that creating jobs and wealth for others benefit themselves. This is not a new finding *per se*. Pastakia (1998) makes a similar conclusion, but is not prepared to label them all social entrepreneurs, but divides them into the two categories of commercial and social entrepreneurs. We suggest that we are able to place the two on an equal footing. Comparing our approach to social entrepreneurship where we point to the outcome as well as the personal gain in both social value and monetary terms for the individual social entrepreneur him-/herself with Davidsson's (2003) definition of entrepreneurship as a societal phenomenon with the introduction of new economic activity that leads to change in the marketplace, the similarities are striking.

At this point we do not agree with Exhibit 1 in this paper, where Steenkamp's (2004) and Rwigema and Venter (2004) make a distinction between For-profit entrepreneurs and Social entrepreneurs. The latter are here known to gain strength from own personal skills and knowledge and have under the circumstances been more or less forced to focus on short-term financial gains, where profit has been the main goal. On the other hand, from other studies we can conclude that 'ordinary' entrepreneurs have focussed on long-term capacity and that entrepreneurs in teams have relied on collective wisdom and experience.

To test our arguments, we can turn the question the other way around: Does our framework of social entrepreneurs as an iterative process apply to 'traditional' entrepreneurship? We would say that indeed it does. Most people would probably agree that individual characteristics in combination with skills of the kinds referred to here are vital to any entrepreneur where familiarity with environmental factors and the building of sustainable relationships are as important. The outcome is also possible to equal with the outcome of 'traditional' entrepreneurship, i.e. where profit-making, social development, legitimacy and rules of the game are essential.

The theoretical concepts 'entrepreneur' and 'entrepreneurship' are not well-known concepts among former disadvantaged groups in South Africa. Even so, in the native tribe of bushmen we find strong entrepreneurial elements where the bushmen make their own handicraft and also sell it, which is an entrepreneurial and appreciated commerce for tourists. On the other hand, the solidarity for friends and families in the community is a taken-for-granted element that is well developed since generations. The idea of "ubuntu" seems to be relevant where ubuntu stands for "the sense of solidarity or brotherhood which arises among people within 'margninalised' or 'disadvantaged' groups" (Mbigi and Maree, 1995:7). The typical African group solidarity is perhaps one explanation for what is going on here, rather than social entrepreneurship. May it be that in the South-African context social entrepreneurship is a new word for an old phenomenon?

As a final note, we recommend the concept social entrepreneurship be used with caution. It is more fruitful to talk about entrepreneurship in different contexts, where different sets of factors play a more or less distinguished role. The social dimension should always be considered important for understanding entrepreneurship. In many cases we use and apply the term entrepreneurship carelessly. The same seems to apply for social entrepreneurship, where we use the concept in a variety of situations when we see the slightest connection to societal development or not-for-profit enterprises. However, we leave open for debate whether we shall conform to a need to clean up, or do we in the end benefit from this variety?

References

Adam, H. and Moodley, K. (1993). *The Negotiated Revolution*. Johannesburg: Jonathan Ball.

Alvesson, M. och Sköldberg, K. (1994). *Tolkning och reflektion: Vetenskaplsfilosofi och kvalitativ metod*. Studentlitteratur

Bornstein, D. (1998). Changing the world on a shoestring, *Atlantic Monthly* 281 (1), pp. 34-39.

Bornstein, D. (2004). *How to Change the World: Social Entrepreneurs and the power of new ideas*. Oxford: Oxford University Press.

Brinckerhoff, P.C. (2000). *Social Entrepreneurship: the art of mission-based venture development*. New York: Wiley & Sons.

Burrell, G. and Gareth M. (1979). *Sociological paradigms and organizational analysis*. London: Heinemann.

Cook, B., Dodds, C., Mitchell, W. (2003). Social Entrepreneurship- False premises and dangerous forebodings. *Australian Journal of Social Issues*. Vol. 38 (1). pp. 57–72.

Davidsson, P. (2003). The Domain of Entrepreneurship Research: Some Suggestions. In Katz, J. and Sheperd, D. (eds). *Advances in Entrepreneurship; Firm Emergence and Growth*, Vol.6, JAI Press.

Dees, J. G., Emmerson, J. and Economy, P. (2001). *Enterprising Nonprofits: A Toolkit for Social Entrepreneurs*. New York. John Wiley and Sons.

Dees, J. G., Emmerson, J. and Economy, P. (2002). Strategic Tools for Social Entrepreneurs: Enhancing the performance of your enterprising Nonprofit. New York. John Wiley and Sons.

Emerson, J. and Twersky, F. (Eds.). (1996). *New Social Entrepreneurs: The Success, Challenge and Lessons of Non-profit Enterprise Creation*. San Francisco: Roberts Foundation.

Filion, L.J. (1998). From Entrepreneurship to Entreprenology. *Journal of Enterprising Culture*. Vol. 6 (1). pp. 1–23.

Harding, R. (2004). *Social Entrepreneurship Monitor – United Kingdom 2004*. London: London Business School.

Hibbert, S.A., Hogg, G., Quinn, T. (2002). Consumer response to social entrepreneurship: the case of the Big Issue in Scotland. *International*

Journal of Nonprofit and Voluntary Sector Marketing. Vo. 7 (3). pp. 288 – 301.

Hjort, D., Johannisson, B. and Steyaert, C. (2003). Entrepreneurship as discourse and life style. In: *The Northern Lights – Organization theory in Scandinavia,* edited by B Czarniawska and G Sevón. Liber, Astrakt, Copenhagen Business School Press, pp. 91-110.

LaBarre, P.Fishman, C., Hammonds,K. H. Warner, F. (2001). Who's Fast Leaders 2002. *Fast Company* 52, pp. 83-128.

Lasprogata, G. A., Cotton, M.N. (2003). Contemplating "enterprise": the business and legal challenges of social entrepreneurship. *American Business Law Journal.* Vol. 41 (1). pp. 67 – 113.

Liberty Learning Centre. 2003. Geography Classroom. (Online) http://www.learn.co.za/content/grade12/geography/regional/political/unit 1/12goT1L1_8.htm

Mair, J., Marti, I. (2004). Social Entrepreneurship: what are we talking about? A framework for Future Research. *Working Paper 546.* IESE Business School. University of Navarra. pp. 1–14.

Mair, J. and Noboa, E. (2003a). Social Entrepreneurship: How intentions to create a social enterprise get formed. *Working paper 521.* IESE Business School. University of Navarra. pp. 1–20

Mair, J. and Noboa, E. (2003b). The Emergence of Social Enterprises and their place in the new organizational landscape. *Working paper 523.* IESE Business School. University of Navarra. pp. 1–13.

Mbigi, L. and Maree, J. (1995). *Ubuntu: The Spirit of African Transformation Management,* Knowledge Resources (PTY) Ltd.

Mort, G.S., Weerawardena, J., Carnegie, K. (2003). Social Entrepreneurship: Towards Conceptualization. *International Journal of Nonprofit and Voluntary Sector Marketing.* Vol. 8 (1). pp. 76–88.

National Strategy for the Development and Promotion of Small Business in South Africa. 1996. Government Gazette. Cape Town: Government Printer. 357(16317).

North, D C 1990 *Institutions, Institutional Change and Economic Performance.* Cambridge, Ma.: Cambridge University Press.

Pastakia, A. (1998). Grassroots ecopreneurs: Change Agents for a Sustainable Society. *Journal of Organizational Change Management.* Vol.11(2), pp. 157-70.

Pomerantz, M. (2003). The Business of Social Entrepreneurship in a "Down Economy". *In Business,* March / April. Vol. 25(2), pp. 25 - 28.

Prabhu, G.N. (1999). Social Entrepreneurship Leadership. *Career Development International* (4).

Reis, T.K., Clohesy, S.T. (2001). Unleashing new resources and entrepreneurship for the common good: A philanthropic renaissance. *New Directions for Philanthropic Fundraising.* Vol. 32 (Summer). pp. 109–143.

Rwigema, H., Venter, R. (2004). *Advanced Entrepreneurship.* Cape Town: Oxford University Press.

Seelos, C and Mair, J. (2004). *Social Entrepreneurship. The Contribution of Individual Entrepreneurs to Sustainable Development.* IESE Business School: Working paper, WP No 553.

Shane, S. and Venkataraman, S. (2000): The Promise of Entrepreneurship as a Field of Research. *Academy of Management Review* 25 (1), pp. 217-226.

State of Small Business Development in South Africa. (2002). Annual Review 2002. Ntsika Enterprise Promotion Agency.

Statistics South Africa, (2003). Census 2001. (Online). http://www.statssa.gov.za/census01/html/default.asp.

Steenkamp, D. (2004). FEBDEV as a Social Enterprise: Supporting staff members and emerging business owners to be social entrepreneurs. Unpublished Report. Cape Town: Foundation for Economic and Business Development.

Steyaert, C. (1997). A qualitative methodology for process studies of entrepreneurship. *International Studies of Management and Organizations*, 27(3):13-33.

Suchman, M.C. (1995). Managing legitimacy: Strategic and institutional approaches. *Academy of Management Review*, Vol.20. No.3, 571-610.

Thomson, J., Alvy, G. and A. Lees (2000) Social entrepreneurship: A new look at the people and the potential. *Management Decision* 5 (6), pp. 328-338.

Thomson, J.L. (2002). The world of the social entrepreneur. *The International Journal of Public Sector Management.* Vol. 15, No. 2, 2002, pp. 412-431.

Visser, K. (1997). Enterprise Education in South Africa. *Papers in Education, Training and Enterprise.* No. 8. University of Edinburgh: Centre of African Studies

Waddock, S. and Post, J.E. (1991). Social Entrepreneurs and Catalytic Change. *Public Administration Review* 51 (5), pp. 393-401.

Chapter 14: Entrepreneurial Intentions in Kenya

The Factors that Facilitate Entrepreneurial Intentions Among the Youth and Nascent Entrepreneurs: Kenyan Case

Daniel Oruoch and Renson Muchiri

Abstract: A business venture is an intentionally planned activity. Literature in social psychology has shown that intentions are the best predictors of planned behaviour. Intentions in turn can be predicted by certain social and psychological factors. This study investigates how certain psychosocial factors impact on an individual's intention to create a business venture. The study was conceived after the realization that there was inadequate literature linking psychosocial factors and intention to business venture creation in Kenya. Consequently, many of the efforts used to promote entrepreneurship focus on provision of financial capital as evidenced by the policies the Kenya government has been putting in place for the youth and women. Using a sample of 380 students and 148 nascent entrepreneurs in Nairobi, Kenya, we confirmed that perceived feasibility and perceived desirability were significant antecedents of intention to venture business creation. We further found that social norms, social support networks and entrepreneurial experiences had indirect significant influence on intentions mediated by the perceptions of desirability and feasibility. As one of the implications of this study we propose that the Kenya government should in addition to facilitating easy access to financial capital, put in place policies and initiatives that impact positively on the social and psychological factors that positively influence entrepreneurial intentions.

Keywords: Intention to Venture, Perceived Desirability, Perceived Feasibility, Social Norms, Social Networks, Enterpreneurial Experience

Introduction

Creating a business venture is not a reflex action but a well-planned act. According to Ajzen's Theory of Planned Behaviour (1991), any planned behaviour can be predicted by the intention to perform that behaviour. Most entrepreneurial scholars therefore argue that to predict the act of starting a business venture, one has to look at the pre-entrepreneurial event, and that is the intention to venture. A number of intention-based models have been proposed and key among them include the Shapero Entrepreneurial Event (SEE) model (Shapero, 1975; Shapero and Sokol, 1982) tested by Krueger (1993) and Ajzen's TPB model (1991). Krueger, Reilly &Carsrud (2000) have compared these two models in terms of their ability to predict entrepreneurial intentions. The results from Krueger *et al* (2000) comparative study offered statistical support for both models. The Shapero's SEE model was found to be slightly superior to Ajzen's TPB model in predicting entrepreneurial intentions (Krueger *et al*, 2000). In this study we adopted a variation of the Shapero-Krueger model.

This study specifically focuses on Kenyan entrepreneurial environment. The study was conceived after the realization that there was inadequate literature linking psychosocial factors and intention to business venture creation in Kenya. Indeed much of the effort by the Kenya government, finance and micro-finance institutions have mainly focused on provision of financial capital. There is therefore need to look at the influence of the social and psychological factors on business creation. Most of the Kenyan communities have strong social and cultural norms which could be exploited to inculcate positive attitudes towards entrepreneurship.

Conceptual Model and Hypotheses

Intention literature argues that intentions have antecedents. According to Ajzen (1991) intentions can be predicted from attitudes towards the behaviour, subjective norms and perceived behavioural control. Shapero (1975) and Shapero & Sokol (1982) hypothesize that an individual's behaviour is driven by inertia until an event interrupts the inertia. The disruption of the inertia triggers a change in behaviour and the choice of alternative behaviour will then depend on the individuals' perceptions of desirability and feasibility towards that alternative coupled with the propensity to act. The perceptions of desirability and feasibility are seen here as antecedents of intentions to a business venture. Krueger (1993) argues that an individual's perceptions that lead to entrepreneurial behavior could be partly derived prior entrepreneurial experiences. Aldrich and Zimmer (1986) have reviewed literatures that show social support networks enhance probability of starting a venture. These literatures identify psychological factors that precede the intention to venture as perceived desirability and perceived feasibility and the social factors to be social norms, social networks and entrepreneurial experience.

In this study we examined the impact of both the social and psychological factors on the intention to business creation in Kenya. Past empirical evidence has revealed that situational and individual variables are poor predictors of entrepreneurial activities (Krueger, Reilly, Carsrud, 2000). Ajzen (1991) avers by stating that an individual's processing of available information mediates the effects of biological and environmental factors. This means that the social factors may not directly affect the intention to venture but they may influence the individual's perceptions. For this study we conceptualized perceived desirability and perceived feasibility to be mediators of entrepreneurial experience, social norms and perceived social support networks on intention to venture. Figure 1 shows the conceptualized model.

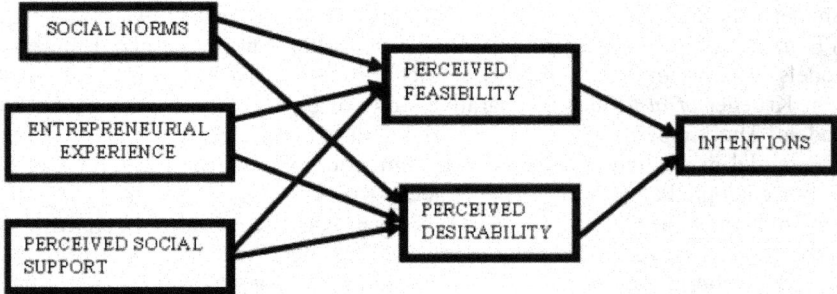

Figure 1: Conceptual Intention Model for Intention to Venture Business Creation - Adapted from Shapero-Krueger Model (Krueger *et al*, 2000)

Intention to Venture Creation

According to Ajzen and Fishbein (1980) intention refers to the degree of commitment towards some future target behavior, for example engaging in some entrepreneurial activity in future. In Social psychological studies intention has been identified to be the single best predictors of planned behaviour. Understanding intentions is therefore important especially where the behaviour involves unpredictable time lag (MacMillan and Katz, 1992). Intentions are not hereditary or inborn but they are formed as an individual interacts with the environment and processes the informational cues. Behavioral intentions are a function of a personal beliefs and information about the probability that performing a particular behavior will lead to a specific outcome (Fishbein and Yzer, 2003). It is believed that the stronger a person's intention to perform a particular behavior, the more successful they are expected to be (Ajzen and Fishbein, 1980). This implies that the intention to venture business creation is a necessary, though not sufficient, condition for one to be an entrepreneur.

How does an individual entrepreneur impact the process in venture creation? Individual differences; for example in attitudes, predisposition, traits, skills and abilities and cognitive differences influence the development of entrepreneurial intentions, opportunity search and discovery, decision processes and subsequent action (Shook, Priem and McGee, 2003). It may take relatively long or a short time after an intention develops before a new venture opportunity is identified and exploited (Shook, Priem and McGee 2003). This research examined intention to venture business as influenced by psychosocial factors, without having a time frame when the intention would be translated into action. Intention-based models contend that venture creation must be preceded by the development of intention to create a new venture, and that by understanding intentions we can better predict venture creation (Shook *et al,* 2003). To understand the intentions to venture business creation, we must look at the factors that drive these intentions. In intention models situational variables interact with perceptions to influence intentions to venture into business (Shapero and Sokol, 1982)

Perceived Desirability

Perceived desirability refers to a person's will power, his or her personal preference, motivation traits and self-determination. It is the most powerful force of human behavior (Brush, 2003). Shapero (1975) defines perceived desirability to be the personal attractiveness to start a business venture. It is the personal bias towards ventures perceived to be more desirable, a bias that grows from perceived personal consequences of the entrepreneurial outcomes and type of venture (Krueger and Brazeal, 1994). Research has shown that perceived desirability has a positive influence on entrepreneurial intention (Mair and Naboa, 2005). Thus;

> H1a: Perceived desirability has a positive influence on intention to venture

Perceived Feasibility

Perceived feasibility is derived from the belief in one's own competence (self-efficacy) and from the belief that the situation will permit us to exercise that capability (Bandura & Wood, 1989). It simply means a belief in oneself that an ideal opportunity is achievable and also, there are back-up resources to make it work (Shapero, 1975 & 1982). In entrepreneurship, perceived feasibility can be looked as the attitude towards the risk involved in an entrepreneurial opportunity. Shapero (1982) argues that resilience in communities requires a supply of individuals who are potential entrepreneurs. Resilience arises from what he refers to as "nutrient-rich environment". "Nutrient" includes both tangible and intangible resources. The tangible resources include physical infrastructure, finances and human capital. Intangible resources include, support networks, social norms that recognize entrepreneurship, self-efficacy, and perceptions, all of which are central to intention toward entrepreneurship (Krueger, 1993; Krueger and Brazeal, 1994). Perceived feasibility is the entrepreneur's belief in his/her ability to put together the required human, social, financial and other physical resources to start a business (Shapero and Sokol, 1982). We would expect that perceived feasibility will therefore have a positive impact on intention to venture into business. Therefore;

> H1b: Perceived feasibility has a positive influence on intention to venture

Social Norms

Social norms refer to the perceived social pressure to behave in a certain way (Ajzen, 1991). Social norms could also refer to the perception of what important people or groups (peer pressure, friends' wishes, and family wishes) think of target behavior (Fayolle, 2000b). These perceptions are influenced by normative beliefs and are relevant to individuals with a strong internal locus of control (Ajzen, 1987) and those with a strong action orientation (Bagozzi &Warshaw, 1992). Further, social norms cover the notion of desirability and feasibility. Shapero and Sokol (1982) suggest that societal beliefs influence attitudes that should predict an individual's intention. The combination of community-social norms and individual trait on perceptions of desirability and feasibility should positively influence intentions. Ajzen (1991) says that perceived behavioural control is function of underlying personal beliefs. If a societal norm is favorable to a kind of behaviour, then we would expect that the perceived feasibility of such behaviour would be high. Perceived social norms would therefore impact positively on perceived feasibility of a venture. The social norms will also play a significant role in an individual's attitude towards a given act like engaging in business for example a person who has been brought up in a family of business people will be more attracted to initiate a business venture. We would thus expect to see social norms impact positively on the perceptions of feasibility and desirability. In the Kenya, a casual observation shows that the communities associated with strong business norms have dominated most of the business establishments. Therefore;

> H2a: Perceived social norms have a positive influence on perceived feasibility

> H2b: Perceived social norms have a positive influence on perceived desirability

Entrepreneurial Experience

Entrepreneurial experience refers to personal experience in a family business, family involvement in a business or participation in start-ups (Ajzen and Fishbein, 1980). Shapero (1982) contends that for intentions to crystallize, it may be first necessary for something to disrupt a person's inertia. Circumstances such as loosing a job may trigger previously unrecognized entrepreneurial abilities. Significant progress has been made in understanding the impact of personal background factors such as prior experience and family background on the development of perception of entrepreneurship and intention to start a business (Krueger, 1993). In his attempt to disentangle the antecedents of perception of desirability and feasibility, Krueger (1993) argued that perceptions that lead to entrepreneurial behavior are derived partly from the entrepreneur's prior entrepreneurial experiences. Prior entrepreneurial experiences refer to the quantity and quality of prior exposure to entrepreneurship (Krueger, 1993). Quantity of exposure refers to personal experience in a family business, family involvement in a business, or participation in a start-up, whereas quality of exposure is the perception of whether those experiences were positive or negative. Shane and Venkataraman (2000) argue that possession of prior information is an influential factor in the discovery of entrepreneurial opportunities. Such prior information could come from the individual's prior entrepreneurial experience. According to Cooper, Woo, and Dunkelberg (1989) people are more likely to exploit opportunities if they developed useful information from previous employment. Prior entrepreneurial experiences influence perceived feasibility, perceived desirability and propensity to act (Shapero and Sokol, 1982), which in turn influence intentions to create an entrepreneurial venture. Although we found no Kenyan literature connecting entrepreneurial experience with intentions, We expect that entrepreneurial experience would positively influence perceptions of feasibility and desirability. Hence;

> H3a: Entrepreneurial experience has a positive influence on perceived feasibility

> H3b: Entrepreneurial experience has a positive influence on perceived desirability

Perceived Support Networks

Perceived support networks refer to the entrepreneurial perception of mentoring, role modeling, bridging, bonding and counseling as being negative or positive towards the perception of feasibility and desirability. In a community setting, the potential entrepreneur may have a large diffuse reference group that includes family and friends. The cultural impact in this instance comes from the community (Krueger *at al*, 2000). In their studies on women entrepreneurs in Nairobi, Njeru & Njoka (2001) contend that most women got support from family, friends and relatives. Aldrich and Zimmer (1986) have reviewed research that shows social ties to resource providers enhance probability of entrepreneurial opportunity exploitation. This means that if one perceives that (s) he has reliable social support networks that would facilitate acquisition of resources (s)he would be more attracted to venture. This is a case where social support networks influence an individual's perception of feasibility and desirability.

Therefore;

> H4a: Perceived social support networks have a positive influence on perceived feasibility

> H4b: Perceived social support networks have a positive influence on perceived desirability

Data and Measures

The Sample

The data was sourced form a sample of 380 university students (170 females) in either junior or senior years in four Kenyan Universities and 148 nascent entrepreneurs (69 females). These are students who are faced with prospects of making important career decisions and this would help us to investigate the entrepreneurial intention before the act. We used convenience sampling, where fifteen research assistants approached the respondents in their classrooms and business premises to fill the questionnaires. The students were from different universities taking business related courses.

Measures

All the six constructs in the conceptual model were measured using multiple-item measures. The measurement items of intention, perceived desirability, social norms and support networks were adapted with adjustment from Fisher and Corcoran (1994); *Measures for Clinical Practice, Vol 2: Adults* and from Peterman and Kennedy (2003); *Enterprise Education: Influencing Students Perception of Entrepreneurship.* Entrepreneurial experience and perceived feasibility lacked sufficient measurements in extant literature, as such, we developed scale items based on the few existing scale items and from relevant theoretical dimensions for each construct. For all constructs we used a five-point Likert scale.

> *Intention to venture creation.* The respondents were asked to respond to five items relating to their entrepreneurial intentions. The Cronbach reliability alpha for intentions was 0.78.

> *Perceived desirability.* Two items were used to measure perceived desirability. The Cronbach alpha was 0.72.

> *Perceived feasibility.* We used three items to measure perceived feasibility. The Cronbach reliability alpha was 0.73.

> *Entrepreneurial experience.* The two items used to measure entrepreneurial experience had a Cronbach reliability alpha of 0.69.

> *Social norms.* A set of four items was used to measure this construct and the Cronbach reliability alpha was 0.87.

> *Social support networks.* The Cronbach reliability alpha was 0.72 for the four items were used to measure social support networks.

Generally, all measures of the six constructs except one yielded Cronbach alphas greater than 0.70. According to Nunnelly (1978) an alpha of more than 0.70 is moderately adequate for the items to be used as a single construct. The Cronbach alphas indicated that the measurement item were reliable enough to measure the respective constructs.

Gender, Age, Institution category and Employment status were included as part of demographic profiling.

Results

Analyses

Construct validity. The Kaiser-Meyer-Olkin measure of sampling adequacy (= 0.84) indicated that factor analysis could be suitable for structure detection. The Bartlett's test of sphericity (p<0.001) was also significant indicating that the minimum standard for factor analysis had been met. We carried exploratory factor analysis and extracted six (6). These six factors explained 65% of the items' variance. The factor residual matrix yielded only three (1%) non-redundant residuals an indication of a good representation of the original data. Table 1 shows the SPSS output of the total variance explained by the six factors extracted.

Table 1. The total Variance Explained by the Extracted Six Factors

Factor	Initial Eigenvalues			Extraction Sums of Squared Loadings		
	Total	% of Variance	Cumulative %	Total	% of Variance	Cumulative %
1	5.220	26.102	26.102	4.762	23.812	23.812
2	2.370	11.849	37.951	1.933	9.667	33.479
3	1.760	8.801	46.752	1.265	6.327	39.806
4	1.432	7.159	53.912	.980	4.900	44.706
5	1.273	6.364	60.276	.811	4.056	48.762
6	1.006	5.028	65.303	.522	2.609	51.371

The pattern matrix (see table 2) confirmed the convergent validity of the items. The cross loadings for all item were low (<0.2) revealing the discriminant validity of the items.

Table 2. The Pattern Matrix

	Factor					
	1	2	3	4	5	6
Intention1		.643				
Intention2		.796				
Intention3		.511				
Intention4		.613				
Intention5		.494				
Desirability1					.737	
Desirability2					.710	
Network1			.649			
Network2			.639			
Network3			.613			
Network4			.592			
Norm1	.585					
Norm2	.854					
Norm3	.909					
Norm4	.802					
Feasibility1				.585		
Feasibility2				.802		
Feasibility3				.648		
Experience1						.599
Experience2						.862

Hypotheses Testing

Preliminary. In our preliminary analysis we fitted a structural equation model with intention as the response and the other five factors as the predictors. This we did to examine the direct effects of each of the five constructs on intention. The results from this model showed perceived desirability ($p < 0.001$) and perceived feasibility ($p < 0.001$) being significant predictors of intention. The other three did not have any significant effect ($p > 0.3$) on intention. The regression weights for this model are shown in table 3.

Table 3. Regression Weights for the Preliminary Model

	Estimate	S.E.	t-value	p-value
Intention ← Feasibility	.790	.107	7.354	< 0.001
Intention ← Experience	-.039	.042	-.929	.353
Intention ← Social networks	-.006	.046	-.135	.892
Intention ← Desirability	.261	.046	5.710	< 0.001
Intention ← social norm	.009	.038	.236	.813

Nevertheless, despite the results we could not conclude that these factors are insignificant in prediction of intention to venture since they could have significant influence on perceived desirability and perceived feasibility that could not be detected by the direct effects model.

Intention model. To examine the antecedents of intention, we fitted the intention model (see figure 1) and conducted confirmatory factor analysis using AMOS. The goodness of fit indices indicated that on the overall the model was a good fit (TLI = 0.968, RMSEA = 0.033). Convergent validity of the items was also confirmed for all items. Table 3 shows the regression coefficients of the intention model.

Table 4. Regression Weights for the Intention Model

		Estimate	S.E.	t-value	p-value
Feasibility ←	Experience	.124	.034	3.609	< 0.001
Desirability ←	Experience	.312	.069	4.536	< 0.001
Desirability ←	Social networks	.004	.078	.051	.959
Feasibility ←	Social networks	.099	.036	2.734	.006
Feasibility ←	social norm	.135	.029	4.590	< 0.001
Desirability ←	social norm	.288	.062	4.623	< 0.001
Intention ←	Desirability	.252	.042	5.943	< 0.001
Intention ←	Feasibility	.771	.099	7.771	< 0.001

The results showed perceived desirability and perceived feasibility to be significant predictors of intention to venture. This provided statistical support for hypotheses H1a and H1b. Moreover, social norms and entrepreneurial experience had a significant influence (p-values < 0.001) on perceived feasibility and perceived desirability. Support for hypotheses H2a, 2b, 3a and 3b was found. However, perceived social support networks did not a significant influence (p>0.1) on perceived desirability but had a significant influence (p < 0.01) on perceived feasibility. The data therefore provided statistical support for H4a but no support for H4b was found.

Overall; these results showed that perceived feasibility and perceived desirability mediated the influence of social norms and entrepreneurial experience on intention to venture. The influence of perceived social support networks on intention was mediated by perceived feasibility mediated but not perceived feasibility.

Discussion

The findings of this study suggest that though social factors of social norms, social support networks and entrepreneurial experience do not have a significant influence on intention, but they do have significant impact on the perceptions of desirability and feasibility. These findings are homologous to the finding of Krueger *et al* (2000). This study shows the intention model explaining 56% of the variance of intentions. Going by the theory of planned behavior (Ajzen, 1991) that intention is the single best predictor of planned behavior, these findings are important since understanding facilitators of intention enhance our understanding of future entrepreneurial behavior. According to Brockhaus & Horwitz (1986, as cited in Krueger *et al*, 2000), understanding intentional behavior helps to explain why many entrepreneurs decide to start business long before discovering entrepreneurial activities. Moreover, individuals with strong entrepreneurial intentions more likely discover entrepreneurial opportunities when they exist than those with weak or no intentions at all. It is therefore important that the government of Kenya and also the organizations seeking to promote entrepreneurship do promote activities that inculcate business norms among the community groups. This would help to enhance the formation of entrepreneurial intentions and hence increase the chances of venture creations.

This research also advocates the strengthening perceptions of feasibility and desirability in promoting entrepreneurial behavior. Some of these perceptions are gained through learning when interacting with the environment. Kenyan educational institutions could promote positive perceptions towards entrepreneurship by incorporating entrepreneurship education in their curriculum. The institutions could offer specific training that promotes these perceptions specific to certain business ventures. For example, in Kenya, entrepreneurial opportunities do exist in the information technology sector and mobile telephony. Such training should be aim at inculcating norms among the trainees and providing avenues of networking with successful entrepreneurs in the industry. This could be done through seminars and liaison with successful entrepreneurs to complement the training. Such activities will help to develop positive attitudes towards entrepreneurship among the trainees and change their mindsets from focusing on white color jobs only.

In recent past the government of Kenya has setup revolving funds for women and the youth with the intention of promoting entrepreneurship among these groups. Whereas the provision of financial capital is noble idea, this research shows that other factors of social and psychological capital need to be considered. This research suggests that the government should also promote initiatives and policies that enhance positive psychological perceptions and hence strengthen the urge to initiate business ventures. The government could work with community-based organisations (CBOs), non-governmental organisations, micro-finance institutions and financial institutions in promoting activities that enhance social networking among nascent entrepreneurs and develop entrepreneurial experience. By simply providing easy access to financial capital the government may only succeed in creating many imitations of the already exploited opportunities instead of creating new venture opportunities. This will only lead to increased competition and when the benefits from these exploited ventures exceeds the cost of pursing them the incentive for people to pursue the opportunity is reduced. This could end up being counterproductive. To identify 'genuine' entrepreneurs, the government should look for initiatives that enhance social networking and promote positive entrepreneurial experiences among the youth and women.

Limitations

Despite the bright picture we may have portrayed in this study we would wish to throw some caution in interpreting the results of this study by shedding some light on the limitations of this study.

a. Research on entrepreneurial intentions is an area that has not been extensively studied by scholars in Kenya. There was therefore limited Kenyan literature to ground the study, which made theoretical validation of the study measurements in the Kenyan case difficult. We however used literature from other parts of the world to theoretically validate the study measurements.

b. This research was concerned with the factors that precede the formation of entrepreneurial intentions. We were therefore not concerned with the connection between entrepreneurial intentions and entrepreneurial behavior. Although intention literature on entrepreneurship argues that intention is the best predictor of entrepreneurial behavior, empirical evidence validating this link is very pertinent in the application of this intention model.

c. This was a cross sectional study that examined the factors that facilitate formation of entrepreneurial intentions. It would be worth to consider stability of these intentions over time. Further, it is important to investigate the longitudinal variation of intentions to determine for example the time lag between the formation of the intentions and the realization of those intentions to business ventures. Investigation of how long the intentions last after formation before dying out would also draw a lot of interest. Of interest would be when intervention should occur to facilitate the transition of intentions to entrepreneurial activities?

d. The findings of this study cannot be generalized to the entire Kenyan population or other cultural settings outside Kenya. This is because the sample was taken from a section of the population centered on the capital city, Nairobi. It is also noted that the larger percentage of the sampled population were college students in their junior and senior years, pursuing business related courses. Further the social and cultural norms vary widely across the various regions in Kenya and as such these results cannot be generalized wholesomely as only one such a region was covered. We recommend that further studies could be done to determine if similar results would be obtained with same model.

In spite of these limitations, the results of this study do offer timely and useful insights into the factors that facilitate entrepreneurial intention to venture creation in Kenya.

Conclusion

This research did find any significant direct effects on intention by the social capital factors of perceived social norms, social support networks and entrepreneurial experience. However, these were found to be antecedents of perceived desirability and perceived feasibility. The social capital factors were found to be partially mediated by perceived feasibility and desirability in their influence on intention to venture creation. The findings of this research therefore reveal that for an individual to develop intentions to venture business creation there must strong perceptions of feasibility and desirability. These perceptions are stimulated by exogenous factors of social capital and the social capital factors do not impact directly on the intent to venture creation.

The available literature on entrepreneurship in Kenya indicates that the study on entrepreneurial intentions towards venture creation has not been put into sharp focus. This study is an initial attempt to open doors for further studies in this area. Further studies could focus on multi-group research on nascent entrepreneurs covering all the geographical areas of the country. Most of the literature on entrepreneurial intentions has used cross sectional data; future research could be done using longitudinal data to establish causal order. The longitudinal studies could be done to establish the relationship between intentions and the different groups' propensity to act.

Acknowledgement

This paper is based on the 3rd year research project of Dr. Daniel Oruoch at Case Western Reserve University. Muchiri Mwangi participated in the authorship by his contribution in the re-analysis and interpretation of data, drafting and critical revision of the paper and also in the submission of the final paper. We are grateful to the professors Michael Avital, Argun, Bob Carlson, Jagdip Singh and Paul Salipante for insightful comments they made in the preparation of the project. Special thanks reserved to Dominic Ojwang for data collection from the various Universities in Kenya and preliminary data analysis. We are indebted to the Mandel Fellowship for the financial support offered to Daniel.

References

Ajzen, I .1991. Theory of planned behavior. *Organizational Behavior & HumanDecision Processes*, 50, 179-211.

Ajzen, I. 1987. Attitudes, Traits and Actions: Dispositional Prediction of Behavior in Personality and Social Psychology. In Berkowitz, Z (Ed), *Advances in experimental Social Psychology*: Vol. 20 (1 – 63), New York: Academic Press.

Ajzen, I and Fishbein, M. 1980. *Understanding Attitudes and Predicting Social Behavior*. Englewood Cliffs, NJ: Prentice-Hall.

Aldrich, H & Zimmer, C., 1986. Entrepreneurship through social networks. In D. Sexton & R. Smilor (Eds.). *The art and science of entrepreneurship.* 3 – 23. Cambridge, MA: Ballinger.

Bagozzi, R.P. and. Warshaw, P.R. 1992. An Examination of the Etiology of the Attitude-Behavior Relation for Goal-Directed Behaviors. *Multivariate Behavioral Research*, 27 (4): 601-634.

Bandura, A., & Wood, R. 1989. Effect of perceived controllability and performance standards on self-regulation of complex decision making. *Journal of Personality and Social Psychology*, 56, (5), 805-814.

Bandura, A. 1986. *Social Foundations of Thought and Action*. Englewood Cliffs, NJ: Prentice-Hall.

Birds B. 1988. Implementing Entrepreneurial Ideas. The Case for Intention. *Academy of Management Review,* 13) 3): 442-453

Brush, G. c., Duhaime, I. M., Gartner, W. B., 2003. Doctoral Education in the Field of Entrepreneurship. *Journal of Management.*, 29.(3): 309 – 331

Brockhaus, R., and Horwitz, P. 1986. Psychology of the entrepreneur. In D. Sexton and R. Smilor,eds., *The Art and Science of Entrepreneurship.* Cambridge: Ballinger, 25–48.

Cooper, A., Woo, C., & Dunkelberg, W. 1989. Entrepreneurship and initial size of firms. *Journal of Business Venturing*, 4:317 – 332.

Dollinger, M. J. 2003. *Entrepreneurship: Strategies and Resources*. New Delhi: Pearson Education.

Dondo, A. and Ongile, G. 2001. Small and Micro-enterprise assistance organizations in Kenya: Quantity of services provided by their support programs *Kenya Rural Enterprise Program*.18.

Deakins, David. 1999. *Entrepreneurship and Small Firms*, 2nd Ed., New York: McGraw Hill.

Diochon, M., Menzies, T. V and Gasse, Y. 2004. *Exploring the Sequence and Duration*
http://www.google.co.ke/search?h/=en$q=Diochon$btng=google+search

Fayolle, A. 2000b. Exploratory study to assess the effects of entrepreneurship programs on student entrepreneurial behaviours, *Journal of Enterprising Culture*, 8(2):169-84.

Fishbein M., Yzer M. C. 2003. Using Theory to Design Effective Health Behavior Interventions. *Communication Theory* 13 (2), 164–183.

Fisher,J. Corcoran K. J. 1994. *Measures for clinical practice*. New York: Free Press Vol. 2. Adults

Gartner, W. B., Shaver, K. G., Gatewood, E., and Kartz, J. A. 1994. Finding the Entrepreneur in entrepreneurship. *Entrepreneurship: Theory and practice,* 19 (3):5 – 9.

Gartner, W. B 1988. Who is the Entrepreneur? Is the wrong question. *American Journal of Small Business,* 12.:11-32

Gartner, W 1985. A Conceptual Framework for Describing the Phenomenon of New Venture Creation, *Academy of Management Review,* 10: 696-706.

Hisrich, R. D and. Brush C. G. 1984. The woman entrepreneur: Management Skills and Business problems. *Journal of Small Business Management* 22 (1).

Kenny, D. .A. 2006. *Mediation* . http://davidakenny.net/cm/mediate.htm.

Kim, M. and Hunter, J. E. 1993. Relationships among attitudes, behavioral intention and behavior. *Communication research,* 20:331–364.

Krueger, N. & D.V. Brazael, 1994. Entrepreneurial Potential and Potential Entrepreneurs, *Entrepreneurship Theory & Practice,* 18.

Krueger, N., Reilly, M. D., & Carsrud, A. L. .2000. Competing models of entrepreneurial intentions. *Journal of Business Venturing, 15,* 411-432.

Krueger, N. 1993. Impact of prior entrepreneurial exposure on perceptions of new venture feasibility and desirability. *Entrepreneurship Theory and Practice* 18(1):5–21.

Lawrence, L. and Hamilton, R. T. 1997.*Unemployment and new business formation.* International small Business Journal. 15.

Macmillan, I. C., Block, Z. Narasimha, P. N. S., 1986. Corporate venturing: Alternatives, obstacles and experience effects. *Journal of Business Venturing* 1(2); 177 – 191

MacMillan, I., and Katz, J. 1992. Idiosyncratic milieus of entrepreneurship research: The need for comprehensive theories. *Journal of Business Venturing* 7:1–8.

Mair, J. and Noboa, E. 2003. Social Entrepreneurship: How Intentions to Create a Social Enterprise Get Formed. *IESE Working Paper* No. D/521.

Newton, K. 1997. Social Capital and Democracy. *The American Behavioral Scientist* 40 (5)

Njeru, E. H. and Njoka, J .M. 2001. Women entrepreneurs in Nairobi: The social cultural factors influencing their investment patterns, negotiating social space*: East African micro-enterprises.* Africa World Press.

Nunnelly, J.C., 1978. *Psychometric Theory 2ⁿᵈ Ed.* New York: McGraw Hill.

Peterman N.E., Kennedy J., 2003. Enterprise Education: Influencing students' perceptions of entrepreneurship. *Entrepreneurship Theory and Practice,* 28(2), 129 – 144(16).

Shane, S and Venkataraman, S. .2000. The Promise of Entrepreneurship as a Field of Research. *Academy of Management Review* 2000. Vol. 25 (1):217 - 236.

Shapero, A. 1984, '*The Entrepreneurial Event,*' in CA Kent, (ed.), *The Environment for Entrepreneurship.* Lexington Books: Lexington, MA,

Shapero A. 1982. Social Dimensions of Entrepreneurship. In C. Kent, D. Sexton and K. Vesper, eds., *The Encyclopedia of Entrepreneurship.* Englewood Cliffs: Prentice-Hall, 72–90.

Shapero A and Sokol L., 1982. *The Social Dimensions of Entrepreneurship.* In C.A Kent and K. H. Vespo (Eds). *The Encyclopedia of Entrepreneurship.* New Jersey: Prentice Hall.

Shapero, A. 1975. The displaced, uncomfortable entrepreneur. *Psychology Today*, November 9, 83-88.

Shook C. L., Priem, R. L., McGee, J. E., 2003. Venture Creation and the Enterprising Individual: A Review and Synthesis. *Journal of Management*, Vol. 29, No. 3, 379-399.

Schumpeter, J. 1934. *Capitalism, socialism and democracy.* New York: Harper & Row.

Spreitzer, G. M. 1995. Psychological Empowerment in the Workplace: Dimensions, Measurements, and Validation. *Academy of Management Journal*, 38 (5).

Chapter 15: Microfinance in Vietnam

The Efficiency of Microfinance in Vietnam: Evidence from NGO Programs

Hong Son Nghiem, Tim Coelli, and Prasada Rao

Abstract: A large amount of donor money and government money is spent on microfinance programs in developing countries around the world. However, there is very little quantitative research available on the relative efficiency of these programs. This research investigates the efficiency of the microfinance industry in Vietnam through a survey of 46 schemes in the north and the central regions. Data Envelopment Analysis (DEA) methods are used to assess the technical efficiency and scale efficiency of the microfinance schemes. Given the lack of previous studies in this industry, we review the various approaches to variable selection used in the financial institutions literature and amend the so-called "production" approach to accommodate the poverty reduction focus of microfinance. The empirical results reveal that the average technical efficiency scores of schemes surveyed is 80%. A second stage regression analysis is used to assess the impact of a variety of environmental variables upon the efficiency of the schemes. The age and the location of the scheme are found to have a significant influence upon efficiency.

Keywords: Microfinance, Efficiency, NGOs, Poverty Reduction

Introduction

Improving efficiency is one of the major challenges of the microfinance industry but little attention has been paid to efficiency assessment (Morduch, 1999). The efficiency of microfinance schemes is an important topic because the degree to which a dollar spent on microfinance programs converts into poverty alleviation will be in part a function of the degree to which these programs operate in an efficient manner. A commonly used approach to the measurement of microfinance efficiency involves the use of financial ratios, which were originally designed for conventional financial institutions. Accounting ratios provide only a partial measure of efficiency, and are unable to take into account issues such as economies of scope and scale. Therefore, this study takes a different approach to efficiency measurement, utilising production frontier, which can provide more useful managerial information than available from traditional methods.

After the financial reforms introduced in the early 1990s the Vietnamese microfinance industry developed rapidly, although 70 per cent of the poor in the country still do not have access to reliable financial services (GSO, 2005). Improving the efficiency of microfinance institutions (MFIs) is one possible way in which to increase the outreach of this sector, as improvements in efficiency will mean that more clients can be served from the available resources. However, there has been no previous research into the efficiency of the Vietnamese microfinance industry. This study seeks to fill the gap in the research by analysing the efficiency of 44 microfinance schemes in the north and central regions of Vietnam. Determinants of efficiency in these programs are also examined using second stage regressions, where efficiency scores are regressed against environmental variables such as infrastructure, locations, and the maturity levels of NGO microfinance programs (NMPs).

The remainder of this chapter is organised into five sections. Section 2 provides a discussion of efficiency measurement methods. Section 3 reviews several previous efficiency studies in microfinance. The data and results of the efficiency analysis are then presented in Section 4, with some concluding remarks made in Section 5.

Methodologies

This section describes the two main approaches to the measurement of efficiency, namely parametric and non-parametric approaches.

The Non-parametric Approach

The non-parametric approach uses mathematical programming techniques to estimate "best practice" frontiers as the "real" frontier is typically unknown. The Data Envelopment Analysis (DEA) technique, popularised by Charnes *et al.* (1978), has been the most commonly used non-parametric method in empirical studies. DEA involves the calculation of efficiency by constructing a piecewise frontier surface (which represents efficient operations) using linear programming applied to the input-output vectors of a sample of firms. Efficiency is then measured as the distance that each inefficient firm lies below this frontier. DEA efficiency scores are normally measured using an input-oriented approach (i.e., reducing inputs while maintaining a particular level of outputs), or an output-oriented approach (i.e., expanding outputs while using the same level of inputs) or non-orientation (i.e. both output expansion and input reduction).

This section briefly describes the DEA technique, as presented in Coelli *et al.* (2005). We use the notation X to represent the $K \times N$ matrix of inputs, consisting of $K = \{1,2,...,k\}$ inputs from $N = \{1,2,...,n\}$ firms; Y denotes the $M \times N$ matrix of outputs, consisting of $M = \{1,2,...,m\}$ outputs from $N = \{1,2,...,n\}$ firms. The input-oriented constant returns to scale (CRS) DEA frontier is defined by solutions to N linear programs:

$$Min_{\rho, \lambda} \; \theta,$$

$$subject \; to:$$

$$-y_i + Y\lambda \geq 0,$$

$$x_i \theta - X\lambda \geq 0,$$

$$\lambda \geq 0,$$

(1)

where λ is a $N \times 1$ vector of weights, $0 \leq \theta \leq 1$ represents the technical efficiency (TE) score, and $1-\theta$ is the proportional reduction in inputs that could be achieved by the *i-th* firm to produce the given level of output.

Similarly, the output-oriented CRS DEA frontier is defined as follows:

$$Max_{\phi, \lambda} \; \phi,$$

$$subject \; to:$$

$$-y_i\phi + Y\lambda \geq 0,$$

$$x_i - X\lambda \geq 0,$$

$$\lambda \geq 0,$$

(2)

where $0 \leq \phi \leq \infty$, $1/\phi$ represents the TE score, and ϕ-1 is the proportional expansion in outputs that could be produced using the given level of inputs. Other parameters are defined as previously.

The CRS frontier assumes that all firms operate at their most productive scale (Coelli *et al.*, 2005). This assumption is relaxed in the variable returns to scale (VRS) model by adding the convexity constraint $N1'\lambda = 1$ (where $N1$ is the $N \times 1$ vector of ones) to the above linear programming problems. Therefore, by comparing TE scores under the CRS and VRS frontiers, one can decompose the TE under the CRS frontier into TE_{VRS} or "pure" technical efficiency and scale efficiency (i.e., $TE_{CRS} = TE_{VRS} \times$ Scale efficiency). In this setting, TE_{CRS}, TE_{VRS} and scale efficiency vary between zero and one.

In order to determine whether the firm operates at increasing or decreasing returns to scale, the non-increasing return to scale (NIRS) frontier is constructed by adding the constraint $N1'\lambda \leq 1$ to the CRS linear programming problem. This constraint ensures a firm is not benchmarked against smaller firms, but can be benchmarked against substantially larger ones. If the TE score of a firm under a VRS frontier does not equal the NIRS TE score, it operates under increasing returns to scale (IRS), while the firm operates at decreasing returns to scale (DRS) if its TE scores under the two frontiers are equal.

One advantage of the DEA technique is that it can provide information about peers of each inefficient firm (peers are those firms with similar input and output mixes to the inefficient firm, but located on the frontier). This peer information is very useful for managerial purposes as managers can improve the efficiency of their institutions by learning from their efficient peers. The main drawback of DEA (and other non-parametric techniques) is that it assumes that there is no random noise in the data.

The Parametric Approach

a) Single Output Production Functions

The parametric approach uses econometric techniques to construct the production frontier. One generally needs to specify distributional forms for the inefficiency error term and a functional form for the parametric production frontier. The inefficiency error component is often assumed to have a half-normal distribution, but this distribution can be criticised on the basis that it implicitly assumes that the modal outcome is the full efficiency. Other more general distributional forms, such as a *gamma* distribution (Yuengert, 1993) or a truncated normal distribution (Berger and DeYoung, 1997) have been tried, but revealed little difference compared to the results obtained from the half-normal distribution.

Parametric frontier productions were first used in efficiency measurement by Aigner and Chu (1968) with a deterministic specification as presented in equation (3), where y_i denotes output, x_{ki} denotes the *k-th* input, and u_i represents the inefficiency component of the *i-th* firm (i=1,2,...,N).

$$\ln y_i = \alpha_0 + \sum_{k=1}^{K} \alpha_k \ln x_{ki} - u_i$$

(3)

The technical efficiency of an i-th firm is defined as the ratio of the observed output to its potential output.

$$TE_i = \frac{y_i}{\exp(x_i \beta)}$$

(4)

where the potential output level, $\exp(x_i\beta)$, is estimated by solving the problem of minimising $\sum_{i=1}^{N} u_i$, subject to the constraint $u_i \geq 0$ (i=1,2,...,N). This model was also estimated by other techniques such as maximum likelihood (Afriat, 1972) and corrected least squares (COLS) (Richmond, 1974), which is basically the ordinary least squares (OLS) estimate adjusted up so that estimated frontiers envelop all observations. However, the model of Aigner and Chu (1968) did not take into account noise and measurement errors. This motivated the development of the stochastic frontier analysis (SFA) technique, which has the ability to include random errors. A SFA may be defined as:

$$\ln y_i = \alpha_{0i} + \sum_{k=1}^{K} \alpha_{ki} \ln x_{ki} + v_i - u_i$$

(5)

where y_i and x_{ki} are as defined above; u_i represents the strictly non-negative vector, representing the inefficiency component with a pre-assumed distributional form, such as half normal, truncated normal or exponential; and v_i is a random error, which is generally assumed to be normally distributed.

The technical efficiency of the *i-th* firm can be estimated using the following conditional expectation:

$$TE_i = E[\exp(-u_i) \,|\, (v_i - u_i)]$$

(6)

The two common functional forms used in SFA studies are the Cobb-Douglas and translog, which is quadratic in logs. The Cobb-Douglas functional form is generally less demanding to both estimate and interpret. In addition, it requires fewer parameters, which is useful for applications with a modest number of observations. The main disadvantage of the Cobb-Douglas functional form is that it assumed implicitly that all firms have the same production elasticities and that the elasticity of substitution between inputs equals one. The translog functional form is less restrictive on production and substitution elasticities but it is more difficult to interpret and involves the estimation of many parameters, which make it inconvenient for applications with few observations (Coelli and Perelman, 1999).

Attempts to weaken the distributional assumptions in the SFA approach were proposed in the distribution free analysis (DFA) method (Berger, 1993) and thick frontier analysis (TFA) method (Berg and Kim, 1994). The DFA method makes no assumption on the distributional form of either the error term or the inefficiency component. However, it requires access to panel data and assumes that the error component has a zero mean and that the inefficiency component is stable over time. The efficiency level of each firm is estimated as the difference between its average residual and that of the firm on the frontier. One disadvantage of the DFA method is that when efficiency is not stable (e.g., shifting over time due to technical changes or other factors), the difference between average residuals of any firm on the frontier does not represent the efficiency of that firm at any one point in time.

The TFA method also assumes no distributional form of the random error and the inefficiency component. Instead, it assumes that randomness is represented by deviation "within" the lowest and highest quartile performance values, whilst the inefficiency component is represented by the difference "between" these quartiles. With this method, best-practice firms do not necessarily lie on the frontier but are close to the frontier. Therefore, the TFA method reduces the effects of outliers but it provides only estimates of the overall efficiency instead of point estimates of efficiency for individual firms.

Although the DFA and TFA approaches do not require assumptions about distributions for the inefficient and noise components, they require new assumptions such as that the efficiency level of a firm remained constant overtime (DFA), or that the efficiency level varies within the first and the third quartiles of the residuals (TFA), both of which may be arguable. In addition, the DFA and TFA approaches require the availability of panel data, which is very rare in the world microfinance industry; no such data exist in Vietnam, to the best of our knowledge; therefore these techniques are beyond the scope of this study.

b)   Multiple Output Industries and Distance Functions

The estimation of production frontiers using parametric approaches becomes more complex in multiple output industries, especially when the aggregation of outputs is not possible. For example, the main outputs of the microfinance industry are number of clients and loans volumes, which are both important and are difficult to aggregate. One can measure the efficiency of multiple output firms using cost or profit functions, where efficiency is measured as the ratio of observed costs and minimised costs (if the cost function is used), or the ratio of observed profits over maximised profits (if the profit function is used). However, the estimation of cost and profit functions requires assumptions of cost minimisation or profit maximisation, which may not be relevant behaviour for public and not-for-profit services such as microfinance. Fortunately, this multi-output issue can be solved using the distance function concept, pioneered by Shephard (1953). Distance functions can be specified with an input-oriented or output-oriented approach. Input distance functions, given the output vector, focus on minimal proportional contraction of the input vector, while output distance functions, given an input vector, seek a maximal proportional expansion of the output vector.

To define the distance functions one must first define the production technology. Based on the notations described in Coelli *et al.* (2005), we define $x \in \mathbf{R}_+^K$ as a vector of inputs, $y \in \mathbf{R}_+^M$ as a vector of output, and the production technology T as:

$$T = \{(x, y) : x \text{ can produce } y\}$$

(7)

Some assumptions are made with the production technology T as follows:

- T is closed and convex;

- Inputs and outputs are strongly disposable: if $(x,y) \in T$ and $(x^*, -y^*) \geq (x, -y)$, then $(x^*, y^*) \in T$;[1]

- Inaction is possible: $(x, 0) \in T$;

- There is no free lunch: $(0, y : y > 0) \notin T$; and

- Unlimited quantity of output cannot be produced: $P(x) = \{y : (x, y) \in T\}$ is bounded from above.

Using these notations, input and output distance functions, respectively, are:[2]

$$D_i(x, y) = \underset{\delta}{Sup} \{\delta > 0 : (x / \delta, y) \in T\}$$

(8)

and

$$D_o(x, y) = \underset{\theta}{Inf} \{\theta > 0, (x, y / \theta) \in T\}$$

(9)

Some properties of distance functions follow directly from assumptions of the production technology T:

1) $D_i(x, y) \geq 1 \Leftrightarrow (x, y) \in T$; and it is linearly homogeneous in x;

2) $D_o(x, y) \leq 1 \Leftrightarrow (x, y) \in T$; and it is linearly homogeneous in y;

3)   Distance functions are non-decreasing in x and y; and

4)   Distance functions equal one if the firm is located on the efficient frontier.

Duality theorems presented in Diewert (1992) and Chambers *et al.* (1998) show that, under certain conditions, output distance functions are equivalent to the cost or profit functions, which are commonly used in efficiency studies in the banking sector. The advantage of distance functions is that they do not need price

---

[1] An alternative assumption is "weak disposability" of inputs and outputs, in which ">" is used instead of "≥". Since x, x^*, y and y^* are vectors, the notation "≥" between two vectors means that all elements on one vector are greater than or equal to the corresponding elements of the other vector with at least one strict inequality.

[2] "*Sup*" stands for "*Supremum*" to allow the case when a maximum does not exist (i.e., $\delta = +\infty$) and "*Inf*" stands for "*Infimum*" to allow the case when a minimum does not exist (i.e., $\theta = +\infty$).

information, and hence, avoid possible issues of price endogeneity or a lack of price information.

The concept of distance functions was further developed into various branches such as the gauge function proposed by McFadden (1978) and directional distance functions, proposed by Chambers *et al.* (1996; 1998). The McFadden gauge function measures the largest radial expansion of a netput vector, which can be specified as:

$$H(-x, y) = \underset{\theta}{Inf} \{\theta > 0 : (-x/\theta, y/\theta) \in T\}.$$

Directional distance functions measure the amount that one can translate the input and output vectors from the current position to the technology frontier in pre-assigned directions $(g^y \in \mathbf{R}_+^M, g^x \in \mathbf{R}_+^K)$, and can be defined as

$$\vec{D}(x, y, g^x, g^y) = \underset{\theta}{Sup} \{\theta : (x - \theta g^x, y + \theta g^y) \in T\}.$$

However, this study will focus on discussing Shephard distance functions since the netput expansion concept presented in gauge functions, which is similar to the profit efficiency concept, may not apply in the microfinance sector. The pre-assigned direction of inputs and outputs in this industry is also difficult due to its multiple objective nature (i.e., the choice of the direction may vary according to different objectives). In addition, by using non-radial contraction of inputs or expansion of outputs, directional distance functions do not have the ability to decompose the overall efficiency into useful managerial concepts of technical and allocative efficiency.

As mentioned previously, there are two functional forms commonly used to represent productions: Cobb-Douglas and translog. A translog input distance function for the case of K inputs and M outputs is specified as:

$$\ln D_{Ii} = \alpha_0 + \sum_{m=1}^{M} \alpha_m \ln y_{mi} + 0.5 \sum_{m=1}^{M} \sum_{n=1}^{M} \alpha_{mn} \ln y_{mi} \ln y_{ni}$$

$$+ \sum_{k=1}^{K} \beta_k \ln x_{ki} + 0.5 \sum_{k=1}^{K} \sum_{l=1}^{K} \beta_{kl} \ln x_{ki} \ln x_{li} + \sum_{k=1}^{K} \sum_{m=1}^{M} \delta_{km} \ln x_{ki} \ln y_{mi}$$

$$i = 1, 2, ..., N,$$

(10)

where *i* denotes the *i-th* firm in the sample and D_{Ii} represents an input distance. The required restrictions for homogeneity of degree +1 in inputs are:

$$\sum_{k=1}^{K} \beta_k = 1$$

$$\sum_{l=1}^{K} \beta_{kl} = 0, \quad k = 1, 2, ..., K$$

$$\sum_{k=1}^{K} \delta_{km} = 0, \quad m = 1, 2, ..., M$$

(11)

and the required restrictions for symmetry are

$$\alpha_{mn} = \alpha_{nm}, \ m,n = 1,2,....M$$
$$\beta_{kl} = \beta_{lk}, \ k,l = 1,2,....K$$

(12)

Distance functions can be used in efficiency measurement under parametric (e.g., SFA), non-parametric (e.g., DEA) and combined approaches (Coelli and Perelman, 1999). Some of these techniques are presented below (we focus on presenting the input-oriented approach because the output oriented approach is conducted analogously).

b1) Stochastic Frontier Analysis (SFA)

The application of the SFA technique to distance functions is conducted by introducing a random error component to the distance functions as in equation (10). In addition, the homogeneity of degree one in an input distance function specified in equation (11) is used to transform it to a relevant format that can be estimated using the SFA method. Recall that a function of homogeneity of degree ω is presented as:

$$D_i(\omega x, y) = \omega D_i(x, y) \text{ for all } \omega > 0$$

(13)

Thus, if we choose one input arbitrarily (e.g., the *k-th*) and replace $\omega = 1/x_K$, this will result in:

$$D_i(x/x_K, y) = D_i(x, y)/x_K$$

(14)

Representing the right hand side of the translog input distance function as represented in equation (10) by a brief format of *TL(x,y)*, we have:

$$\ln(D_i / x_{Ki}) = TL(x_i / x_{Ki}, y_i)$$

or

$$-\ln(x_{Ki}) = TL(x_i / x_{Ki}, y_i) - \ln(D_i)$$

(15)

With the introduction of the random error ε_i, the transformed translog input-oriented distance function in the final form of equation (15) becomes:

$$-\ln(x_{Ki}) = TL(x_i / x_{Ki}, y_i) - \ln(D_i) + \varepsilon_i$$

(16)

It is shown that the equation (16) can be estimated by the SFA method with the composite error term including a non-negative component $-\ln(D_i)$, representing efficiency, and a random error ε_i.

b2) Corrected Ordinary Least Squared (COLS)

The COLS method was proposed by Greene (1980), while its application to distance functions was introduced later by Lovell *et al.* (1994) and Grosskopf *et al.* (1997). This method applied OLS to the transformed distance function using the homogeneity of degree one characteristics as presented in equation (15). In addition, the largest positive residual is added to the intercept, making the frontier envelops all the data points. The inefficiency of each firm is calculated as the distance between observed data and its radial expansion to the frontier.

b3) Parametric Linear Programming (PLP)

The PLP technique was proposed by Aigner and Chu (1968) with single-output deterministic Cobb-Douglas production functions. The technique was expanded to translog output distance functions by Fare *et al.* (1993). Coelli and Perelman (1999) argued that the translog was less restrictive on elasticity of substitution and scale properties, and hence preferable to the Cobb-Douglas functional form. Applying the PLP technique to an input-oriented translog distance function specified in equation (10) requires the solving of the following linear programming problem:

$$\min \sum_{i=1}^{N} \ln D_{Ii}$$

$$Subject\ to:$$

$$\ln(D_{Ii}) \geq 0, \quad i = 1, 2, ...N$$

(17)

plus the homogeneity and the symmetry constraints in equations (11) and (12).

In summary, there are several methods for efficiency analysis using the production frontier approach. A number of the above-mentioned methods have been applied widely in the banking industry while only a few studies were conducted in the microfinance sectors. More details of efficiency studies in financial institutions are presented in the next section.

A Review of Efficiency Studies of Financial Institutions

Microfinance institutions offer services (e.g., credit, savings and insurance) similar to those of other types of financial institutions such as commercial banks and credit unions. However, there is a sharp contrast in the number of efficiency studies in microfinance versus other types of financial institutions: for example, while the amount of research on financial institutions is very large, there are only a handful of studies on microfinance efficiency. Therefore, it is useful to review efficiency measurement studies on commercial banks and credit unions in addition to studies on microfinance institutions, with the view to applying relevant lessons to the microfinance sector.

Commercial Banks

A comprehensive review of efficiency measurement studies in financial institutions provided by Berger and Humphrey (1997) found 130 banking studies conducted mainly in the 1990s. The authors also revealed relatively equal proportions of non-parametric and parametric methods used, dominated by DEA and SFA techniques, respectively.[3] In addition, the authors found that non-parametric methods have lower average efficiency scores than those of parametric estimates. Random noise in data may contribute to this difference. The relationship between results obtained from parametric and non-parametric techniques revealed generally weak correlation, although the correlation is much stronger when comparing results obtained from the different techniques within each category.

One of the earliest studies of efficiency measurement in the banking sector is that of Sherman and Gold (1985), who applied the DEA method to measure the efficiency of 14 bank branches. The authors emphasised the advantage of DEA compared with the traditional accounting standard in measuring efficiency of multiple-input, multiple-output industries. They described two approaches in classifying outputs in the banking sectors: production and intermediation. The production approach considers financial institutions as the producers of services to their clients. The intermediation approach argues that financial institutions play the role of intermediating funds between savers and borrowers. The authors argued that the production approach provides more useful information to the operations of banks in their study.

Within the above two approaches in banking efficiency studies, one of the most controversial issues is the classification of deposits, which arguably has the characteristics of both inputs and outputs. For example, deposits can be classified as an output if the production approach is used (i.e., deposits are the result of saving services) but it is considered an input if the intermediation approach is selected (i.e. deposits are part of input funds). To overcome this issue, Hunter and Timme (1995) and Berger et al. (1997) analysed two separate models and compared their respective efficiency measures. They found a strong correlation between the efficiency scores evaluated by the two approaches. However, the efficiency scores were higher when deposits were classified as an output, which is not surprising because, ceteris paribus, the production approach will result in a larger amount of outputs and less input quantity (i.e., deposits are shifted from the input side to the output side when moving from the intermediation to the production approach). In addition, the banking sector may have the dual roles of both producers of services and intermediators between savers and borrowers. Therefore, some studies such as Berger and Humphrey (1991) and Bauer et al.

---

[3] Among 69 non-parametric studies surveyed, 62 applied DEA, five applied free disposable hull (FDH), one used the Index Numbers (IN) method, and one study used the Mixed Optimal Strategy (MOS) method. The 60 parametric studies included 24 SFA, 20 DFA and 16 TFA.

(1993) included both characteristics of deposits (i.e., interest paid on deposits are included in inputs while deposit quantity is included in outputs). One arguable point in this choice is that it may take similar amounts of labour to process deposits of different sizes: and therefore the number of deposits accounts may be a better proxy for deposit outputs.

Since the mid-1980s, the number of efficiency studies in the banking sector increased rapidly, making it one of the most popular areas in efficiency measurement research (Tavares, 2002). One point to keep in mind when reviewing efficiency studies is that regional or cross-country comparisons may produce misleading information unless a common frontier is constructed. For example, results from studies reviewed by Berger and Humphrey (1997) showed that the average efficiency scores of commercial banks in the United States (US) and other countries were 79 and 75 per cent, respectively. However, this does not necessarily mean that US banks were more efficient since the average figure for other countries included country-specific studies (i.e., using one frontier for each country). Using a common frontier, Fecher and Pestieau (1993) and Pastor *et al.* (1997) found that US banks were least efficient among the respective set of 11 OECD and 8 developed countries. This is a useful lesson for our study, that a common frontier should be used to compare the efficiency levels of microfinance programs in different regions.

Another useful lesson learnt from banking studies was that it is necessary to check for the robustness of results among different methods and input/output combinations. In addition, it is necessary to use flexible functional forms in the parametric approach and integration of random noise in the non-parametric approach to mitigate their respective limitations. Banking studies that used flexible functional forms include Berger and DeYoung (1997), and Berger and Mester (1997); those employing bootstrap techniques include Ferrier and Hirschberg (1997) and Simar and Wilson (1998).

Credit Unions

Credit unions can be considered a transition between microfinance and commercial financial institutions. Credit unions provide similar financial services as commercial banks but as their roles focus on intermediating between savers and borrowers among members, profit maximisation assumption may not be relevant (Smith *et al.*, 1981). Compared to credit unions, microfinance institutions often have a smaller scale and focus more on rural areas. However, lessons learnt from credit union studies could be useful for microfinance applications.

One of the earliest production frontier studies on credit unions was that of Fried *et al.* (1993; 1996), who applied the FDH method to examine the efficiency of credit unions in the US. The authors argued that credit unions aim to maximise services given their resource constraints, and hence, the production approach to output variable selection was arguably more relevant. They found that credit unions were relatively efficient in providing financial services to their clients, with average scores ranging from 80 to 83 per cent. The relatively high efficiency scores estimated by the FDH were not surprising as this method enveloped the data closer, compared to DEA frontiers. However, some authors are sceptical about the choice of the FDH method in their analysis because there is no strong economic ground to relax the convexity assumption (Thrall, 1999).

In contrast to Fried *et al.* (1993, 1996), Brown and O'Connor (1995) selected the intermediation approach for credit unions, arguing that the market value of outputs may not be higher than that of inputs, and thus the notion of "production" may not be relevant for this industry. They applied a translog cost function to measure the economies of scale of credit unions in Australia. The study found significant evidence of diseconomies of scale for small credit unions (ranked by asset sizes) but no such evidence was found in medium and large credit unions. One possible reason for the diseconomies of scale issue could be the subsidy from host companies in the form of provision of office space and arrangements for payroll deductions. However, the use of cost functions may be questionable because cost-minimising assumptions may conflict with the multiple-objective nature of credit unions.

A recent study conducted by Paxton (2006) considered the dual roles of credit unions as producers of services and intermediators between savers and producers. She applied the DEA technique to 350 non-bank financial institutions in rural Mexico, most of which were credit unions. The author found that the efficiency of credit unions was sensitive to choice of approach. On average, the technical efficiency of credit unions was 58 and 14 per cent under the intermediation and production approaches, respectively. This finding was in contrast to our expectation that the production approach would generate higher efficiency scores, *ceteris paribus*. The possible reason was that her choice of inputs and outputs were not comparable (the intermediation approach involved 3 inputs and 3 outputs while the production approach included only 2 inputs and 2 outputs). Mathematically, the intermediation approach produced higher efficiency scores due to its relatively larger input-output dimension in linear programming. It is also possible that the low efficiency scores in this study were due to the use of a single frontier for different types of financial institutions. Because of issues such as information asymmetry, efficient financial institutions may not wish to provide their services to some segments of the population, leaving room for those having an informational advantage to sell their 'inefficient" services; therefore using a separate frontier for each type of financial institution may result in higher efficiency scores.

Microfinance

The measurement of efficiency using production frontiers is still quite rare in microfinance. To date, there has been only a handful of efficiency studies in the microfinance sector, including a study of the Grameen Bank by Hassan and Tufte (2001) and two international studies by Gutierrez-Nieto *et al.* (2006; 2007).

Hassan and Tufte (2001) applied a Cobb-Douglas stochastic cost function to estimate the cost efficiency of the Grameen Bank and then used Tobit regressions in the second stage to identify determinants of the efficiency. They used the production approach, which defines microfinance as a process that uses standard inputs such as labour and capital to produce outputs such as number of loans and number of clients. In particular, the three output variables used in their study were the numbers of loans, savings volumes, and the number of members, and the two input variables were labour and capital. The study found that most of the 186 branches of the Grameen Banks in the 1989–1991 period were highly efficient, with average technical efficiency scores varying from 94 to 97 per cent. Determinants of cost efficiency were investigated using second-stage regressions with regressors including infrastructure (electricity, road, and density of banks and schools) and characteristics of MFIs (age of institutions, asset values, and sex of target clientele). The study found that female-only branches were more efficient than male-only and mixed branches. As one may expect, branches located in areas with good infrastructure are more efficient than branches located in remote areas. Education for members significantly affects the efficiency of a branch because it allows members to have more control over their own transactions. The age and size of a branch have insignificant influences on its cost efficiency. The cost minimisation assumption used in Hassan and Tuft (2001) may not reflect the multiple objectives of microfinance, especially the social objective of serving the poor. As forcefully argued by Pestieau and Tulkens (1994), assessing and explaining the performance of multiple-objective institutions is more complex, and production frontier techniques are generally a more adequate choice for use in measuring the performance of such organisations.

Gutierrez-Nieto *et al.* (2007) used DEA in combination with the principal component analysis (PCA) technique to measure the efficiency of 124 MFIs from around the world. The production approach was selected as the authors argued that deposit service, the main component of the intermediation approach, plays minor roles in MFIs studied. Their DEA model included two inputs, namely labour and operating expenses; and three outputs, namely interest rate income, loan volume and the number of loans. They also conducted DEA models with all combinations of inputs and outputs to check the robustness of the main results. The determinants of the efficiency of microfinance institutions were analysed using PCA with all DEA models. The results revealed that location and type of MFIs are the main components affecting the efficiency levels of MFIs. An arguable point in the study by Gutierrez-Nieto *et al.* (2007) is their use of all possible combinations of the selected two inputs and three outputs, in which many combinations were formed by just one input and one output; thus the use of the DEA method will provide limited additional benefit relative to accounting ratios, other than adjusting for scale.

Gutierrez-Nieto *et al.* (2006) expanded their data to 430 MFIs and used separate models for financial and social objectives. The two models shared three inputs (total assets, operating costs, and number of employees) but used a different set of outputs. The two outputs for the social objective model included the number of women borrowers and the number of poor clients, while the two outputs for the financial objective model included the total loan volume and the financial revenue. Although the authors revealed that most MFIs were efficient in both aspects, the use of separate models for each objective weakens the main advantage of DEA in benchmarking multiple-objective production units.

Gutierrez-Nieto *et al.* (2006) also tried two specifications using one output (either number of women clients, or number of poor clients) and the same set of three inputs. They found a high correlation between efficiency scores of the two models, which suggests that MFIs that efficiently serve women also have positive contribution to poverty reduction. The authors found no clear relationship between the age of MFIs and their social efficiency level, which is against the expectation of the conceptual model proposed in Chapter 3 of this study that mature MFIs could be more efficient in serving the poor.

In summary, efficiency studies using the production frontier approach were widely applied in the banking sector whilst such studies in credit unions and microfinance limited. An important factor in efficiency measurement of financial institutions was the choice of production or intermediation approaches, which was often made on a case-by-case basis. The characteristic of microfinance is to deliver financial services on a small scale to the poor rather than maximising financial transactions between all savers and borrowers; hence the production approach is arguably more relevant than the intermediation approach. In addition, methods involving behavioural assumptions such as profit maximisation may not be relevant to the not-for-profit nature of credit unions or microfinance programs.

Empirical Analysis

The descriptive statistics of the main variables from the institutional survey, presented in Table #1, show that the operational scale varies greatly among NMPs surveyed due to a large variation in key variables, such as number of members, and loans and saving volumes. The loan interest rates and saving interest rates do not vary greatly across schemes. On average, the loan interest rate is 1.28 per cent per month, which is higher than the interest rate charged by the VBP at 0.6 per cent per month. However, compared with the interest rate charged by local moneylenders (which varies from two to five per cent per month), the interest rates charged by NMPs were reasonable.

Table 1. Descriptive Statistics

Variable	Unit	Median	Mean	Std. Dev.	Min	Max
Groups	Numbers	89	381.84	710.52	5	3900
Members	Persons	776	2413.77	3707.72	68	19508
Borrowers	Persons	681	2259.11	3663.22	48	19608
Savers	Persons	660	2337.77	3732.83	18	19508
Loan interest rate	% per month	1.2	1.28	0.22	0.8	1.7
Deposit interest rate	% per month	0.6	0.61	0.13	0.4	0.85
Outstanding loans	VND'000	673000	2.06E+06	3.43E+06	31000	2.00E+07
Saving volume	VND'000	48697.5	445782.11	1.05E+06	2225	6.35E+06
Income	VND'000	108720	335296.29	596547.02	5580	3.60E+06
Interest cost	VND'000	2947.39	36455.66	92120.54	172.68	571206
Other financial cost	VND'000	9540	10368.68	6503.92	382	35000
Wages	VND'000	127200	151658.2	106028.78	40800	564000
Other operating cost	VND'000	14550	10528.74	6408.92	130	22846
Head quarter staff	Persons	3	2.82	1.69	1	9
Local staff	Persons	8	20.91	37.75	2	220
Year in operations	Years	7	6.61	2.92	1	12
Poorest areas	1=yes, 0=no	0.5	0.5	0.51	0	1
Car accessibility	1=yes, 0=no	1	0.89	0.32	0	1
Electricity	1=yes, 0=no	1	0.82	0.39	0	1
Distance to township	Km	5	6.33	4.28	0	16.75
Northern regions	1=yes, 0=no	1	0.61	0.49	0	1
Ethnic minority	1=yes, 0=no	0.00	0.39	0.40	0.00	1.00
Sustainability objectives	1=yes, 0=no	0.00	0.32	0.47	0.00	1.00
Max loan size	VND'000	2000	2819	3042	500	15000
Repeating clients	Per cent	95.00	75.10	37.19	0.00	100.00

Note: Unless otherwise specified, all results in this chapter are own calculations from the survey data

Cost and income information shows that wage costs are almost three quarters of total costs. Interest costs contribute only a minor proportion of the total costs because most loan funds are supplied by donors with no interest. Information on staff numbers is provided; however, this information is questionable in many cases because some microfinance workers also have another full-time job and hence are unlikely to work full time on microfinance activities. For example, most local staff of NMPs are also staff of the Women's Union; therefore, they only receive bonuses from NMPs as additional income from their main jobs. The variation in the number of groups reflects the fact that NMPs operating in remote regions tend to have smaller group sizes than those operating in densely populated areas.

Input-Output Choice

As mentioned previously there are two common approaches used in efficiency measurement of financial institutions, namely, the production approach and the intermediation approach. We follow the production approach, essentially because it is a more appropriate choice to make in the case of microfinance as the focus is more on providing a service to a large number of poor people, rather than trying to negotiate large loans with rich clients. In addition, the production approach considers deposits as an output since deposits are a product of the savings mobilisation activities (in the intermediation approach it is considered as an input since deposits are part of the loanable fund). Also, the intermediation approach considered volume of transactions (e.g., volumes of savings and loans) as outputs, which may create a downward bias for the efficiency of some NMPs that focus on serving smaller transactions. Since it takes a similar amount of time and resources to process small transactions as to process larger transactions, those serving small transactions look less efficient if the volume of transaction is selected as outputs.

Despite considerable time and effort, the dataset from the institutional survey still suffers from incomplete data on several important variables, such as subsidies received and depreciation on fixed assets. Some financial inputs, such as bad debts, contained many zero values, as NMPs have no bad debt and these zero-value input variables can cause computation problems in the DEA method. In addition, there is a very high correlation between the number of clients and the number of female clients, and between the number of savers and the number of frequent savers, so that it may not provide additional benefits to estimate different models with alternative choices between these variables. The final choice of variables for this study, therefore, includes two inputs, namely labour costs and non-labour costs, and three outputs, including number of savers, number of borrowers and number of groups (see Table #2). Labour cost is selected as an input instead of number of employees because it accounts for possible differences in labour quality across schemes and mitigates the difficulties of taking into account part-time labour.[4]

Among the three selected outputs, the number of groups is included in an attempt to accommodate the social objective of microfinance: to reach the poor who are often located in isolated villages in difficult terrain. In these remote areas it is more difficult for microfinance members to travel to attend regular group meetings. Hence, the number of groups tends to be greater in schemes that operate in remote areas (compared with schemes having the same numbers of clients operating in more convenient locations).

The environmental factors that may explain efficiency differences include age of the program and characteristics of the village, including poverty status, availability of grid electricity, accessibility by car, distance to town, and the dummy variable for the North region. It is expected that the age of NMPs would

---

[4] The use of this labour cost variable includes an implicit assumption that wage rates do not differ significantly across regions, which would be a reasonable assumption.

have a positive effect on efficiency levels as the high set-up cost has diminished and the savings revenue would rise as they reach more clients. More importantly, it is expected that together with the passage of time, the proportion of members deposits to total loanable funds would increase, which would create a greater feeling of ownership in NMPs, and hence, could contribute to improvements in efficiency, as suggested by the quotation of Milton Friedman stated in the beginning of this chapter.

Table 2. Variables selected and their definitions

	Names	Definitions	Units
Inputs	Labour costs (X1)	Wages for head-quarters staff, and allowances for local staff.	VND'000
	Non-labour costs (X2)	All other operational and financial costs, measured in thousands of VND.	VND'000
Outputs	Borrowers (Y1)	Total number of clients, who borrowed from NMPs at least once in the survey period.	Persons
	Savers (Y2)	Total number of members deposited voluntary and/or compulsory savings at least once in the survey period.	Persons
	Groups (Y3)	Total groups available at the NMPs.	Groups
Environments and characteristics	Age of NMPs	Time since NMPs have operated officially to the time the survey was conducted.	Years
	Poor areas	If the areas are in the Government's list of poorest areas.	Yes/No
	Electricity	If the areas are connected to the national electricity network.	Yes/No
	Car accessibility	If the project areas of the NMPs can be accessed by cars.	Yes/No
	Distance to town	The distance from the project areas to the district capital.	Km
	Ethnic minority clients	If the project serves clients of ethnic minority groups.	Yes/No
	Financial sustainability	A dummy variable representing if obtaining financial sustainability is one of the objectives of the programs.	Yes/No
	Repeating borrowers	The per centage of members who borrowed more than once in the last 12 months.	Per cent
	Max loan size	The maximum amount that a member can borrow.	VND'000

Regarding the environmental variables, it is expected that NMPs operating in more favourable conditions, such as access to electricity, good roads and proximity to townships (i.e., district capitals), will be more efficient as convenient locations and infrastructure would help to reduce transaction costs. The expected sign of the regional dummy parameter would be ambiguous since NGOs operating in these regions often have similar selection criteria for project sites, such as poor, remote areas with limited access to formal financial services (one NGO can have projects in both regions). The reason to include this dummy is to test if other regional characteristics (culture characteristics, government policies) affect the performance of microfinance.

Results and Discussions

This section presents our results on the efficiency analysis of NMPs surveyed using the DEA technique and second stage analysis on efficiency determinants. In addition, there is a sensitivity analysis using alternative estimation techniques, choices of data and treatment for sample variability. In general, NMPs surveyed were relatively efficient, recording an average technical efficiency score of 75 per cent, and the results are relatively robust among alternative techniques and input/output combinations.

a) Efficiency Estimates

Results from the DEA models using two inputs (labour and non-labour costs) and three outputs (number of borrowers, number of savers and number of groups) are presented in Table (detailed results for all NMPs are presented in Table A2-1 in Appendix 2).[5] As can be seen, the overall efficiency of the NMPs surveyed was very modest at 20.8 per cent, suggesting that NMPs can improve their performance by 80 per cent. Table also shows that scale inefficiency plays a significant role in the low performance of most NMPs. On average, NMPs surveyed achieved only 29 per cent efficiency with regard to their operational scale. The large gap in the operational scale of NMPs (the largest NMP in the sample serves 20,000 clients while the smallest has only 70 clients), may contribute to an "unrealistic" figure that the least inefficient NMP can improve their scale efficiency by 98.7 per cent (i.e., the minimum scale efficiency is 1.3 per cent). The detailed results show that with the exceptions of NMP No. 2 and No. 21,[6] other programs operate at increasing returns to scale, and hence, can improve performance by expanding operations. This finding is consistent with studies reviewed by Berger and Humphrey (1997) where scale differences often account for very low average efficiency performance of banks and credit unions.

Although there is substantial room for improvement in scale efficiency, it may be difficult for inefficient NMPs to adjust their scale, at least in the short run. Therefore, the technical efficiency measure provides more relevant information for NMPs. Table #.3 shows that the average technical efficiency of NMPs surveyed is 75 per cent; hence on average inefficient NMP can save up to 25 per cent of inputs while being able to produce the existing level of outputs. However, the third quartile of the TE score is very high at 94.6 per cent, suggesting that a number of NMPs operate closely to the efficient frontier. In addition, the first quintile of TE score is 56.8 per cent, which is reasonably close to the central tendency, given that the DEA method does not take into account measurement errors. Therefore, the level of technical competence may not vary considerably among NMPs surveyed. This finding is not surprising because most NMPs surveyed share similar characteristics such as operating in poor, rural areas and often using staff from the local Women's Union.

---

[5] Results of the main DEA model were obtained using the DEA computer Program (DEAP) version 2.1, written by Coelli (1996a).
[6] Because of the confidentiality agreement, we do not disclose names of NMPs associated with their efficiency performance in this book.

Table 3. Efficiency of microfinance programs (main results)

Statistics	Overall efficiency	Technical efficiency	Scale efficiency
Mean	0.208	0.748	0.291
Standard deviation	0.249	0.203	0.301
Minimum	0.013	0.413	0.016
1st quartile	0.057	0.568	0.061
Median	0.112	0.755	0.147
3rd quartile	0.241	0.946	0.458
Maximum	1.000	1.000	1.000

One advantage of the DEA technique is that it can provide information about peers (i.e., those NMPs on the efficient frontier) that an inefficient NMP could learn from to improve its efficiency. The results of this study revealed that five NMPs (No. 2, 5, 9, 21 and 35) are often referred to as peers for inefficient NMPs. Among the five influential players, only NMP No. 2 and No. 21 also achieve scale efficiency. However, it is interesting to note that NMP No. 2 is referred to as a peer only seven times (see Table #.4), while NMPs No. 5 and No. 9, which are relatively smaller scale, were the peer of 30 and 29 inefficient NMPs, respectively. Therefore, it is possible that the input-output combination of NMP No. 2 was not relevant for many inefficient NMPs: NMP No. 21 was the most influential, appearing 38 times as a peer for inefficient NMPs despite it being only 50 per cent the size of NMP No. 2. Therefore, the size of NMP No. 21 and its input-output combination may be most relevant for inefficient NMPs. A closer examination revealed that this influential NMP has been in operation for more than 10 years, and more importantly, the principal aim of its donors was to build a successful demonstration model; hence, its efficiency level at the survey period may be due to the large amount of support it received in the set-up period.

Table 4. The most influential NMPs

NMPs No.	Peer counts	Overall efficiency	Technical efficiency	Scale efficiency
2	7	1.000	1.000	1.000
5	30	0.041	1.000	0.041
9	29	0.016	1.000	0.016
21	38	1.000	1.000	1.000
35	9	0.060	1.000	0.060

b) Second-stage regressions

Factors determining the efficiency of NMPs can be analysed using several methods such as sub-samples, one-stage estimation (i.e. include environmental variable in efficiency estimates), and two-stage estimation (i.e. regress efficiency scores against environmental variables) (Coelli et al., 2005). This study focuses on the two-stage approach but the one-stage estimation is implemented for sensitivity analysis.

Before conducting the second stage analysis, it is necessary to discuss some issues related to this approach. Tobit regressions have been applied widely in second stage analysis because a number of DEA efficiency scores equal one. However, a Monte Carlo experiment by Simar and Wilson (2007, p. 48) showed that estimates from truncated regressions were fairly close to the truth whilst results obtained from Tobit regressions were, according to the authors, "catastrophic". Therefore, truncated regressions are selected for the second stage analysis in this study.

Another concern with the second stage approach is the interdependency of efficiency estimates (i.e., changing the position of one firm in the frontier can cause changes in the efficiency estimates for other firms), and hence, the standard regression approach is irrelevant. This issue can be mitigated using the bootstrap method to construct estimates from a pseudo population. There are a few studies in the literature, particularly Xue and Harker (1999), Hirschberg and Lloyd (2002), Casu and Molyneux (2003) and Simar and Wilson (2007), that have applied this approach. The bootstrap procedure in the first three studies applied a data generating process (DGP) proposed by Xue and Harker (1999), which considered that random noise has a normal distribution.

Table 5. Determinants of efficiency

Variables	Truncated regressions		Tobit regressions	
	Coefficients	z-ratios	Coefficient	z-ratios
Age	-0.054	-1.330	***-0.093	-2.470
Age squared	0.002	0.710	**0.006	2.060
Poorest areas (Y/N)	***-0.257	-3.970	***-0.161	-3.020
Electricity (Y/N)	*0.155	1.650	0.070	1.020
Car accessibility (Y/N)	*-0.201	-1.850	-0.138	-1.610
Town distance (km)	***0.039	3.800	**0.017	2.470
Ethnic minority (Y/M)	**0.150	2.040	*0.114	1.970
Sustainability (Y/N)	*-0.113	-1.810	***-0.158	-2.700
Repeating borrowers	0.001	1.370	*0.002	2.030
Max loan size	-9.2E-06	-0.930	**-2.3E-05	-2.320
Constant	***0.860	5.460	***1.044	7.160

Note: ***, ** and * represent, respectively, 1, 5 and 10 per cent significant level.

We have tried a simulation experiment based on the DGP introduced by Simar and Wilson (2007), which is more relevant to the nature of efficiency scores (i.e., bounded between zero and ones). However, the results of both the single bootstrap procedure (i.e., resampling directly from original efficiency estimates) and the double bootstrap procedure (i.e. efficiency estimates were corrected using the bootstrap procedure in Simar and Wilson (1998)[7] before bootstrapping the second stage estimates) do not generate significant estimates. In addition, we observed that the results from Tobit regressions provide consistent estimates as

---

[7] The DGP of this bootstrap procedure will be discussed in Section 5.4.3.2, where various means of sensitivity analyses for efficiency estimates are presented.

compared to the truncated regression. Therefore, we do not report the bootstrap results of second-stage regressions as they are the subject of further investigation. As can be seen in column 1 of Table , both age and age-squared received unexpected signs, which suggested that NMPs can be less efficient as they become more mature; however, this reduction in efficiency over time may be plausible. From a practical viewpoint, NMPs often lack a funding capacity to meet the increasing credit demand of clients, and so they kept providing small loan sizes. As clients become wealthier, they may leave microfinance programs to seek larger loans from commercial financial institutions, thanks to their now improved financial knowledge and experience. In the meantime, the NMPs seek new clients, who may not have the equivalent confidence and capacity to make use of microfinance services. Even when new clients are not vulnerable, the theory on information asymmetry suggests that the peer-monitoring system becomes weaker when demand for funds become more satisfied (i.e., if members can easily switch to other institutions, borrowers have less incentive to monitor and repay for defaulting members). Economic theory also suggests that, as the level of competition increases (e.g., the arrival of commercial institutions in the microfinance market), NMPs will have to use more resources in order to keep existing clients, as well as serving newer clients. All these factors can lead to the possible decline of efficiency of NMPs.

The sign of the age-squared variable suggests that the marginal effect of technical efficiency increases over time (i.e., becomes less negative). In particular, when the age of a the NMP reaches $0.054/(2*0.002)=13.5$ years the marginal effect becomes zero. One possible factor making this happen is the increase of ownership over time (i.e., the share of members' funds in the total loanable fund increase). Due to the low level of saving mobilisation, the restriction to mobilise saving within members, and the relatively young age of NMPs (less than 12 years), deposits from members were only 30 per cent of the total fund, on average. Therefore, most people still considered microfinance funds were a kind of external gift from NGOs. The weak level of ownership can lead to detrimental effects on efficiency, especially when NGOs hand over microfinance programs to local authorities.

The poor area dummy variable relates to a location in one of the poorest communities in Vietnam. It is expected that this would reduce efficiency levels because these areas are often located in remote areas, and this can lead to higher transaction costs. Both truncated and Tobit regressions confirmed this expectation significantly.

A similar story is shown by the dummy variable for the availability of grid electricity, as both the truncated and Tobit regressions supported the expectation that NMPs in villages with grid electricity are more efficient. However, only results produced by truncated regressions were statistically significant. One possible factor supporting this result is that NMPs operating in areas connected to the grid electricity may be able to apply labour-saving equipments such as computers and fax machines and hence the productivity of services can be higher compared to those operating in other regions.

Three other environmental variables, including car accessibility, distance to township and the dummy variable for members of ethnic minority groups (i.e.

those who are often poor and live in remote areas) also received significant but unexpected estimates. In particular, villages that are accessible by car have low efficiency in their NMPs. In contrast, NMPs are more efficient if they operate in areas further from townships and in areas with ethnic minority groups. These results are not as expected: it was thought that it would be more expensive to deliver financial services with difficult infrastructure and terrain (e.g., far away from township and no car access). Ethnic minority groups (with the exception of the Chinese) often lack essential skills to integrate into mainstream economic activities (Baulch *et al.*, 2002). Therefore, NMPs operating in ethnic minority areas often need to spend more resources supporting activities such as training in numeracy, literacy and production techniques (Che, 2002), which should make them less efficient than others. One possible reason for this counter-intuitive result is that NMPs operating in remote areas, where ethnic minority groups often reside, face less competition from other financial service providers, and hence, they can attract larger number of clients with less effort than those operating in other areas, *ceteris paribus*.

The most important characteristics of NMPs, such as maximum loan size, the attitude towards financial sustainability and the proportion of repeating borrowers, have almost no influence on the efficiency of NMPs as the estimated parameters were very close to zero. This finding, similarly shown by all alternative estimates, may be due to the fact that NMPs in the survey share similar characteristics such as loan size and interest rates. It is also shown that NMPs with financial sustainability objectives are less efficient. One may argue that the sustainability objective drives NMPs to apply tougher screening and monitoring devices to select clients. In addition, NMPs that really care about sustainability would have to spend more resources on recruiting and training independent staff (i.e., not depending on local staff of MOs) and on establishing a sustainable organisation (e.g., transfer NMPs to PCFs) after the termination of their microfinance projects. These effort are time and resource consuming, which could make them appear less efficient in the short-run (recall that NMPs in this study had been in operation for 12 years at most). It is also possible that mature NMPs become less efficient due to the reduction of subsidy from donors after the set-up period.

Conclusions

In this chapter, we have analysed the technical efficiency of microfinance schemes in the north and the central regions of Vietnam using the DEA technique. The study uses the traditional production approach in defining input and output variables for use in analysing the efficiency of NMP surveyed. However, we amended the approach by including an extra variable, the number of groups, to help capture the social aspect of microfinance activities.

DEA results produced an average technical efficiency score of 75 per cent, suggesting that there is scope for efficiency improvements in many of these schemes. In addition, most NMPs surveyed were very inefficient in operational scale but this issue is difficult to address given the limited funding from donors and poor performance on saving mobilisation from members.

A second stage analysis, using truncated and Tobit regressions, revealed that NMPs may be less efficient as they become more mature. It is possible that the departure of capable clients and the arrival of more vulnerable clients may have caused the decline of efficiency among mature NMPs. Other environmental variables (e.g., location and infrastructure) and program characteristics (e.g., maximum loan size and attitude for financial sustainability) confirmed the expectation that NMPs operating in favourable environments are more efficient.

References

Afriat, S. N. 1972. "Efficiency Estimation of Production Functions". *International Economic Review*, 13, 568-598.

Aigner, D. J. and Chu, S. F. 1968. "On Estimating the Industry Production Function". *American Economic Review*, 58, 826-839.

Battese, G. E., and Coelli, T. J. 1995. "A Model for Technical Inefficiency Effects in a Stochastic Frontier Production Function for Panel Data". *Empirical Economics*, 20(2), 325-332.

Bauer, P. W., Berger, A. N., and Humphrey, D. B. 1993. "Efficiency and Productivity Growth of US Banking". In H. O. Fried, C. A. K. Lovell & S. S. Schmidt (Eds.), *The Measurement of Productive Efficiency: Techniques and Applications* (pp. 386-413). Oxford: Oxford University Press.

Baulch, B., Truong, T. K. C., Haughton, D., and Haughton, J. 2002. "Ethnic minority development in Vietnam: a socioeconomic perspective". Policy Research Working Paper No 2836: The World Bank.

Berg, S. A. and Kim, M. (1994). "Oligopolistic Interdependence and the Structure of Production in Banking: An Empirical Evaluation". *Journal of Money, Credit and Banking*, 26(2), 309-322.

Berger, A. N. 1993. ""Distribution Free" Estimates of Efficiency in US Banking Industry and Tests if the Standard Distribution Assumption". *Journal of Productivity Analysis*, 4, 261-292.

Berger, A. N. and DeYoung, R. 1997. "Problem Loans and Cost Efficiency in Commercial Banks". *Journal of Banking and Finance*, 21(6), 849-870.

Berger, A. N. and Humphrey, D. B. 1991. "The Dominance of Inefficiencies over Scale and Product Mix Economies in Banking". *Journal of Monetary Economics*, 28, 117-148.

Berger, A. N., & Humphrey, D. B. (1997). Efficiency of financial institutions: International survey and directions for future research. European Journal of Operational Research, 98(2), 175-212.

Berger, A. N., Leusner, J. H. and Mingo, J. J. 1997. "The Efficiency of Bank Branches". *Journal of Monetary Economics*, 40(1), 141-162.

Berger, A. N. and Mester, L. J. 1997. "Inside the Black Box: What Explains Differences in the Efficiencies of Financial Institutions?". *Journal of Banking and Finance*, 21(7), 895-947.

Brown, R. and O'Connor, I. 1995. "Measurement of Economies of Scale in Victorian Credit Unions". *Australian Journal of Management*, 20(1), 1-24.

Casu, B. and Molyneux, P. 2003. "A comparative study of efficiency in European banking". *Applied Economics*, 35(17), 1865-1876.

Chambers, R. G., Chung, Y. and Fare, R. 1996. "Benefit and Distance Functions". *Journal of Economic Theory*, 70(2), 407-419.

Chambers, R. G., Chung, Y. and Fare, R. 1998. "Profit, Directional Distance Functions, and Nerlovian Efficiency". *Journal of Optimization Theory and Applications*, 98(2), 351-364.

Charnes, A., Cooper, W. W. and Rhodes, E. 1978. "Measuring the efficiency of decision making units". *European Journal of Operational Research*, 2(6), 429-444.

Coelli, T. J. 1996a. "A Guide to DEAP version 2.1: Data Envelopment Analysis (Computer) Program". Working Paper 96/08 Centre for Productivity and Efficiency Analysis, Department of Econometrics, The University of New England, Australia.

Coelli, T. J. 1996b. "A Guide to FRONTIER Version 4.1: A Computer Program for Stochastic Frontier Production and Cost Function Estimation". Working Paper 96/07, Centre for Efficiency and Productivity Analysis, Department of Econometrics, The University of New England, Australia.

Coelli, T. J. and Perelman, S. 1999. "A Comparison of Parametric and Non-parametric Distance Function: With Application to European Railways". *European Journal of Operational Research*, 117, 326-339.

Coelli, T. J. and Perelman, S. 2000. "Technical Efficiency of European Railways: A Distance Function Approach". *Applied Economics*, 32(15), 1967-1976.

Coelli, T. J., Rao, D. S. P., O'Donnell, C. J. and Battese, G. E. 2005. *An Introduction to Efficiency and Productivity Analysis* (2nd ed. ed.). New York: Springer Science.

Diewert, W. E. 1992. "Duality Approaches to Microeconomic Theory". In K. J. Arrow & M. D. Intrilligator (Eds.), *Handbook of Mathematical Economics*, Volume 2 (535-599). Amsterdam: North-Holland.

Fare, R., Grosskopf, S., Lovell, C. A. K. and Yaisawarng, S. 1993. "Derivation of Shadow Prices for Undesirable Outputs: A Distance Function Approach". *The Review of Economics and Statistics*, 75(2), 374-380.

Fecher, F. and Pestieau, P. 1993. "Efficiency and Competition in O.E.C.D. Financial Services". In H. O. Fried, C. A. K. Lovell & S. S. Schmidt (Eds.), The Measurement of Productive Efficiency: Techniques and Applications (pp. 374-385). Oxford: Oxford University Press.

Ferrier, G. D. and Hirschberg, J. G. 1997. "Bootstrapping Confidence Intervals for Linear Programming Efficiency Scores: With an Illustration Using Italian Banking Data". *Journal of Productivity Analysis*, 8(1), 19-33.

Greene, W. H. 1980. "Maximum likelihood estimation of econometric frontier functions". *Journal of Econometrics*, 13, 27-56.

Grosskopf, S., Hayes, K. J., Taylor, L. L. and Weber, W. L. 1997. "Budget-Constrained Frontier Measures of Fiscal Equality and Efficiency in Schooling". *The Review of Economics and Statistics*, 79(1), 116-124.

Gutierrez-Nieto, B., Serrano-Cinca, C. and Mar Molinero, C. 2006. "Social Efficiency in Microfinance Institutions". Working Paper N0. 93, Kent Business School, University of Kent, UK.

Gutierrez-Nieto, B., Serrano-Cinca, C. and Mar Molinero, C. 2007. "Microfinance institutions and efficiency". *Omega: International Journal of Management Science*, 35(2), 131-142.

Hassan, M. K. and Tufte, D. R. 2001. "The X-Efficiency of a Group-Based Lending Institution: The Case of the Grameen Bank". *World Development*, 29(6), 1071-1082.

Hirschberg, J. G. and Lloyd, P. J. 2002. "Does the Technology of Foreign-invested Enterprises Spill over to other Enterprises in China?". In P. J. Lloyd- & X. G. Zang (Eds.), *Modelling the Chinese Economy*. London: Edward Elgar Press.

Hunter, W. C. and Timme, S. G. 1995. "Core Deposits and Physical Capital: A Reexamination of Bank Scale Economies and Efficiency with Quasi-fixed Inputs". *Journal of Money, Credit and Banking*, 27, 165-185.

Lovell, C. A. K., Richardson, S., Travers, P. and Wood, L. L. 1994. "Models and Measurement of Welfare and Inequality". In W. Eichhorn (Ed.), *Resources and Functionings: A New View of Inequality in Australia*. Berlin: Springer.

McFadden, D. 1978. "Cost, Revenue, and Profit Functions". In M. Fuss & D. McFadden (Eds.), *Dual Approach to Theory and Applications*. Amsterdam: North Holland.

Morduch, J. 1999. "The Microfinance Promise". *Journal of Economic Literature*, 37(4), 1569-1614.

Pastor, J., Perez, F. and Quesada, J. 1997. "Efficiency Analysis in Banking Firms: An International Comparison". *European Journal of Operational Research*, 98, 396-408.

Paxton, J. 2006. "Technical Efficiency in the Rural Financial Sector: Evidence from Mexico". *Journal of Developing Areas*, 39(2), 101-119.

Pestieau, P. and Tulkens, H. 1994. "Assessing and Explaining the Performance of Public Enterprises". *Finanz Archiv*, 50(3), 293-323.

Richmond, J. 1974. "Estimating the Efficiency of Production". *International Economic Review*, 15, 515-521.

Shephard, R. W. 1953. *Cost and production functions*. Princeton: Princeton University Press.

Sherman, H. D. and Gold, F. 1985. "Bank branch operating efficiency : Evaluation with Data Envelopment Analysis". *Journal of Banking & Finance*, 9(2), 297-315.

Simar, L. and Wilson, P. W. 1998. "Sensitivity Analysis of Efficiency Scores: How to Bootstrap in Nonparametric Frontier Models". *Management Science*, 44(1), 49-61.

Simar, L. and Wilson, P. W. 2007. "Estimation and inference in two-stage, semi-parametric models of production processes". *Journal of Econometrics*, 136(1), 31-64.

Smith, D. J., Cargill, T. F. and Meyer, R. A. 1981. "An Economic Theory of a Credit Union". *The Journal of Finance*, 36(2), 519-528.

Tavares, G. 2002. "A Bibliography of Data Envelopment Analysis". Working
    paper. Rutgers Center for Operational Research, Rutgers University,
    New Jersey.
Thrall, R. M. 1999. "What Is the Economic Meaning of FDH?". *Journal of
    Productivity Analysis*, 11, 243-250.
Xue, M. and Harker, P. T. 1999. "Overcoming the Inherent Dependency of DEA
    Efficiency Scores: A Bootrap Approach". Working Paper No. 97-17:
    Financial Institution Center, University of Pennsylvania.
Yuengert, A. M. 1993. "The Measurement of Efficiency in Life Insurance:
    Estimates of a Mixed Normal-Gamma Error Model". *Journal of Banking
    and Finance*, 17(2-3), 483-496.

Chapter 16: Educational Centers and Microfinance in India

Anganwadi Centers: An Exploratory Study Suggesting Linkages between Educational Services and Microfinance

Ricardo Lozano

Abstract: Through this study, the potential of providing microfinance services through the already existing, government sponsored, educational centers targeting low-income populations in southern India is explored. During the summer of 2007, 31 Anganwadi centers were observed and workers were interviewed at these centers. Government officials were also interviewed at both, Integrated Child Development Services, and the Tamil Nadu Corporation for Development of Women. Based on Dunford and Rueda's models for the delivery of microfinance and education services combined, this study suggests a bound/linked model in which two independent entities work together for the provision of these services. The study suggests practical ways for the implementation of the model.

Keywords: Education and Microfinance, Education and Development, Economic Development, Anganwadi, Balwadi, Chennai, India

Introduction

Education and Microfinance, particularly in less developed countries, share some similarities. In some contexts, both target low-income populations and focus their efforts on individual development and empowerment. Through time, microfinance institutions have attempted to integrate education into their portfolio of products and services; however, at the time the study was conducted, the researcher was not aware of other studies aiming at providing microfinance services through already existing educational systems.

This chapter explores the potential of delivering microfinance services through the educational programs provided by Integrated Child Development Services (ICDS) in the city of Chennai, state of Tamil Nadu, in southern India. During the summer of 2007, 31 randomly selected centers were observed in Chennai. Interviews were also conducted with the Assistant Director for Training and the Joint Coordinator for Training of ICDS, and also with the Joint Director/Project Officer of the Tamil Nadu Corporation for Development of Women Magalir Thittam Project (branch of the state government responsible for promoting and expanding microfinance services in India).

Inspired by Dunford (2007) and Rueda's (2006) models for the integration of microfinance and education, this chapter suggests the implementation of bound/linked services, with two independent institutions contributing their areas of expertise, as a viable way to deliver microfinance and education services combined.

In the following sections, this chapter provides background and specific information in the areas of (1) education, (2) microfinance, (3) linkages between education and microfinance, and (4) specific recommendations for the implementation of a model linking microfinance services to government sponsored educational programs in India.

Education

Educational Initiatives: From Global to Local

Initiatives promoting the education and development of children have existed for years. Some of them have been promoted by international organizations and are cross-national in their scope. Other initiatives have been promoted by country or state governments with a regional or local focus. At the global level, the United Nations Declaration of the Rights of the Child of 1959 declares that:

> The child is entitled to receive education...which will promote his general culture and enable him, on a basis of equal opportunity, to develop his abilities, his individual judgment, and his sense of moral and social responsibility, and to become a useful member of society...The child shall have full opportunity for play and recreation, which should be directed to the same purposes as education; society and the public authorities shall endeavor to promote enjoyment of this right.

At the national level, the Government of India, in accordance with international initiatives, has mandated, through its Constitution, the provision of mechanisms securing "that children are given opportunities and facilities to develop in a healthy manner, and in conditions of freedom and dignity". Additionally, India has a specific national policy on children which, in 1974, declared children as "supremely important assets". India's National Policy on Children laid the foundation for the Integrated Child Development Services (ICDS) program, introduced in 1975.

India's Integrated Child Development Services

With 40,000 centers nationwide, and providing services to over 4.8 million expectant and nursing women, and over 23 million children under the age of six, ICDS is, according to UNICEF, the largest integrated early childhood program in the world. Its main purpose is to improve the health, nutrition, and development of children. This is accomplished through the distribution of health, nutrition and hygiene education to women, non-formal preschool education to children, supplementary feeding, growth monitoring, and links to primary healthcare services such as immunization and vitamin supplements.

ICDS services are delivered through community-based *anganwadi* centers. As stated above, these centers not only provide services and education for children, but also are places where low-income pregnant and nursing women attend weekly meetings where they receive education and training in health, nutrition and hygiene. In short, the *anganwadi* center provides the meeting ground for women to come together with workers to promote awareness and action for development and empowerment. The centers promote a holistic development on the individual based on the assumption that education, in order to be effective and make a difference in the life of an individual, must be accompanied with services that ensure their health and wellbeing.

ICDS in Chennai

In 1975, 33 experimental ICDS projects (every project running approximately 100 centers) were begun in India. Three of these projects were launched in the southern state of Tamil Nadu; two in rural areas in Dharmapuri and Madurai, and one as an urban project in the city of Chennai. The main deciding factors contributing to the location of these centers in urban Chennai were:

- Heavily populated urban slums
- Migration of rural population into urban settlements
- Problems with overpopulation, poor sanitary conditions, water scarcity, and spread of diseases

By 1997, the number of projects in Chennai had expanded to 12, strategically located so that each served a population of about 100,000. According to the Ministry of Women and Child Development, Tamil Nadu is already fully covered under ICDS. *Anganwadi* centers are ICDS' mechanism for the promotion and distribution of health and educational services to children and pregnant and nursing women. Figure 1 illustrates the organizational structure that makes the delivery of ICDS services possible.

Figure 1: Organizational Structure which Makes the Delivery of ICDS Services Possible.

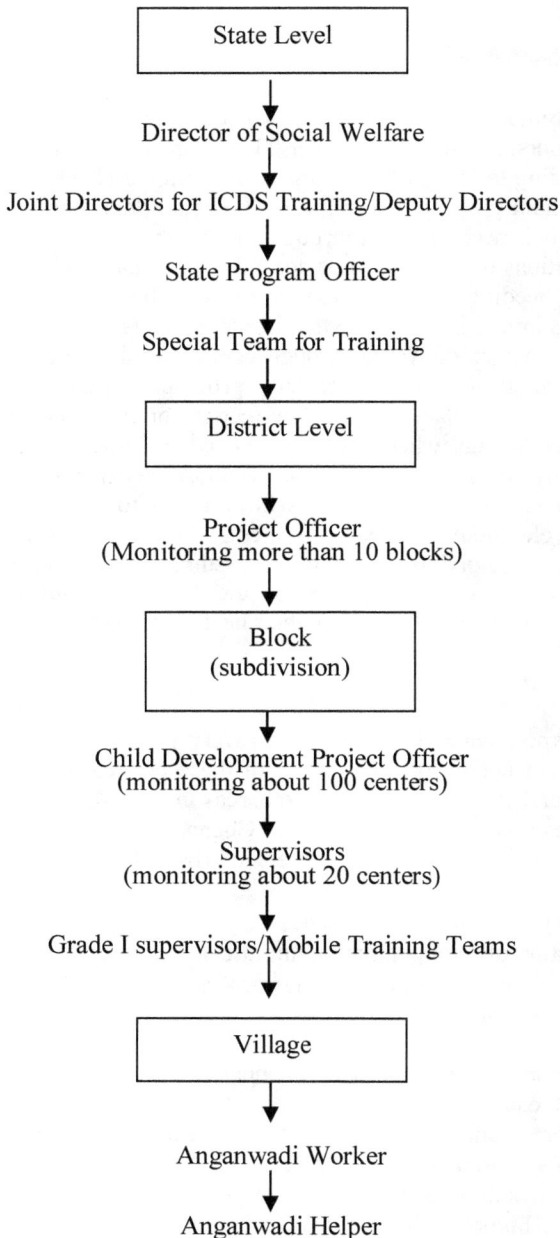

```
                    ┌─────────────────────┐
                    │     State Level     │
                    └─────────────────────┘
                              │
                              ▼
               Director of Social Welfare
                              │
                              ▼
     Joint Directors for ICDS Training/Deputy Directors
                              │
                              ▼
                  State Program Officer
                              │
                              ▼
                Special Team for Training
                              │
                              ▼
                    ┌─────────────────────┐
                    │    District Level   │
                    └─────────────────────┘
                              │
                              ▼
                     Project Officer
              (Monitoring more than 10 blocks)
                              │
                              ▼
                    ┌─────────────────────┐
                    │        Block        │
                    │    (subdivision)    │
                    └─────────────────────┘
                              │
                              ▼
            Child Development Project Officer
                (monitoring about 100 centers)
                              │
                              ▼
                      Supervisors
               (monitoring about 20 centers)
                              │
                              ▼
        Grade I supervisors/Mobile Training Teams
                              │
                              ▼
                    ┌─────────────────────┐
                    │       Village       │
                    └─────────────────────┘
                              │
                              ▼
                  Anganwadi Worker
                              │
                              ▼
                  Anganwadi Helper
```

At the state level, ICDS' structure is as follows: The Director of Social Welfare is responsible for monitoring and coordinating the administrative, logistical, and training efforts that take place throughout the state. These areas (administrative, logistical and training) are led by specialists that conceptualize and develop specific action plans to be implemented.

At the district level, Project Officers monitor approximately 10 blocks (specific sections of the city) with close to 100 centers per block. Every Project Officer oversees the centers through Supervisors that monitor approximately 20 centers each. Among the Supervisors, there are also Grade I Supervisors and Mobile Training Teams that ensure that *anganwadi* Workers and Helpers receive the training needed for the operation of these centers.

Anganwadi workers and helpers are trained through a curriculum initially provided by the federal government. However, states are expected to draw their particular State Training Action Plan (STRAP), which must be approved by the Federal Government before financial support is released. Once the funding is provided by the Federal Government, project trainers train *anganwadi* workers in groups of 25 to 30 (trainers are also trained through regional institutes).

The *anganwadi* worker training consists of on-the-job training during 26 working days, and refresher courses once every 2 years. Trainers also assess needs to be integrated in subsequent sessions. The training addresses specific topics such as management, development of the skills required by the position, integrated management of neonatal child illness, and infant and young child feeding.

Through time, there have been attempts to integrate financial services through *anganwadi* meetings in the form of Women's Working Groups and Mothers' Support Groups. These groups were introduced by the Government of Tamil Nadu in conjunction with the World Bank, but the initiative eventually became extremely complex to manage, and in time, abandoned. At present, ICDS does not promote any type of services, nor training, in the area of microfinance.

Anganwadi centers are managed by a worker and a helper; both women. Essentially, the worker coordinates the entirety of the activities taking place at the center. The responsibilities of a worker are wide-ranging, from teaching children's classes, to keeping attendance and immunization records, home visits, coordinating appointments for hospital visits, and overseeing nutrition/meal plans. The helper is responsible for most of the implementation of the program and the logistics of the center. Her main activities are cooking, serving meals, cleaning, and assisting the worker as needed.

After observing 31 randomly selected *anganwadi* centers in urban Chennai[1], it was concluded that the services provided are very homogeneous throughout the city: There are, in average, 20 children under 2 years of age served per center and an average of 24 children ages 2 to 5. There is an average of 7 pregnant women receiving services and training at the center and approximately 8 nursing mothers per center.

Days are very clearly and homogeneously structured throughout the centers in the city. From Monday through Saturday, workers and helpers arrive to the centers before 9 am, when parents start bringing their children in. The first three hours of the day are devoted to the development of social skills through playing,

---

[1] The observations were conducted during the month of July, 2007.

as well as reading and writing. At noon, meals are served to all children, mainly by the helper. After their noon meal, children nap for approximately an hour. When they wake up, workers and helpers play and sing with them until their parents pick them up, between 2 and 3 in the afternoon. If parents do not pick up their children on time, the center's helper usually takes them home. If parents are not home, she leaves the child with a trusted neighbor, or waits for their return.

The daily meals served at the centers consist mainly of rice and a supplement. Three times per week the child receives a boiled egg supplement (recently increased from two). In addition to the egg supplements, the meals are supplemented with lentils, potatoes, and other vegetables, once a week. A few weeks before these observations were conducted, ICDS began installing gas stoves in *anganwadi* centers. Prior to the installation of these stoves, helpers cooked over fire at the centers' kitchens. Most centers do not have electricity or bathrooms in them. When needed, teachers and helpers get them from neighbors willing to share their facilities or their electricity through extension cords stretched to their houses.

One afternoon a week, usually on Wednesdays, pregnant and nursing women attend the center to pick up nutrition supplements to be used for cooking at home. If they are unable to come to the center, helpers personally deliver them to their houses. Apart from picking up their supplements, women also spend time at the centers attending meetings where they are taught classes on nutrition, health, and hygiene, usually taught by the center worker. In addition to the services provided to children and nursing and pregnant women, 77% of the centers visited also provided health and hygiene classes to adolescent women.

Apart from the many intended purposes of *anganwadi* centers, communities also utilize the facilities as meeting places for local affairs such as fishermen associations or artists' fan clubs.

Research has demonstrated that *anganwadis* have had a positive impact on the survival, growth, and development of young children. According to the National Nutrition Monitoring Bureau, the percentage of children suffering from severe malnutrition has significantly declined from 15.3% during 1976-1978 to 8.7% during 1988-1990. Due to the effectiveness demonstrated by ICDS programs, the Indian government has made a commitment to make these services available to all citizens in need of them.

Microfinance

On 15 December 1998, the General Assembly of the United Nations, by Resolution 53/197, proclaimed 2005 as the International Year of Microcredit. The resolution requests the year to be "a special occasion for giving impetus to microfinance programs throughout the world". Resolution 53/197 also invites governments, the United Nations system, non-governmental organizations, the private sector, the media, and all involved, to engage in strengthening the existing microfinance institutions (MFIs), so that credit and related services for self-employment and income-generating activities may be made available to an increasing number of people living in poverty.

Microfinance is the result of the standardization and adaptation of simple but innovative financial and business practices emerging from places like Bolivia and Bangladesh. Its simplicity has made microfinance appealing to individuals who can easily understand its principles, and reap its benefits in their everyday lives. This is certainly an advantage over sophisticated, complex finance methods adapted to poor societies in less developed countries (Armendáriz de Aghion & Morduch, 2005). In short, microfinance may be defined as the provision of appropriate financial services to low-income individuals with the specific purpose of alleviating poverty (Kosiura, 2001). The main goal of microfinance is to promote the investment of capital in income generating activities through new business endeavors or the expansion of already existing ones (Morduch, 1999).

History of Microfinance

Microfinance, as a way to promote financial services among the poor, is not a new idea. According to Global Envision, informal community-supported financial programs and services have existed for centuries; from *tandas* in Mexico to chit funds in India. Moreover, formal institutions serving the poor have also operated for decades, usually known as rural banks, credit unions, and cooperatives. In more recent years, experiments with small amounts lent to the poorest of the poor in different parts of the world have taken place, providing the foundation for what we presently know as Microfinance Institutions (MFIs). Some of these experiments began in places like Mexico, Venezuela, India, and Bangladesh. In time, these experiments became formal institutions providing microfinance products and services throughout the world. Among the most successful microfinance institutions worldwide are ACCION International in Venezuela, COMPARTAMOS in Mexico, the Self Employed Women's Association (SEWA) Bank in India, and the Grameen Bank in Bangladesh.

Group Lending

Microfinance institutions provide their services largely based on the idea of group lending: the idea of poor individuals with no collateral forming small groups with the purpose of obtaining loans from MFIs. Joint liability has proven to be the solution to the problem of nonexistent collateral that had limited the poor from accessing high-quality financial services.

Another benefit of joint liability, and probably the reason why it is so popular among MFIs, is its ability to reduce the risks of adverse selection (unknown characteristics of the borrower), moral hazard (unknown actions of the borrower), costly state verification (unknown outcome), and enforcement (unknown borrower's willingness to repay) faced by these Institutions. In practical terms, the immediate benefits of joint liability are (1) the reduction in transaction costs, which are particularly high when lending small amounts of money to the poor (as individuals come together in groups, loan offices use their resources more efficiently as they serve groups of clients, instead of working with them individually), and (2) access to information about potential clients that, without the sophisticated information systems available in developed countries, would be nearly impossible to obtain (Ghatak and Guinnane, 1999).

Microfinance in Tamil Nadu: The Corporation for Development of Women's Magalir Thittam Project

Tamil Nadu Corporation for Development of Women's (TNCDW) Magalir Thittam Project, is the branch of the state government responsible for providing the funding, training, and infrastructure necessary for the development of self-help group-based microfinance. A self-help group (SHG) may be defined as a type of joint liability microfinance group. TNCDW Magalir Thittam Project's main objectives are (1) the improvement of the social and economic standards of poor women through promoting the formation of SHGs, and (2) the supervision of non-governmental organizations (NGOs) and Microfinance Institutions (MFIs) working with these groups.

Initially the TNCDW's Magalir Thittam Project thought it beneficial to train *anganwadi* teachers and helpers on issues related to microfinance. This training is still available (on a voluntary basis) for interested *anganwadi* teachers and helpers. However, it is not in the interest of the corporation to intentionally focus their efforts on *anganwadi* centers. The corporation does not work exclusively with ICDS in the formation of SHGs, and consequently, TNCDW's Magalir Thittam Project provides its services to many different NGOs and MFIs; ICDS is viewed simply as another entity that may request their services if they so desire. In short, TNCDW's Magalir Thittam project does not have a particular focus on reaching out to ICDS' *anganwadi* centers for the formation of SHGs.

Linkages between Microfinance and Education

Education is known to be one of the most important preexisting conditions for economic growth and development (Easterly, 2002; Lindauer & Pritchett, 2002; Pack & Saggi, 2006; Rodrik, 1995). However, research in this area, although existent, is not abundant. But when specifically studying the linkages between microfinance and education, the availability of literature is even more deficient, consisting in a few valuable reports, mainly from practitioners conducting pilot studies in the field. Among them are MkNelly and Dunford (1988, 1999), observing the impact of credit with education on mothers and their young children's nutrition in Ghana and Bolivia; Quaegebeur and Marthi (2005), focusing on the linkages between microfinance and education with a particular emphasis on parental involvement in India; and Banerjee and Duflo (2006), conducting research on issues of absenteeism among school teachers in India and Kenya.

When looking at potential ways to link microfinance and education, researchers must analyze the variables involved in the process (e.g. MFIs, investors, personnel, and the needs of the community, among others), and the possible ways to combine these variables in such a way that the outcomes are positive and the available resources used efficiently. *Anganwadi* group meetings provide an appropriate setting for microfinance to take place. The fact that *anganwadis* serve groups of low income women, locates them in a strategic position, since MFIs target the exact same segment of the population. Additionally, *anganwadis* are excellent places where the problems of adverse selection, moral hazard, costly state verification, and enforcement faced by MFIs are minimized. These problems are minimized since groups are formed by women who already know each other resulting in self-selection. In short, the structure provided by ICDS through *anganwadi* centers is ideal for the provision of microfinance services.

During the visits to these centers, it was observed that a few independent non-governmental organizations, microfinance institutions, and money lenders provided informal financial services to women attending meetings there. However, none of these was believed to have a clear plan of action to provide services exclusively to anganwadi centers; instead, it seemed to have been the effort of independent, visionary loan officers seeking to expand their operations by reaching to an *anganwadi* center coincidently located in their target area. In spite of these efforts to independently provide microfinance services to *anganwadi* centers, only 32% of them reported to have any kind of financial activity taking place in their premises. Figure 2 represents the existing model in which different entities partially reach out to *anganwadi* centers seeking to provide financial services to their members. As shown in figure 2, this is yet to reach the fullest of its potential, as none of these entities possesses a clear strategy for reaching out to them. The fact that these entities touch on *anganwadi* centers is merely coincidental and mostly based on the location of the centers within individual loan officers' territories.

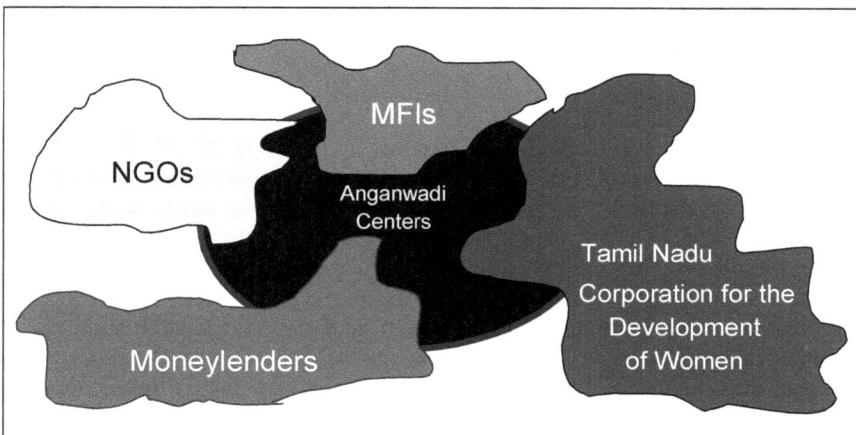

Figure 2: Existing model in which different entities provide microfinance services with no particular focus on ICDS' *Anganwadi* Centers.

The following sections present potential models for the integration of microfinance and education and suggest specific ways for the distribution of microfinance services through *anganwadi* centers.

The Models

Although credit is a very important resource in the overcoming of financial challenges, credit *per se* does not provide the necessary tools to eradicate poverty (Rueda Fernández, 2006). Dunford and Rueda, aware of the unmistakable benefits of tying microfinance with educational products and services, propose three potential models for their delivery: Bound/linked services, parallel services, and unified service. Following are Rueda's definitions, advantages and disadvantages of the three different models used in the delivery of traditional and non-traditional microfinance products and services:

- Bound/linked Services refer to the creation of strategic allegiances with other institutions. This model suggests services being provided through uniting two different organizations with knowledge and experience in different and independent areas of service. The greatest strength of this model is each organization maintaining its specialty; the main challenge, the lack of control, supervision and communication between them.
- Parallel Service involves different and specialized personnel from an individual institution providing both, financial and non-financial services. Its main strength is having highly specialized and motivated personnel; its weakness, high operational costs.
- Unified Service refers to the same personnel from a single institution providing both financial and non-financial services. Contrary to the parallel service, this model's strength is found in its low operational costs. Its weakness is the potential for inadequate results, as few individuals are capable of providing high quality services in two areas at the same time.

The Integration

Given the nature of both, *anganwadis* and MFIs, the most feasible model to be pursued for this potential merger is bound/linked services; two different and independent institutions partnering together in providing education and microfinance services at a single location. Parallel and unified services are virtually impossible for *anganwadis* and MFIs, since both of them lack the necessary knowledge, experience and resources to deliver education and microfinance services at the same location and by the same institution or personnel.

According to Rueda, the main disadvantage of the bound/linked services model is the lack of follow-up and control in the non-financial area. When partnering with *anganwadis*, MFIs would greatly benefit from the already existing and very homogeneous structure, excellent follow-up, and control provided by the centers, especially in the non-financial area, their area of expertise. Having a strong and homogeneous delivery system, *anganwadis* are the perfect partner for an MFI in search of distribution channels for financial services. Weekly meetings may be added to the existing *anganwadi's* schedule, or the existing meetings may be extended for a certain period of time in which microfinance services may be provided. These meetings, as suggested by the bound/linked services model, would be led by a loan officer from an MFI independent from ICDS, releasing *anganwadi* workers and helpers from additional responsibilities.

Recommendations for Implementation

As stated earlier in this chapter, TNCDW Magalir Thittam Project is the provider of the funding, training, and infrastructure necessary for the development of SHG-based microfinance in Tamil Nadu. The Project's main goal is to support MFIs and NGOs in the formation of SHGs. Since the Project's scope is rather ample, it is understandable that ICDS is nowhere at the top of their priority list with regards to the expansion of their services. TNCDW Magalir Thittam Project operates based on the demand of their services by MFIs and NGOs. *Anganwadi* workers and helpers do not possess the capacity to expand their activities to new areas such as microfinance.

On the other hand, ICDS provides health, nutrition, and hygiene services for the poor throughout India. Apart from the education of children, *anganwadi* centers promote weekly meetings where women gather to learn about issues of health, nutrition, and hygiene. When other services, such as microfinance, have been attempted to be added to the centers through the same personnel, the result has been the overwhelming of the workers.

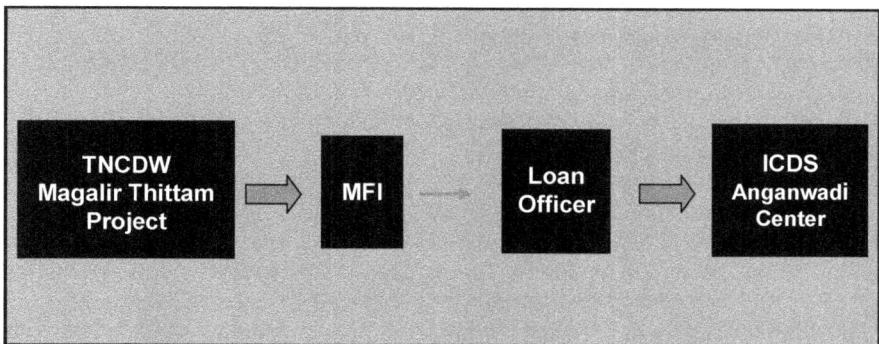

Figure 3: Recommendation for the provision of microfinance services by well-established MFIs with the support of TNCDW Magalir Thittam Project, and through the distribution channels provided by ICDS' Anganwadi Centers

A bound/linked service promoting a partnership between independent institutions is, in this context, a viable solution to the challenge of linking microfinance and education. This study suggests contacting a well-established, trustworthy MFI to direct loan officers to anganwadi centers. The role of TNCDW Magalir Thittam Project would be to provide the MFI and the individual loan officer with the means necessary for the development of SHGs at the centers. The role of ICDS would be to allow loan officers from recognized MFIs to hold meetings at the centers. The *anganwadi* worker would only be expected to keep the center open during the meetings and would also be encouraged to participate as a member of the SHG. Figure 3 represents the model suggested in which TNCDW Magalir Thittam Project would provide its services and expertise to MFIs with a specific focus on *anganwadi* Centers.

Conclusion

This chapter suggests the formation of a link/bound service model, with two independent organizations working together in the delivery of microfinance and educational services combined at a single location. The model suggests the Tamil Nadu Corporation for Development of Women, Magalir Thittam Project to provide its support to a well establish Microfinance Institution. The microfinance institution will, in turn, supply loan officers to Integrated Child Development Services' *anganwadi* centers for the distribution of microfinance services. The activities at the centers will not be disrupted by the MFIs activities and the centers will continue with the provision of educational services as they normally do.

This model is beneficial for both, *anganwadi* center workers and loan officers. *Anganwadi* workers will not be expected to perform any activities in addition to their already heavy work load, and loan officers would easily find markets for their services, understanding the existence of demand for them.

References

Armendáriz de Aghion, Beatriz, and Jonathan Morduch. *The Economics of Microfinance*. Cambridge: The MIT Press, 2005.

Banerjee, Abhijit and Esther Duflo. *Addressing Absence*. Poverty Action Lab at the Massachusetts Institute of Technology, 2002.

Dunford, Christopher. "Microfinance as a Vehicle for Educating the Poor," Freedom from Hunger, http://www.freedomfromhunger.org/programs/microfinance.php, (accessed June 14, 2007).

Easterly, William. *Inequality Causes Underdevelopment: New Evidence from Commodity Endowments, Middle Class Share, and Other Determinants of Per Capita Income*. Center for Global Development (2002).

Ghatak, Maitreesh and Timothy Guinnane. "The Economics of Lending with Joint Liability: Theory and Practice," *Journal of Development Economics* 60 (1999): 195-228.

Global Envision. "The History of Microfinance." http://www.globalenvision.org/library/4/1051/ (accessed June 27, 2007).

Government of India. "National Policy for Children." Department of Social Welfare. http://nicp.nisd.gov.in/pdf/npc/pdf (accessed June 24, 2007).

Kosiura, Hala. *Microfinance Workshop*. Warsaw: Microfinance Center, 2001

Lindauer, David and Lant Pritchett. "What is the Big Idea? The Third Generation of Development Advice." *Economía: Journal of the Latin American and the Caribbean Economic Association* 3.1 (2002): 1-39.

Ministry of Women & Child Development. "Child Development," Government of India, http://wcd.nic.in/childdet.htm (accessed June 27, 2007).

Mknelly, Barbara and Christopher Dunford. *Impact of Credit with Education on Mothers and their Young Children's Nutrition: Lower Pra Rural Bank Credit with Education Program in Ghana.* Freedom from Hunger, 1998.

MkNelly, Barbara and Christopher Dunford. *Impact of Credit with Education on Mothers and their Young Children's Nutrition: CRECER Credit with Education Program in Bolivia.* Freedom from Hunger, 1999.

Morduch, Jonathan. "The Role of Subsidies in Microfinance: Evidence from the Grameen Bank," *Journal of Development Economics* 60 (1999): 229-48.

Pack, Howard and Kamal Saggi. *The Case for Industrial Policy: A Critical Survey.* World Bank Policy Center, 2006.

Quaegebeur, Margot and Srivatsa Marthi. *Linkages Between Microfinance and Effective Education with a Focus on Parental Involvement.* Institute for Financial Management and Research, 2005.

Rodrik, Dani. "Getting Interventions Right: How South Korea and Taiwan Grew Rich." *Economic Policy* 20 (1995): 53-107.

Rueda Fernández, Isabel. "The Marginal Cost of Integrating Microfinance with Education using the Unified Approach," Crédito con Educación Rural (CRECER), 2006.

UNICEF. "India-Integrated Child Development Services (ICDS)." http://www.unicef.org/earlychildhood/files/india_icds.pdf

United Nations Department of Economic and Social Affairs. "UN Resolution: International Year of Microcredit 2005." United Nations. http://www.gdrc.org/icm/iym2005/un-resolution.html

United Nations Office of the High Commissioner for Human Rights. "Declaration of the Rights of the Child," United Nations, http://www.unhchr.ch/html/menu3/b/25.htm, (accessed June 21, 2007).

www.ingramcontent.com/pod-product-compliance
Lightning Source LLC
Chambersburg PA
CBHW060251220326
41598CB00027B/4065